Introduction to Religions of the African Diaspora

Introduction to Religions of the African Diaspora

Stephanie Y. Mitchem

BLOOMSBURY ACADEMIC
NEW YORK • LONDON • OXFORD • NEW DELHI • SYDNEY

BLOOMSBURY ACADEMIC

Bloomsbury Publishing Inc, 1359 Broadway, New York, NY 10018, USA
Bloomsbury Publishing Plc, 50 Bedford Square, London, WC1B 3DP, UK
Bloomsbury Publishing Ireland, 29 Earlsfort Terrace, Dublin 2, D02 AY28, Ireland

BLOOMSBURY, BLOOMSBURY ACADEMIC and the Diana logo are
trademarks of Bloomsbury Publishing Plc

First published in the United States of America 2026

Copyright © Bloomsbury Publishing Inc, 2026

For legal purposes the Acknowledgments on p. x constitute an extension of this copyright page.

Cover design: Diana Nuhn
Cover photo taken by Stephanie Y. Mitchem in Oyo, Nigeria, 2015.

All rights reserved. No part of this publication may be: i) reproduced or transmitted in any form, electronic or mechanical, including photocopying, recording or by means of any information storage or retrieval system without prior permission in writing from the publishers; or ii) used or reproduced in any way for the training, development or operation of artificial intelligence (AI) technologies, including generative AI technologies. The rights holders expressly reserve this publication from the text and data mining exception as per Article 4(3) of the Digital Single Market Directive (EU) 2019/790.

Bloomsbury Publishing Inc does not have any control over, or responsibility for, any third-party websites referred to or in this book. All internet addresses given in this book were correct at the time of going to press. The author and publisher regret any inconvenience caused if addresses have changed or sites have ceased to exist, but can accept no responsibility for any such changes.

Library of Congress Cataloging-in-Publication Data
Names: Mitchem, Stephanie Y., 1950- author
Title: Introduction to religions of the African diaspora / Stephanie Y. Mitchem.
Description: 1st. | New York : Bloomsbury Academic, 2026. |
Includes bibliographical references and index.
Identifiers: LCCN 2025035724 (print) | LCCN 2025035725 (ebook) |
ISBN 9798881806729 hardback | ISBN 9798881806736 paperback |
ISBN 9798881806743 ebook | ISBN 9798881867621 pdf
Subjects: LCSH: African diaspora–Religion
Classification: LCC BL2400 .M58 2026 (print) | LCC BL2400 (ebook)
LC record available at https://lccn.loc.gov/2025035724
LC ebook record available at https://lccn.loc.gov/2025035725

ISBN: HB: 979-8-8818-0672-9
PB: 979-8-8818-0673-6
ePDF: 979-8-8818-6762-1
eBook: 979-8-8818-0674-3

Typeset by Deanta Global Publishing Services, Chennai, India
Printed and bound in the United States of America

For product safety related questions contact productsafety@bloomsbury.com.

To find out more about our authors and books visit www.bloomsbury.com and sign up for our newsletters.

Contents

List of Figures vi
Preface vii
Acknowledgements x

Introduction 1

1 Origin Stories 21

2 Growing African Diasporan Religions (ADR) 53

3 Evolving African Diasporan Religions (ADR) 79

4 Afrikan Indigenous Religions (AIR) 99

5 Candomblé 121

6 Vodou/Haiti and Lucumí/Cuba 143

7 Widening the Lens: ADR in the United States 177

Conclusion: Horizons 203

Bibliography 213
Index 221

Figures

1.1 Alhambra, Granada, Spain 27
1.2 Map of Trafficked Africans' Routes 35
1.3 Major African Coastal Areas for Transportation of Africans 36
1.4 Site of Spirit Attenuation Well, Badgary, Nigeria 44
2.1 Egyptian Divinities 71
2.2 Kemetic Symbols 73
3.1 42 Laws of Ma'at 93
4.1 Bakongo Cosmogram 103
4.2 Chart of Orisa/orixas/orishas 108
5.1 Festival of the Sisterhood of the Good Death, Cachoeira, Brazil 136
6.1 Example of Veve, in Honor of Lwa Erzulie Freda 151
6.2 Callejon De Hamel, Havana, Cuba 169

Preface

I began my doctoral studies with questions that came from thinking through Black Americans' religious lives and meanings. Through life experiences that aligned with my studies, I came to understand that religions carry cultures or, perhaps, cultures carry religions. That is, the connections between cultures and religions can be understood anthropologically. For instance, distinctive Black religious practices such as "jumping the broom" as a celebration of marriage surfaced from cultural views and were carried into church settings. However, some religions believe that their theologies and practices are "universal" and therefore above culture. Nonetheless, the mergers between religions and cultures are real and can be seen in Black Americans' folk healing practices, which defy reduction to simple superstition.[1]

In Black communities, there has been consistent ease in blending religious belief and practice to match needs. The idea of a sharp separation between body and soul is not prominent; instead, faith and religion have been embodied. The body itself has been celebrated, not subjected to forms of asceticism and shame. The ancestors are not just people from a given nuclear family; they are drawn from the breadth of the communities that give shape to identity and humanity. I have seen many Black people, regardless of confessed faith, pour wines, liquors, and waters in memory of those who fell too soon. These practices might be referenced as underlying spiritualities, drawn from some cultural sources; such folkways do not comfortably fit into Abrahamic religions' structures. Therefore, my curiosity about religions grew.

I was fortunate to live in Detroit, Michigan, a city rich in Black religious traditions and cultures. I received an alternative education that challenged mainstream canonical norms. Controversial authors such as Frances Cress Welsing[2] and Ivan van Sertima,[3] whose names are seldom used in college classrooms, presented different views of history, race, and religion, which challenged readers to think critically. Religions with Black points of view flourished: the Shrine of the Black Madonna and the Nation of Islam thrived alongside Rev. Charles C. Adams[4] and Martha Jean the Queen.[5] Religion was embodied and infused with the history of a people.

Myriad questions took me to the Diaspora and the continent of Africa. What has informed Black religious and spiritual lives? What meanings might cross different Black Diasporic communities? How did Black cultures form in lands far away from the continent of Africa, priming Black understandings of self and community? These and other questions gave rise to my study of spiritualities of the African Diaspora. From my starting point to this moment, I have been amazed by the creativity and ingenuity of Black peoples across the globe, who found beauty and grace amid unimaginable injustices and violence, through an array of spiritualities that affirmed their humanity and goodness. This book introduces some of the meanings of the religions of the African Diaspora.

Scholars have studied and taught religions of the African Diaspora in many ways and from multiple intellectual perspectives, including studying abroad, which has enriched our understanding of such religions. *Introduction to Religions of the African Diaspora* reflects the pedagogical and travel experiences that inform courses about Black religions that I have taught for many years in Detroit. I have taken groups of students to different religious houses, including the Shrine of the Black Madonna and a Nation of Islam Mosque. On several occasions, I took students to Bahia, Brazil, where we spoke with Candomblé practitioners. On-the-ground experience is integral to understanding African and African Diasporan religions and countering misinformation. Today, I inform my students in South Carolina that to enroll in one of my courses is to embark on a journey we take together. In an ideal world, we would travel for a year, going from one site to another, learning about and discussing Black religious life in ways we cannot by reading texts, looking at photos, or viewing videos. Since we cannot travel extensively, I draw on my own travels to provide context and representations, if only in brief slices, of the diversity and richness of religions of the African Diaspora.

In this book, the journey continues . . .

Notes

1 Stephanie Y. Mitchem, *African American Folk Healing* (New York: New York University Press, 2007).
2 Frances Cress Welsing, *The Isis Papers: The Keys to the Colors* (Chicago: Third World Press, 1991).

3 Ivan Van Sertima, *They Came Before Columbus: The African Presence in Ancient America* (New York: Random House Trade Paperbacks, reprint, 2003).
4 Prince of the Pulpit: Detroit pastor emeritus Rev. Charles Gilchrist Adams dies at 86," Detroit Free Press, November 29, 2023, https://www.freep.com/story/news/local/michigan/detroit/2023/11/29/rev-charles-g-adams-dies/71749141007/, accessed September 11, 2025.
5 "Steinberg, Martha Jean 'The Queen,'" *Detroit Historical Society*, https://detroithistorical.org/learn/encyclopedia-of-detroit/steinberg-martha-jean-queen, accessed March 7, 2025.

Acknowledgments

This book has been a labor of love that many people have helped bring to life: To my family, especially my fierce ancestors, who kept me on the right road;

The students I've taught over the years who have really lived through my development of this material;

The many people who patiently answered my initial questions as I traveled, helping me to broaden my views—so that I could ask the right questions;

The College of Arts and Sciences, University of South Carolina, which generously supported this endeavor;

The Noble Esthetic, LLC, whose creativity brought my ideas to life with their illustrations;

Ambassador Olúwo Mógàjí Òkítí Adéṣínà Ọlátúnjí-Arẹ̀sà at Ilé Arẹ̀sà International and Ambassador Olóyè Ìyánifá Ifáṣèyí Ọlátúnjí-Arẹ̀sà at Oricounseling.com who provided invaluable historical and theological information and guidance;

Richard Brown, my editor at Bloomsbury with whom I have shared ideas over many coffees; and Cup and Quill Editing and Publication Services, LLC. Above all, I thank Olodumare, who brought me here.

Introduction

Chapter Outline

African and Diasporan Spiritualities	2
Old Ways of Thinking: Africa, Diaspora, and Religion	3
Redirecting Our Thinking	7
Black People	13
The Journeys	15

The African Diaspora and its religions extend across the globe, and a moment to appreciate the scope of this study is needed. Multiple languages, cultures, and nationalities inform multiple religions across the Diaspora; there is no single place or people that encompasses all Africa-based or -derived religions and spiritualities. African Diasporan religions reflect their own histories, politics, and geographies that have a connection to the continent of Africa. Through forced migrations, Africans forced from their homes during periods of colonization carried their histories and memories to new lands, which informed the religious traditions that arose amid oppressive political realities. Today, citizens of African countries travel to the West for different reasons, thereby complicating the meanings of this Diaspora.

One text cannot offer a comprehensive discussion of religions throughout the continent of Africa or its Diaspora with the depth that every country and people merit. My aim, then, is to introduce a few of these spiritualities in their respective cultural and historical contexts. African and Diasporan spiritualties are first to consider.

African and Diasporan Spiritualities

The diversity among African and African Diasporan spiritualities and religions can be misread or defined as chaotic. The following is an opening description that presents some aspects of these religions and spiritualities when they are centered in African concepts.

General Characteristics

- All life is viewed cyclically, seen in the changing of seasons or death and birth. As such, the circle becomes an important sign and symbol. A Bantu proverb states: "A human being is a rising and setting sun around the world," indicating the cyclical nature of each human being. From such a base, the idea of ancestor reverence respects this flow and is a component of each human person. There are connections among the deceased, the living, and the unborn, particularly within family groupings. Family, in its widest sense, is to be honored.
- As with many indigenous groups, African religions and spiritualities emphasize earth-based spiritualities, understood as connected to nature and its natural rhythms. The universe is a source of wonder. The earth itself is seen as living, and humans are taught the value of honoring the earth's rhythm and therefore embrace it—synergy rather than dominance.
- In this framework, all these beings are connected and thus can relate to and communicate with one another if they choose to honor that potential.
- Divinity in African mindsets is not confined within a church building but is understood to be present in all life. Bodies of water, trees, and humans may share in or hold some aspect of divinity.
- In Indigenous or Diasporan traditions, named divinities may include a primary deity as well as other powerful deities. Western religionists have used the label polytheism to ridicule African and Diasporan traditions. However, multiple concepts of the divine reflect more sophisticated forms of communal and personal worship. These beings become integral components in the reciprocal relationships

between humans and the universe. The aim of the worship and these relationships is to improve the life and character of the practitioner.
- Communities employ the oral transmission of the traditions in these religions and spiritualities. Such learning occurs over time through the interrelationships among community members. Proverbs, wise words, stories, parables, and tradition-specific practices help people identify and connect to their own spiritual truths. The concept of sin reflects perceived imbalances in interrelationships among community members, which invites self-reflection. Such reflection may influence a person's sense of personal responsibility for these imbalances and deepen their faith.

The above characteristics are shared by many African spiritualities and religions, but this list is not comprehensive. Instead, these serve as starting points for readers seeking to deepen their understanding of African religious concepts, spiritualities, and faiths that are the focus of this book.

The next step is to review and address certain deficiencies in earlier scholarship related to Black people and their religious ideas. This step is necessary because the negatives celebrated in that work created other sets of relationships that still have an impact. Western scientific and religious intellectual history shaped negative views of Africa and Black people through scholarship that inaccurately represented their spiritualities. To move forward, it is necessary to look back and then redirect our thinking.

Old Ways of Thinking: Africa, Diaspora, and Religion

Religions and spiritualities are assumed to reflect the intelligence of different people and groups. The ideas they develop will reflect the experiences they deem as mystical. But such credit is not regularly given to African and Diasporan religious thought. Western intellectual history has consistently presented negative views of Black people's intelligence generally, with Black religions serving as evidence of simple minds. This has salted the grounds of academia and the broader society with persistent racist stereotypes.

Two European authors provide examples of this persuasive pattern. Georges Cuvier (1769–1832), a naturalist and zoologist who was also considered one of the foremost early geologists, questioned the humanity of Black people based on their appearance. Cuvier wrote, "The Negro race is confined to the south of the Atlas. Its complexion is black, its hair frizzy, its cranium compressed, and its nose crushed; its prominent muzzle and its large lips obviously bring it closer to the apes: the tribes that compose it have always remained barbarous."[1] Other authors shared similar views, which were already well established in Europe when Charles Darwin (1809–1882) began to make his mark as a notable intellectual figure. Darwin's work on human evolution and racial hierarchy[2] affirmed his place in the lineage of scholars who defined an evolutionary view of all races, positioning White Europeans as the pinnacle and most definitive example of human development.

Despite Darwin's commitment to using a scientific method, his work was informed by the Great Chain of Being ideation that originated in the work of Plato and Aristotle. This hierarchy positions God at the top, followed by angels, humans, animals, and so on. Darwin expanded the hierarchy to reflect his perceptions of racial hierarchies. For example, on one of Darwin's exploratory journeys, his group encountered a group of soldiers who were hunting runaway enslaved Africans. When the group was found, Darwin wrote: "The whole were seized with the exception of one old woman, who, sooner than again be led into slavery, dashed herself to pieces from the summit of the mountain. In a Roman matron, this would have been called the noble love of freedom: in a poor negress it is mere brutal obstinacy."[3] As Darwin saw it, a Black person who chose not to submit to enslavement was obstinate and emotional rather than noble and thoughtful. Such definitions by Darwin and other European scholars were integral in crafting ongoing negative views of Black people.

Cuvier and Darwin were not the first to dehumanize Black people and vilify their intelligence. The seventeenth-century period, known as the Enlightenment, generally upheld the primacy of science and eschewed metaphysical considerations. In contrast, seemingly unscientific African belief patterns reflected a more holistic view of the universe. Even as Enlightenment thinkers tried to push religion into a quiet corner, African and Diasporan traditions still hold the Divine in all of life. As Martin G. Bernal asserted, "What stands out about the African tradition is the conception of God in terms of bios, that is what African philosophers tend to call "life-force," but what may also be called "vitality."⁴ The Divine, in other words, cannot be contained in a church building.

As European and American scientists proceeded with their negative constructions of Black people, Christians who approved of enslavement developed theological views that affirmed their beliefs. For instance, Thornton Stringfellow claimed,

> It (enslavement) is from God himself; it (scripture) authorizes that people, to whom he had become king and law-giver, to purchase men and women as property; to hold them and their posterity in bondage; and to will them to their children as a possession forever; and more, it allows foreign slaveholders to settle and live among them; to breed slaves and sell them.⁵

White male enslavers used Christianity to define their own roles as reflective of biblical teachings and to view themselves like Abraham, with their flocks, wives, and slaves. That is, in the eyes of such men, patriarchy was divinely appointed.

Regrettably, these theoretical and religious constructions did not disappear with the abolition of slavery or the arrival of the twentieth century. Indeed, such ideas persist in the twenty-first century. A 2023 poll of Black Americans by the Pew Research Center demonstrates that "a substantial portion of Black Americans say they often come across news about Black people that is racist or racially insensitive."⁶ While the Pew poll focused on reasons that news coverage of Black people is deemed racially fraught, the authors cite an earlier study wherein "Black Americans have expressed similar levels of pessimism about the prospects of achieving equality in the U.S. . . . with just 13% (of those respondents) in 2021 saying that equality for Black people is extremely or very likely."⁷ Continued beliefs in a racial hierarchy still inform some people's beliefs, leading them to exclude and disregard Black people from myriad sectors and as candidates for various opportunities. For those who still believe that Black people are stupid, it follows that they regard Black religious thought as unrefined or as evidence of Black people's lack of intelligence. The impact of Darwin's work on racist evolutionary concepts is still evident in its influence on the study of religions.

Some scholars of comparative religions applied Darwin's concepts of evolution to their analyses of religious traditions, which constructed and affirmed the merit of a hierarchy of religious belief and practice. The hierarchy positions what is defined as indigenous pantheism at the bottom of an imagined evolutionary scale, with Western monotheism at the top and the most evolved. In the language used to construct this hierarchy, race is implicit rather than explicit. Neither the nature nor function of this evolutionary scale is benign. That is, the hierarchy relies on and reproduces negative implications about the intelligence and sophistication of followers of African Diasporan religions; it also loops back to affirm the designation of Black people as ignorant. At the same time, Christianity is considered the most evolved religion. This assessment of Christianity serves as a false standard against which African and Indigenous spiritualities are deemed primitive.

Bias toward a Eurocentric canon influences Western scholars when studying African or Diasporan religions. Scholarship about religion can become a mechanical recitation of beliefs and practices: the main divinity is so and so, these are the commandments and believers do the following. Such details may be important, but if the research is context-free, the analyses or conclusions may be erroneous. How we study Greek mythology provides a sharp contrast to the ways that African Diasporan religions and spiritualities are approached.

In the United States, Greek mythology is not an optional course, taught in a single term as a weird religion. On the contrary, Greek myths are taught in K-12 classes based on the understanding that the United States and its European foundations derive from Greco-Roman roots. Stories about Zeus, Hera, and other divinities, along with their mythological and cultural contexts of origin, are integrated into various classes including literature, languages, religion, and history. Greek or Latin languages or philosophies and study abroad programs to Greece or Italy, or religious studies become part of what is known as classical studies. Greco-Roman divinities' names are used to identify medical conditions, space flights, or planets. These myths are adapted into various pop culture movies and television programs. The message is clear: learning about Greek myths is valuable for numerous reasons and highly relevant in various contexts.

In contrast, Western writers have relied on African religious components to create images that are the stuff of nightmares—voodoo, zombies, mummies, and evil magicians. The composition of such figures betrays the legacy of racist stereotypes and depictions of Black people as depraved, animalistic, and barely human that informs them. While scholars have attempted to move away from the canonical control of Eurocentric mindsets and earlier research, such shifts have not been without pain or consequence.

Some of the earliest academic re-conceptualization of history and the role of Africa was met with derision by the mainstream academic community. Bernal's *Black Athena*[8] challenged the primacy of Greco-Roman roots of European history, instead positing the influence of African thought as foundational to the Greeks'. Unfortunately, the work had research flaws, leading to bizarre arguments and disagreements over issues such as the race of Cleopatra. These debates obscured the value of Bernal's effort to shift the scholarly focus and led to the dismissal of his foundational questions about African contributions. Ultimately, the dogmatic "truth" of Eurocentrism prevailed.

Such theories rely on isolated descriptions and prejudicial wording to objectify African and Diasporan spiritualities. These problems are apparent in some museum collections, where everything labeled as "African" is grouped in one space, with neither rhyme nor reason for the assemblage of materials: a comb is placed next to a mask, next to a stool, next to a funerary jar. It is not possible to understand African religions through disconnected arrangements of artifacts and their accompanying descriptions. The complexities of African religions and spiritualities defy simplistic renderings.

Redirecting Our Thinking

Early questions about the quality or absence of African studies were raised in the 1930s by Carter G. Woodson. According to Woodson, even in Black colleges, educators "direct no attention to the philosophy of the African. Negroes of Africa have and always have had their own ideas about the nature of the universe, time, and space, about appearance and reality, and about freedom and necessity.... There were many Africans who were just as wise as Socrates."[9] With a sharper tone, Woodson challenged the form of Christianity that promoted oppression:

> If Negroes got their conception of religion from slaveholders, libertines, and murderers, there may be something wrong about it and it would not hurt to investigate it. It has been said that the Negroes do not connect

morals with religion. . . . Certainly the Whites with whom the Negroes have come into contact have not done so.[10]

Woodson's perceptive charges called attention to significant absences in studies of Africa and its Diaspora.

Since then, the body of African Studies scholarship has expanded. Scholars are gradually reshaping the fundamental aspects of research in the field and moving toward more realistic, informed, and accurate analyses of African and Diasporan religions. Their efforts are bringing the scholarship that comprises the tapestry of African Diaspora religions into dynamic clarity. Viewing African and its Diasporan religious thought in its contexts as lived and living traditions invites new and important questions: How are African religions connected to the Diaspora? What is different, and who is involved? What are some of the purposes of African spiritualities in the Diaspora? How have African religious ideas changed through colonization or interactions with Black people from the Diaspora? Has colonization influenced religious beliefs and practices on the African continent and in the Diaspora? If so, how?

To begin this study of religions of the African Diaspora, three terms need to be framed in the context of their respective usage: religion, African Diaspora, and Black people. Each term's meaning is fluid, which can be confusing or lead to misinterpretation. Religion, as it has been historically understood in Western contexts, leads to misunderstandings of African-derived religions. The concept of African Diaspora requires clarification regarding its relationship to the African continent. The term Black people is significant in the context of the Diaspora and the African continent itself.

Religion

One of my contacts in Nigeria emphasized that the Western idea of religion does not align with African traditional faith practices. Even the term African traditional religion is inadequate because it may indicate that African spiritualities can be fit within Western ideas of religion. As the short description of African/Diasporan spiritualities at the beginning of this introduction indicates, they should not be viewed as equivalent to or compared to Western and Abrahamic religions.

The root of the problem lies in the Western idea of religion itself. Douglas Jacobsen and Rhonda Hustedt Jacobsen define the issue in this way:

> Rather than being part of the natural world, religion is seen as bringing order to the natural world and as tapping into spiritual power that comes from beyond the natural world. More recently, in the modern era of the last several centuries, religion has come to mean a single facet of life that exists separately from the rest of ordinary, nonreligious, secular life.[11]

However, as Jacobsen and Hustedt emphasize, most people do not live exclusively secular or religious lives; instead, they live somewhere between the two. Drawing on the work of other scholars, they question whether the word "religion" has lost its usefulness and if a new vocabulary needs to be developed to allow more nuanced descriptions of the various attitudes and activities for which "religion" is not always adequate.[12] The exclusionary and limiting definition of religion did not arise overnight. It has its own history.

Prior to the Protestant Reformation in the sixteenth century, the Roman Catholic Church controlled all aspects of life, encompassing the scientific/metaphysical (which they saw as one category) along with the social and political, and the control of the Church was above all. That control was evident as Columbus wandered into lands unknown to him in 1492, funded by Spain. Upon his return to Spain, Pope Alexander VI declared any land not occupied by Catholics to be "discoverable" by Christians for the benefit of the monarchs of Europe. This papal declaration was among those that comprised the Doctrine of Discovery, which Pope Francis renounced in March 2023.[13] Nonetheless, the damage to lands, peoples, and lives was already done. The Doctrine of Discovery enabled inequity to be built into Western Christianity. The significance of these events will be explored further in Chapter 1.

In 1517, Martin Luther nailed his ninety-five Theses to the doors of a church in Wittenberg, Germany, and over the next 150 years, the Reformation transformed the shape of Europe. While Martin Luther's protest was aimed at the abuses within the Catholic Church, the Reformation paved the way for the creation of the modern nation-state, one that was separated from religious control. The reinvention of the university and higher education wrested science from the control of the

Catholic Church as the European Age of Enlightenment began in the late 1600s and continued into the early 1800s. Before the Protestant Reformation, the academic slogan was "Philosophy is the handmaiden of theology," and theology was considered the queen of sciences.

As the Age of Enlightenment began, philosophy took the lead, totally replacing theology with a quest for reason. Philosophers such as John Locke and Thomas Hobbes re-envisioned the social contract and called for empirical approaches to life. Religion was moved from the center to the margins. After the Protestant Reformation, religion was relegated to a private category, separated from the public and political spheres. The public-private split gave religion a place to claim as its own sphere: home and family were considered the realm of morality and, thereby, the realm of religion. As Naomi Goldenberg argues, "Religions are the remainders of former sovereignties that continue to operate in specified jurisdictional spheres with different measures of autonomy within contemporary governments. Religion thus evolves as a tool of statecraft for the containment and management of distinct and possibly rebellious groups whose status and authority have been reduced by a newer ruling order."[14] The social split between the public and private spheres of life is a particularly Western invention.

Religion has been an extremely effective tool of colonialism, as reflected in the writing of David Walker (1796-?). Walker was a free Black man born in the South, who eventually moved to Boston, Massachusetts, where he self-published an *Appeal to the Coloured Citizens of the World* in 1829. He was a devout Christian, but his understanding of Christianity stood apart from that of White enslavers. While attending a religious service in South Carolina, Walker recounts what follows: "To my no ordinary astonishment, our Reverend gentleman got up and told us (coloured people) that slaves must be obedient to their masters or be whipped—the whip was made for backs of fools."[15] Walker, who called only Jesus his "Master," expressed shock at such rhetoric: "To hear such preaching from a minister of my Master, whose very gospel is of peace and not of blood and whips, as this pretended preacher tried to make us believe. What the American preachers can think of us . . . I have never been able to define."[16] Walker gave an example of how religion was used as a "tool of statecraft for containment and management," as Goldenberg stated. However, Walker's writing can be seen as a prologue to the development of Black Christian theologies, as he defined the gospel as one of peace rather than bloodshed. Effectively, in this lineage, Christianity became one of the religions of the African Diaspora.

The African Diaspora

African Diaspora is a complex term. In its simplest form, the term refers to Black people scattered all over the globe who can trace their ancestry to the continent of Africa. However, this definition is incomplete. Currently, many people migrate from the African continent, but their experiences are not always resonant with those were who forcibly migrated generations ago. The definition also does not do justice to the complexities of what happened over generations to Black people dispersed through other travels or through their connections with other cultures or nations.

The most comprehensive definition of the African Diaspora encompasses at least the histories of migration, transnational and national political contexts, cultural developments and retentions, social and economic structures, and the relationships between dispersed peoples and their host lands. As Rita Kiki Edozie et al. succinctly state, "Diaspora studies analyze communities of descendants' collective, common identity and transnationality among host lands and homelands, while also examining settled dispersed communities' existence in and contribution to adaptations, transformations, making diasporic host lands over several generations, and most often forging hybrid multi-cultures."[17] Given such breadth, it is no surprise that there has been significant growth in the field known as Diaspora Studies, wherein scholars explore these and other relationships and questions.

Among the lingering questions are the following. First, can a study on the "African Diaspora" rightly claim to include the African continent? Second, is there really a link between people of the Diaspora and those of the continent? In the late 1950s, two scholars, E. Franklin Frazier and Melville J. Herskovits, took opposing sides on these questions. Frazier, a preeminent Black American sociologist, argued that the Southern plantation system and Christianity eradicated any African consciousness among Black Americans. In contrast, Melville Herskovits, a White American anthropologist, analyzed Black American and West African funeral rites, among other facets of culture, and concluded that what was known as "folk" culture was a synthesis of West African and European traditions. Over the past half-century through the analyses of Diasporan studies, the Frazier-Herskovits argument has been quieted, but not completely laid to rest. As Paul E. Lovejoy stated:

> An "African-centered" focus, in contrast to one centered in Europe or the Americas, reveals the often neglected and misunderstood impact of the African background upon the societies of the Americas and hence the relationship of slavery to modernity itself. It challenges the assumption that not much African history is relevant to the study of the Atlantic because the enslaved population was too diverse in its origins to sustain the continuities of history; or the corollary that the enslaved population, newly arrived from Africa, as comprised of autonomous individuals with such mixed experiences that they rapidly assimilated into the "new" societies of the New World, whether characterized as "American" or "Creole."[18]

Additionally, some people on the African continent might challenge Black Americans who call themselves "African American," asserting that Black Americans have no "right" to refer to themselves as African since they were not born there. On the other side, some Black Americans argue that Africans who move to the United States have no right to call themselves African American since they did not experience enslavement. Were I not to mention different positions among Africans and their descendants regarding such matters, this study would lack important context. However, as far as this text is concerned, African Diasporan spiritualities came from the continent of Africa.

Further, as mentioned earlier, the lack of context regarding African Diasporan religions fuels stereotypes about the alleged mindless, ignorant, superstitious actions of Black populations. Such stereotypes stem from the residue of historical devaluation of the beliefs of Indigenous and Black people. Such devaluation and dismissal were part of a damning pattern in European colonization that continues today.

> Few studies of the classic African diaspora present Africa as a place not just from which people departed, a memory, or a generalized entity, but as both a historic and present complex and diverse and changing continent whose peoples have participated in creating the world today.[19]

There are important links among African-born and Diasporan people, one of which is religion. Another link that can sometimes be masked but is always powerfully present is race.

Black People

Race is itself a constructed category that plays a divisive role among humans. One author made clear the roots of this manufactured controversy:

> Black people did not create themselves as a "race." Race is an ideology, not a biological reality. It arose at a particular time in history, for particular reasons, in an effort to resolve the contradiction of a freedom-loving society that held large parts of its population in bondage. The claim? That the enslaved were a different, lesser form of humanity. It was enslavers who deemed their African captives a "race."[20]

Race is not a biological reality, yet it has held tremendous power to shape global, social, and political realities. Racism and White privilege work hand in glove. As historian Robin D. G. Kelley claims, "Racism is not about how you look, it is about how people assign meaning to how you look."[21]

There is another important language shift across the Diaspora as many Black people are beginning to refer to themselves as melanated people. This is Diasporan-driven, referencing centuries of being dehumanized because of skin color in primarily White-controlled societies. The point of this shift has been to identify the skin as having melanin, rather than an old racially fraught identifier, changing how Black people assign meaning to themselves. Discussions of melanin were brought to the fore in the 1990s as psychiatrist Dr. Frances Cress Welsing published her theories about melanin in the book *The Isis Papers*.[22] Those who use the word today are not necessarily claiming to support Cress's melanin theories. Instead, the word can often be found in hip-hop lyrics, with the younger generation of melanated people leading the transformation.

Melanated also can cut through any sense of whose skin tone is darker, showing the connections between all who are deemed "Black" in the Diaspora. Melanin is also a genetic component of Brown, Native, and Indigenous people. This identifier can become a shared experience in conversations about oppression, rather than the term "people of color." Throughout this book, occasionally I will interchange the terms Black and melanated people, pointedly in conjunction with the Diaspora.

Additionally, racism assigns meanings to Black or African religions and spiritualities. As a result, race mixes with religion in strange ways.

Consider that religion, generally, aims to liberate and uplift people. Yet, the forms of religion that were preached to those Black captives centered on compliance, at best. Evelyn Brooks Higginbotham distinguished the pre- and post-Emancipation membership in Black Baptist churches. "With emancipation from slavery the freedpeople deserted the White-controlled churches that had previously commanded their membership ... No longer were blacks forced to hear sermons on obedience to White masters."[23] Black-owned and -operated Christian churches grew in the United States, with some work to establish missions on the African continent. To be clear, many of the churches and their outreach efforts were conflicted by their status in the United States: to seek separate status, to assimilate to the mores of the United States, or to view those on the continent through the eyes of White people in the United States.

These internal conflicts about being raced persons continued for decades. The theologian and preacher, Howard Thurman, stated this lack emphatically in 1949: "The masses of men live with their backs constantly against the wall. They are the poor, the disinherited, the dispossessed. What does our religion say to them? The issue is not what it counsels them to do for others ... but what religion offers to meet their own needs."[24] But in 1964, as other social movements were furthering Black religious thought, another Black preacher and theologian, Joseph R. Washington, found the idea of Black religion as simply a form of "folk" religion but not Christianity. It came from the experiences of being enslaved, he stated, a dysfunctional form of religion "born in polygamy:" "There is no Negro Protestantism, Negro Christianity, or Negro church."[25] While Thurman and Washington are from the United States, a similar tension can be found across the African Diaspora as people think about what their religion may mean for themselves and their communities.

One way to explain this tension within Black religions is identified by Evelyn Brooks Higginbotham when she refers to the "politics of respectability" based on the history of Black Baptist women's efforts after Emancipation to uplift their communities. "A politics of respectability ... equated public behavior with individual self-respect and with the advancement of African Americans as a group."[26] In this view, spirituality and forms of religion would be integral to the healing work of self-definition and liberation; therefore, a study of African and Diasporan religions will reflect some of the community's tensions.

The Journeys

This *Introduction* provides excursions into religions of the African Diaspora in three ways. First, the chapters that follow explore multiple definitions and characteristics of African religions and spiritualities. The chapters examine historical contexts, general features of most spiritualities, and some aspects of certain traditions, as well as the differences between what happens on the continent and in the Diaspora. Such differences make the mapping of these traditions complex and interesting.

Next, I draw from a variety of sources, deliberately including academics and practitioners, with an emphasis on the voices from the African continent and its Diaspora. In other words, there is a journey across the scholarship of the field, including historical, established, and newer thinkers. Historical thinkers raised questions and opened the field. Established academicians laid one set of paths to these studies that may or may not have aligned with understandings of traditional practitioners. Certainly, newer scholars bring unique modes of analyzing Africa, the Diaspora, and their spiritualities.

The third excursion is the most obvious: religions of the African Diaspora represent global phenomena. No single country or region owns these spiritualities, even as different cultures reshape beliefs and practices.

The process of thinking through the shapes of religions of Africa and its Diaspora begins with Chapter 1, which focuses on the Afrikan/African continent in the context of history and global relationships. The sixteenth century saw the sharpening of differences between the West and Africa, as well as the inhabitants of each. The name that we call the continent today provides a reminder of the differences. From a historical perspective, the name "Africa" is a European misspelling of a word derived from an African context; there is no letter "c" in many West African alphabets. The substitution of "c" for "k" occurs in European spellings of other words as well, such as "Congo" instead of "Kongo." So the first question this chapter tackles is what was Afrika before the arrival of Europeans? The fraught relationships between Africa and the West did not begin in the sixteenth century and I point to events of an earlier time: how might the eighth-century conquests of the Moors have shaped the understanding of "religion"? By the sixteenth century, new questions form: how did colonialism reshape understandings of Black religions and of Black people? How does colonialism, in its past or present form, continue to exert its influence?

Chapter 2 provides a general overview of African religions and spiritualities, elaborating on the characteristics introduced in this introduction. These culturally derived understandings, fueled by the growth of Pan-Africanism, began to center Black people's self-definitions on their own terms. Two twentieth-century African Diasporan religions originated in the United States with a similar focus: the Moorish Science Temple and the Pan-African Orthodox Christian Church. Around the same time, scholarship on ancient Egyptian religion and philosophy opened new doors to Kemetic studies. Thus, African Diasporan Religions (ADR) evolved again with a focus on the African Indigenous Religion (AIR) of Egypt.

Chapter 3 considers some general features of AIR but focuses primarily on the ADR Ausar Auset. Ausar Auset retrieved ancient Egyptian philosophies, reclaiming these traditions and adapting them to modern, Pan-African contexts. Chapter 4 highlights three Afrikan religions from the Afrikan West or West Central area: BaKongo, Ifá, and Vodun. These three are roughly from the current Republic of Congo, Nigeria, and Benin. These traditions were woven into the psyches of captured Africans and carried with them across the Atlantic. While these three were not the only Afrikan traditions that were conveyed into the Diaspora, they are highlighted because the influence on the development of other ADR was traceable.

No country or region parallels traditional Afrikan religious thought as closely as Brazil's Candomblé. Chapter 5 explores some aspects of this rich religious tradition within the context of Brazilian history and social structures. Thereafter, Chapter 6 turns to Vodun and Lucumí. Vodun developed in Haiti, and Lucumí in Cuba. They have shared histories through rebellion. Each played a significant role in the political life of their respective countries, particularly in independence movements.

Chapter 7 turns to African Diasporan spiritualities in the United States which, like other ADR, are reflected in Black people's sociopolitical realities. Hoodoo and Voodoo are the earliest ADR planted in the US. Other African spiritualities developed, thanks to music and dance with African philosophies that sought the "African God."

The conclusion to *Religions of the African Diaspora* builds upon the themes explored in previous chapters. It briefly explores the expanding parameters of the African Diaspora and the future forms of African spiritualities. Such a reflection on the meanings of Afrikan spiritualities throughout history to the present invites the reader to engage in further studies.

I offer this text as a starting point for readers, introducing them to some of the frameworks necessary to understand the complexities involved in studies of these lived and living religions. It is my hope that it becomes a doorway for further explorations of religions of the African Diaspora.

Notes

1. Cited in "Cuvier's History of Life," *Strange Science*, https://www.strangescience.net/cuvier.htm, accessed September 30, 2023.
2. Charles Darwin, *The Descent of Man and Selection in Relation to Sex* (London: John Murray, 1871).
3. Charles Darwin, *Journal of Researches into the Natural History and Geology of the Countries Visited during the Voyage of H.M.S. Beagle Round the World* (London: John Murray, 1860), http://darwin-online.org.uk/content/frameset?itemID=F20&viewtype=text&pageseq=1.
4. Ibid., 397.
5. Thornton Stringfellow, "A Scriptural View of Slavery," in *Slavery Defended: The Views of the Old South*, ed. Eric L. McKitrick (Englewood Cliffs: Prentice-Hall, Inc., 1963), 92–3.
6. Pew Research Center, "Black Americans' Experiences with News," September 2023, https://www.pewresearch.org/journalism/2023/09/26/black-americans-experiences-with-news/, 21.
7. Ibid., 23.
8. Martin G. Bernal, *Black Athena: The Afroasiatic Roots of Classical Civilization*, vols. 1–3 (New Brunswick, NJ: Rutgers University Press, 1987).
9. Carter G. Woodson, *The Mis-education of the Negro* (Trenton, NJ: Africa World Press, 1988), tenth printing, 137.
10. Ibid., 73.
11. Douglas Jacobsen and Rhonda Hustedt Jacobsen, *No Longer Invisible: Religion in University Education* (New York: Oxford University Press, 2012), 11.
12. Ibid., 13.

13 "The Catholic Church formally 'repudiates those concepts that fail to recognize the inherent human rights of Indigenous peoples, including what has become known as the legal and political "doctrine of discovery" . . . the church acknowledges that these papal bulls did not adequately reflect the equal dignity and rights of Indigenous peoples.'" Cited in Clay S. Jenkinson, "What the Repudiation of the Doctrine of Discovery Means for Indian Country," *Governing*, April 9, 2023, https://www.governing.com/context/what-the-repudiation-of-the-doctrine-of-discovery-means-for-indian-country#:~:text=On%20March%2030%2C%202023%2C%20Pope,discovered%20on%20behalf%20of%20Christendom.

14 Naomi Goldenberg, "The Religious is Political," in *The End of Religion: Feminist Appraisals of the State*, ed. Kathleen McPhillips and Naomi Goldenberg (New York: Routledge, 2021), 15.

15 David Walker, *Appeal in Four Articles to the Coloured Citizens of the World*, introduction by Sean Wilentz (New York: Hill and Wang, 1965, 1995), 39.

16 Ibid.

17 Rita Kiki Edozie with Glenn A. Chambers and Tama Hamilton-Wray, "Diasporas of the Blackworld: Re-sculpting Themes, Expanding Scopes, and Recreating Disciplinary Representations," in *New Frontiers in the Study of the Global African Diaspora: Between Uncharted Themes and Alternative Representations*, ed. Rita Kiki Edozie et al. (Lansing: Michigan State University Press, 2018), 5.

18 Paul E. Lovejoy, cited in "Diasporas of the Blackworld: Re-sculpting Themes, Expanding Scopes, and Recreating Disciplinary Representations," Rita Kiki Edozie et al, *New Frontiers in the Study of the Global African Diaspora: Between Uncharted Themes and Alternative Representations*, ed. by Rita Kiki Edozie, Glenn A. Chambers, and Tama Hamilton-Wray (Michigan State University Press, 2018), 9.

19 Rita Kiki Edozie, Glenn A. Chambers, and Tama Hamilton-Wray, "Diasporas of the Blackworld," in *New Frontiers*, 8.

20 Jamelle Bouie, "Black Like Kamala," *The New York Times*, August 14, 2020, https://www.nytimes.com/2020/08/14/opinion/kamala-harris-black-identity.html?smid=em-share, accessed January 12, 2022.

21 Robin D. G. Kelley, cited on "Race," a website created by the American Anthropological Association, https://understandingrace.org.

22 Frances Cress Welsing, *The Isis Papers: The Keys to Colors* (Chicago: Third World Press, 1991).

23 Evelyn Brooks Higginbotham, *Righteous Discontent, The Women's Movement in the Black Baptist Church, 1880–1920* (Cambridge: Harvard University Press, 1993), 53.
24 Walter Earl Fluker and Catherine Tumber, editors, *A Strange Freedom: The Best of Howard Thurman. On Religious Experience and Public Life* (Boston: Beacon Press, 1998), 133.
25 Joseph R. Washington Jr, "Folk Religion and Negro Congregations: The Fifth Religion," in *African American Religious Studies*, ed. Gayraud S. Wilmore (Durham: Duke University Press, 1989), 50.
26 Higginbotham, *Righteous Discontent*, 14.

1
Origin Stories

Chapter Outline

Introduction	21
Afrika Before Africa	22
Colonialism and Religions	31
On the Continent	36
Then the Diaspora	43

Eurocentric historians argue that Europe gave civilization to Africa, which is a complete inversion of the truth. The first civilized Europeans were the Greeks, who were chiefly civilized by the Africans of the Nile Valley. The Greeks transmitted this culture to the Romans, who finally lost it, bringing on a dark age of five hundred years. Civilization was restored to Europe when another group of Africans, the Moors, brought this dark age to an end, recivilizing the Christian barbarians of Europe. . . . Moorish monarchs dwelt in splendid palaces, while the crowned heads of England, France, and Germany lived in big barns, lacking both windows and chimneys, with only a hole in the roof for the emission of smoke.[1]

Introduction

The prefatory paragraph may give pause to an educated Western reader; we did not learn such history. Our current understandings of the continent known as Africa are complicated by layers of colonization, underreporting, politics, and misrepresentation. For example, in the

West today, an internet search for "travel to Africa" will return assorted sites that sell safaris. The sites include many photographs of animals and landscapes but very few photographs of African people. Changing the search term to "cultural tours in Africa" yields sites related primarily to Egypt and Morocco, replete with photos of landmarks, skylines, and grinning tourists. Again, images of African people are notably absent.

Throughout this book, I will sometimes spell the name of the continent "Afrika" because many Afrikan groups do not have the letter "c" in their alphabet. The different spellings keep us mindful that Africa may spell its name and see itself differently. A "k" instead of a "c" is deceptively minor; in fact, it signifies an extraordinarily complex history. This chapter excavates other differences that evolved collectively into scaffolding that undergirds current political and social realities. Narratives related to such differences represent "origin stories," sagas that continue to the present, that will be reflected in the developments throughout the following chapters.

This chapter addresses the ways in which Europe's general colonizing project omitted untold histories related to early Afrika from Western worldviews. The processes of rendering Afrikan lives invisible were inherent to Europe's general colonizing projects. Columbus's adventures in the late 1400s, funded by European royalty, were pivotal in mobilizing the hunt for resources from other people's lands. Columbus's work in the Mediterranean established a template for the West's engagement with the African continent and led to its expansion through the Partitioning of Africa in the 1800s. Colonialism instigated multiple shocks in Afrikan-Western relationships, and the effects are still evident today, particularly in the West's deep resistance to and misunderstanding of African spirituality and religiosity.

Afrika Before Africa

Most world history courses taught in the United States tend to highlight China as an ancient kingdom and brush by Africa in a rush to get to Greece and Rome. Egypt is the one exception in such courses, although it is seldom recognized as part of the continent of Africa. Indeed, references to Egypt as Middle Eastern divorce it from the continent altogether. Furthermore, ideas of kingdom and empire revolve primarily around stories of European royalty, with only a sprinkling of stories about Egyptian Pharaohs.

In world history classes with a Western perspective, Africa often has been referred to as the "dark continent" with people who had no written language and were stereotyped as primitive. The resultant skewed view of the world was evidenced in the mid-1970s when a skeleton named "Lucy," proven to be more than three million years old, was discovered in Ethiopia.[2] The Arizona State University Institute of Human Origins celebrated the fiftieth anniversary of this discovery in 2024: "A celebration of the extraordinary discovery of "Lucy," which provided the first documented proof that our human ancestors walked upright on two feet at least as early as 3.2 million years ago."[3] That the discovery of the skeleton was surprising reflects the dearth of information about the history of the African continent in the West.

The absence of information combined with misinformation created problems for achieving a clearer understanding of the world and its people. As historian Michael Gomez states in the starkest terms, world histories are generally united in the

> consistent omission, their collective silence on early and medieval Africa, of saying anything of substance about it, with the exception of Egypt, Nubia, and North Africa. West Africa is certainly left out of the narrative of early human endeavor, and only tends to be mentioned . . . in conjunction with European imperialism . . . none [of these histories] is invested in ongoing research in Africa, where developments have been considerable.[4]

Two examples of the missing histories make the case regarding developments that are seldom, if ever, referenced in Western world history classes.

The Kanuri people emerged as a distinct group in 3000 BCE in areas that today are called Nigeria, Niger, Chad, and Cameroon. The Kanuri or Kanem-Bornu Empire developed between the ninth and thirteenth centuries of the Common Era. Mai Humai, the first Saifawa king, converted to Islam during the eleventh century, which strengthened the growth and development of the Kanem-Bornu Empire. Islam became the foundation on which Mai Humai built the monarchy and established alliances with other groups, thereby strengthening the Empire's reach. African historian Isaac Samuel described the amount of land encompassed by the Empire: "At its height in the 13th century, the empire's influence extended over a broad swathe of territory stretching from southern Libya in the north to the border of the Nubian kingdoms in the east to the cities of the eastern bend of the Niger river in the west."[5]

The size of the empire necessitated new forms of organization and governance with Islamic identity, as shown in Isaac Samuel's description:

> According to al-Maqrizi (d. 1442) the armies of Kānem *"including cavalry, infantry, and porters, number 100,000."* The ruler of Kānem had many kings under his authority, and the influence of the empire was such that the political organisation of almost all the states in the lake Chad basin was directly or indirectly borrowed from it. While little is known of its internal organisation during this period, the development a fief-holding aristocracy, an extensive class of princes (*Maina*), appointed village headmen (*Bulama*), and a secular and religious bureaucracy with *Wazir, Khazin, Talib,* and *Qadis* that are known from Bornu and neighbouring states were likely established during the Kanem period.[6]

Mali provides another history of a legendary ruler who built an imperial presence across the continent of Africa. Mansa Musa succeeded to the Malian throne around 1312 CE. He intended to become a transcontinental power and undertook a fabled Pilgrimage to Egypt. With a retinue of thousands, he carried so much gold that the local Egyptians thought the Malian supply was inexhaustible.[7] Mansa Musa's Pilgrimage expanded the empire: "By means of his Islamic bona fides, Musa expanded Mali's spatial dimensions from the eastern Niger buckle to the Atlantic Ocean, uniting the Niger, Senegal, and Gambia valleys in unparalleled fashion."[8] The erasure of such histories ensures that twisted views about the African continent and its people continue.

Both the Mai Humai and Mansa Musa developed imperial structures that managed huge territories and diverse peoples. These are examples of established empires with distinctly African characteristics whose histories have been overshadowed by Western views of empire. As Gomez stated: "What unites world and imperial histories . . . is their consistent omission, their collective silence on early and medieval Africa, of saying anything of substance about it, with the exception of Egypt, Nubia, and North Africa. West Africa is certainly left out of the narrative of early human endeavor."[9] Despite such omission and silence, communities of Afrikan people were moving around the continent, establishing kingdoms while carrying their spiritualities and divinities with them, thus enabling both religious and political innovation. As a bridge to a closer examination of Afrikan religions, it is necessary to examine the forces that fueled the exclusions of Afrikan empires and religions.

Before Columbus

Shortly before the ascension of Mansa Musa, several foundations were laid that indelibly marked relationships between Afrika and Europe, especially through the fifteenth-century explorations of Christopher Columbus. Prior to Columbus's travels in 1492, significant portions of the Iberian Peninsula were conquered by Muslims from northern Morocco, beginning in CE 711.

> In 711, Tariq ibn Ziyad, the Berber conqueror of Al-Andalus, and his warriors landed at Gibraltar. Legend has it that the Prophet Muhammad appeared to Tariq as he slept onboard the vessel that carried him across the straits from the northern tip of Africa to the southern promontory of the Iberian Peninsula. The Prophet, leading a ghostly host of his companions from Mecca and Medina, armed with swords and bows, greeted Tariq and enjoined him to go forward in his mission. At the end of the voyage, Tariq awoke and told his men of the portentous dream.[10]

The battles to capture parts of the Peninsula were aided by building alliances where needed. For example, the Goths or Visigoths had held portions of the Peninsula and persecuted Jews. The Jews took the side of Tariq and "proved themselves staunch allies of the Moslems in the campaign, and . . . afterwards enjoyed great consideration at the hands of the conquerors. The Moors admitted them to their intimacy."[11] Thus, they utilized these alliances to capture and hold significant portions of the Peninsula.

The Moors, also called Berbers, refer to themselves as the Amazigh. The Amazigh and other African Muslim groups that arrived in subsequent years expanded their rule through much of the Iberian Peninsula, bringing new social and cultural structures. The land was called Al-Andalus. During the centuries that the Muslims held power, several Caliphates or states were established across Al-Andalus. Trade with eastern lands, including India, became possible because the Africans had already established land and water routes to the east of Spain. Nonetheless, while there were tremendous social benefits, there were also stresses.

In every case, the conquered population posed challenges not only for security and administration but also for political ideology, social status, and religious identity, and not only in the immediate postconquest era but also throughout the history of the regime. Political and religious leaders and local communities of Christians, Muslims, and Jews continuously adapted to shifts in political, economic, social, and cultural conditions in ways that, in turn, affected intercommunal relations.[12]

Over a period of nearly 800 years, from the time that Northern Africans invaded and held portions of the Iberian Peninsula until the time of Columbus in the Mediterranean, religion was firmly established as a political tool and a weapon. Religious pressure from northern Spain was integral to that tension as the Spanish rulers fought to drive out the Muslims: "The medieval expansion of northern Christian societies at the expense of Al-Andalus was driven by non-centralised political orders which operated under the rule of monarchies whose authority and scope were only partial. The dynastic pretensions of kings were subordinated to the task of conquering, the legitimacy of which was conferred by the Church."[13]

Jews, Muslims, and Christians who lived in Al-Andalus often found ways to coexist and benefit one another despite the tension. New products were made available to Spain from various parts of the world, including spices, cloth, and oils. New forms of architecture and art were introduced to Spain, many of which remain in place today. Science and philosophy crossed religious lines. Astronomy was one area where the scientific meeting of the minds could be seen, as Bernard Goldstein pointed out: "Astronomy was a neutral meeting ground for scholars who were sharply divided on religious questions. The practice of holding scholarly meetings among participants of different religious commitments began in Baghdad in the ninth and tenth centuries. . . . However, later in the Middle Ages, such encounters rarely took place except in the Iberian Peninsula."[14] One of the greatest philosophers of that age came from Al-Andalus: "The Andalusian philosopher Ibn Rushd or Averroes (c. 1126–1198) has long enjoyed a reputation as a rationalist thinker of the classical Arabic tradition, a view held by his few readers in the Arabic tradition as well as by readers in the Latin West."[15] Large portions of the architecture, art, science, and philosophy that developed during this period have influenced Western intellectual history, even if the Afrikan sources are not recognized.

Unfortunately, the Africans' rule was sometimes destabilized by internal struggles and ongoing battles with Spanish rulers who sought to claim the entire Peninsula. By 1492, northern Spain had succeeded in driving out the Muslims, with their structures still standing. Among the many visible remnants of the Muslim presence is the castle of Alhambra. It was originally built as a fortress in the eighth century because of its strategic location and gradually expanded into interconnected buildings with distinctive Muslim architecture and design.[16]

This is significant because those who conquer an area often will tear down the structures of the defeated. Not so with the Alhambra: Isabella and Ferdinand moved into the luxurious palaces and began expansions. Subsequent Spanish royals held court there.

But the acceptance of a people's property and artwork is not the same as acceptance of the people themselves. At the urging of the pope, the brutal religious purity and reclamation process called the Inquisition was expanded. Both Jews and Muslims were targeted for expulsion, torture, or

Figure 1.1 Alhambra, Granada, Spain, photo courtesy of Stephanie Mitchem.

execution unless they converted to Catholicism. Religion was central to the Europeans' understanding of power over other people.

The absence of African connections and the need to build dynasties led Queen Isabella and King Ferdinand of Spain to consider their options. They sought to establish trade routes to India, lured by the promise of riches, particularly gold, in other lands. Christopher Columbus had bounced between Portugal and Spain for over a year, trying to find funding for an expedition to India. Columbus believed that by traveling west, he would eventually arrive in India, thereby avoiding the African routes to the east. Isabella and Ferdinand agreed to fund Columbus's expedition as an investment in new streams of wealth.

Columbus and the Ongoing Aftermath

"In 1492, Columbus sailed the ocean blue," a children's rhyme rings out. What the rhyme does not capture is that Columbus did not find what he sought. That is, he was seeking India or China, and as mentioned earlier, he believed that by traveling west, he would end up in the east; he died believing he had achieved his goal. This explains why, when he and his ships landed in the Caribbean, he called the people he encountered "Indians."

Columbus was not the first European to travel to other lands and deem the people he encountered "barbarians" and "savages." Such ideas were well-documented and firmly established in Europeans' minds through the accounts of various explorers. Columbus reported his "discoveries" in a letter:

> Of all I have taken possession for their Highnesses by proclamation and display of the Royal Standard without opposition. To the first island I discovered I gave the name of San Salvador, in commemoration of His Divine Majesty, who has wonderfully granted all this. The Indians call it Guanaham. The second I named the Island of Santa Maria de Concepcion; the third, Fernandina; the fourth, Isabella; the fifth, Juana; and thus to each one I gave a new name.[17]

The name of the land according to the people, Guanaham, was ignored by Columbus which he renamed San Salvador. Renaming is itself a form of claiming. Columbus also named the people themselves, referring to them as "Indians." In the same letter, he defined some of the Indigenous people as simple-minded because they had minimally defended themselves when the Europeans landed, and they did not resist the claiming through the "display of the Royal Standard." Columbus describes how he

> Gave a thousand good and pretty things that I had to win their love, and to induce them to become Christians, and to love and serve their Highnesses and the whole Castilian nation, and help to get for us things they have in abundance, which are necessary to us. They have no religion nor idolatry, except that they all believe power and goodness to be in heaven. They firmly believed that I, with my ships and men, came from heaven, and with this idea I have been received everywhere, since they lost fear of me.[18]

Columbus planned to give them "good and pretty things" to gain their trust and then persuade them to become Christians and "serve" the Spanish monarchy. Columbus defined the indigens as "having no religion," yet claimed they believed he and his men had "come from heaven," a place of power and goodness. Columbus's statements were contradictory; people without spiritual belief do not have concepts of heaven.

However, Columbus's objective was not to find out what the people believed. Indeed, his gift-giving was evidence of his failure to consider the recipients' cultural values regarding giving and receiving. The "pretty things" Columbus and his men handed out meant little to them. The use of such baubles was consistent with Columbus's strategies on earlier journeys when he "had observed how pleased barbarians were with trinkets on which civilized Europeans set small value, such as the little bells that falconers placed on hawks. Before setting off on his voyage, he laid in a store of hawk's bells."[19] Columbus's effort to manipulate the people he called "Indians" by giving them trinkets is evidence of his belief that they lacked the intelligence to recognize his tactics for what they were.

The Europeans did not see the indigenous people they encountered as human, as having values, as having intelligence. There is a pathological cultural deception masked as logic, from the perspectives of the European adventurers, that they had a right to rename and claim the people and the lands. As Edward Morgan stated, "The New World did not replace the Old." Rather, Morgan continued, the "Old determined what men saw in the world and what they did with it."[20] Further, it was important for the "Old World" or Europeans to make these determinations, which would, in turn, allow them to define themselves not only as more powerful and important but also as higher on the scale of humanity than those in the lands they sought to colonize. Why did they do so? Because their God, they said, decreed it. The perceived superiority of Christianity was affirmed and underlined by papal proclamations. In the same logic chain, it follows that the Europeans would be the ones to define the people they met, extract their resources, and claim "ownership" of the lands and the resources within.

The concept of private ownership of land, resources, and other humans was not new, but it was developed in novel ways between 1500 and 1800. Two factors catalyzed this concept: the development of secular national governments and the Industrial Revolution. Nations separated from religious control and required funds to operate; the Industrial Revolution brought the bourgeoisie into prominence in both political and social spheres. Private ownership came to be enshrined in European and American philosophy, religion, and law.

Indigenous people themselves had other ideas of ownership and land use. These views were different from those of the Europeans in the Caribbean and in Afrika. In Afrika, "kingdoms flourished on the continent and people lived in harmony with their environment in a cultural and spiritual relationship that held up a picture of sustainability that appears alien and exotic in today's world."[21] The different understandings of owning and personal property were stark divisions between the conceptualizations and cultures of indigenous peoples and the West.

For Europeans, Christianity confirmed the righteousness of their claim to the land. Hispaniola was a starting point that continued through the centuries of colonization.

> Invaders conned the continent (of Africa) with a Bible in one hand and a musket in the other . . . While we will not belabour that analysis, it is nevertheless important to note that by the nineteenth century, there was a convergence of thought in Europe that sought to proclaim the conquest of territories as a matter that was inevitable and God-given.[22]

The ideas that Columbus carried were part of his national culture; he did not invent these notions of conquest, religion, and superiority. Centuries of turmoil on the Iberian Peninsula added to the European identity crises of the fifteenth century. Columbus gathered related ideas and employed them to characterize explorations of the world he called "new." This is clearly seen in the treatment of the Indigenous people, the first small group brought back as "slaves" by Columbus. Such oppressive treatment of the indigenous people was expanded on the islands by governors who replaced Columbus:

> If we may believe Bartolomé de Las Casas, a Dominican priest who spent many years among them, they [the Indigenous people] were tortured, burned, and fed to the dogs by their masters. They died from overwork and from new European diseases. They killed themselves. And they took pains to avoid having children. Life was not fit to live, and they stopped living. From a population of 100,000 at the lowest estimate in 1492, there remained in 1514 about 32,000 Arawaks in Española. By 1542, according to Las Casas, only 200 were left. In their place had appeared slaves imported from Africa. The people of the golden age had been virtually exterminated.[23]

Although the concept of "race" had not yet been clearly formulated in the fifteenth century, the seeds of defining non-Europeans as "barbarians" and "savages" had been planted, becoming the groundwork for later constructions of racial categories.

While enslavement existed throughout the medieval world and on the African continent, its form was not the same as what would come from the Europeans. That is, "[a]lthough there was internal slavery in African societies, this phenomenon had never formed the basis of the social system, and there was often social mobility within this structure. These were not 'slaves' in the European sense in which human beings totally lost their freedom."[24] The European establishment of slavery, framed by the chattel principle, redefined people who were not White and European as subhuman and their cultures as inferior. Underlining these constructions were the forces of colonialism and religion.

Colonialism and Religions

Columbus, a citizen of his time, understood his Catholic religion as a central aspect of his life. Roman Catholicism believed in God-granted power over all earthly government. Therefore, Isabella, Ferdinand, or any other Catholic ruler had to be approved and crowned by the pope to be granted authority. Religion became a greater factor when northern Afrikans' religion, Islam, upset the Europeans' sense of self as they conquered major portions of the Iberian Peninsula, beginning in 711 CE. Islam and Judaism were viewed as heretical and became markers of Catholic rights and superiority. Jews in northern Spain had suffered persecution for a hundred years before the Inquisition formally began in 1478 under the direction of one pope. Ferdinand and Isabella, as rulers of Castile and Aragon, expanded the Inquisition in 1492 after the defeat of the last of the Andalusian Caliphates. Columbus would have seen persecutions and the Inquisition as evidence of his view of the world.

The Inquisition was considered holy and was used to drive out those decreed heretics using inhumane brutality. Jews were told that they had to depart Spain the morning after they were given a notice to leave. As an option, they could choose to convert to Catholicism. If they did not leave or convert, they would face torture and execution. Some Muslims were granted exemptions to maintain the buildings they had constructed; otherwise, they were also required to leave. The Inquisition was controlled by a religious order that the pope granted power, authorizing the extraction of confessions from those who were not suitably devout Catholics. The rationale in religious terms was that Catholicism was the one true religion, and everything else was evil. Simultaneously, controlling populations and silencing political opposition were effective methods for maintaining governmental control, which the rulers of European countries employed. The Inquisition was carried to some later-established colonies, including Peru, Mexico, Panama, Bolivia, and Ecuador.

Columbus reflected this religiously superior mindset, which was apparent in a letter he wrote after his first voyage: "Our Redeemer has given victory to our most illustrious King and Queen, and to their kingdoms rendered famous by this glorious event, at which all Christendom should rejoice . . . with fervent prayers for the high distinction that will accrue to them from turning so many peoples to our holy faith."[25] Religion had already been a tense and conflict-ridden topic throughout the centuries in Al-Andalus; after 1492, it became a weapon.

When Columbus returned with stories of potential profit and a few "Indians," Pope Alexander VI gave a blessing, proclaiming the first document of discovery, which granted authority for continued conquest and control.

> By the authority of Almighty God conferred upon us in blessed Peter and of the vicarship of Jesus Christ, which we hold on earth, do . . . give, grant, and assign to you and your heirs and successors, kings of Castile and Leon, forever, together with all their dominions, cities, camps, places, and

villages, and all rights, jurisdictions, and appurtenances, all islands and mainlands found and to be found, discovered, and to be discovered towards the west and south. . . . in the direction of India or towards any other quarter.[26]

Alexander was the first but would not be the last pope to write a document of discovery.

In their travels to other lands, Europeans were both fascinated and horrified by the dress of the Indigenous people they encountered. As one scholar emphasized, body reading remains constitutive of Western thought: "The reason that the body has so much presence in the West is that the world is primarily perceived by sight. The differentiation of human bodies in terms of sex, skin color, and cranium size is a testament to the powers of 'seeing.' The gaze is an invitation to differentiate."[27] Nakedness was viewed as signs of ignorance, of bestiality, and of low morals. The natives needed baptism, and they needed European-style clothes. So, Indigenous people in hot climates were stuffed into wool suits and corsets and forced to become Christian, even as their lands were taken. The Christian gospel includes a directive to "Go and make disciples of all nations" (Mt 28:19). In this scripture, the word "make" becomes vindictive. Christianity in the Inquisition, the Doctrine of Discovery, and colonization, with all forms of oppression, had strayed far from the visions presented by Jesus.

The Protestant Reformation, which began in the 1500s, aimed to correct the abuses within the Catholic Church's internal structure and certain aspects of its theology. However, the need to control others who were not of the same religion and the need to use religion as a tool of colonization continued. Accordingly, "The worldview of the Pilgrims and the Puritans was profoundly shaped by the dominant European perspective . . . There arose a narrative of European supremacy. The Doctrine of Discovery provided a theological foundation for the assertion of White superiority."[28]

Colonizing Lands, Colonizing People

Conquest meant division and disunity across the continent [of Africa]. Conquest meant the splintering of nations and kingdoms into different blocs;

it meant the amalgamation of disparate units into new wholes in a tensile state that promised no peace. Conquest and division laid prostrate vast civilisations in Africa, the Americas and Asia, siphoning off resources to fuel the industrial revolution in Europe.[29]

Christopher Columbus's tomb in Spain is inside the Seville Cathedral. It is marked by a life-sized sculpture with four Spanish kings carrying Columbus's casket. The kings from Aragon and Castile are in the front, their heads held high with pride because they had funded Columbus's travels. The kings from Navarre and Leon hold the rear of the casket. Their heads are lowered, ashamed at not having funded the trips and, by extension, not reaping the rewards of colonization. The Age of Colonization had begun in earnest, and Africa moved up on the Europeans' lists.

Columbus went west to arrive in the east, landing in the Caribbean in 1492, but seventy years earlier, Portuguese explorers had traveled south. They were attempting to reach India and its fabled riches by circumnavigating the African continent. Portugal primarily explored the western coast of Africa and some of the islands they happened upon. However, when Pope Alexander VI (who was Spanish) granted Spain control of all non-Christian lands, Portugal was upset. They held a declaration from an earlier pope that granted them additional rights to land, which Alexander's declaration subsequently overturned. Despite their efforts, Pope Alexander VI would not change his decree. So, Portugal entered into the Treaty of Tordesillas with Spain in 1494, dividing the world between the two countries and contravening the papal document. This treaty represents a practice that would become normalized, where Europeans "divide" and claim the lands of other peoples, globalizing colonization.

The patterns for colonialism were laid. The components that developed from Columbus's travels and the Doctrine of Discovery included: negatively defining natives' cultures; renaming Indigenous people; claiming ownership and exclusive use of the lands; and defining Europeans as White and superior. Treaties among Europeans, such as the Treaty of Tordesillas, for lands that were not theirs, were backed up with many forms of violence, which was exemplified by the gradual extermination of the people that Columbus initially encountered. Christian religions, beginning with Catholicism and later different Protestant sects, became tools that reinforced these ideas. All those who were not Christian were defined as heretical and, therefore, evil or criminal. The same tool, religion, has been used as a justification for destruction with the excuse, at least we brought you Christianity.

Whether on the continent of Afrika or in the Diaspora, the Africans' senses of self were disrupted as they were defined by adherents to the Doctrine of Discovery. Their split-screen stories are two sides of the same coin: interconnected, globalized colonization. The sociopolitical and religious impacts of colonization on both the African continent and in its Diaspora indicate there were other complications when Black people from across the globe aimed to reconnect with their heritages. Descendants of forcibly exported Africans may hold utopian images of Africa that may not match the realities on the ground; media portrayals of Black Americans may give those on the continent stereotypical expectations that are lumped in with White Americans. Yet, neither Africans nor those in the Diaspora have benefited from all the disruptions of Africans' sense of self: the colonizers were the beneficiaries. (See Figures 1.2 and 1.3.)

Two questions invite exploration. What became of Afrika with colonization? How did colonization shape the Diaspora?

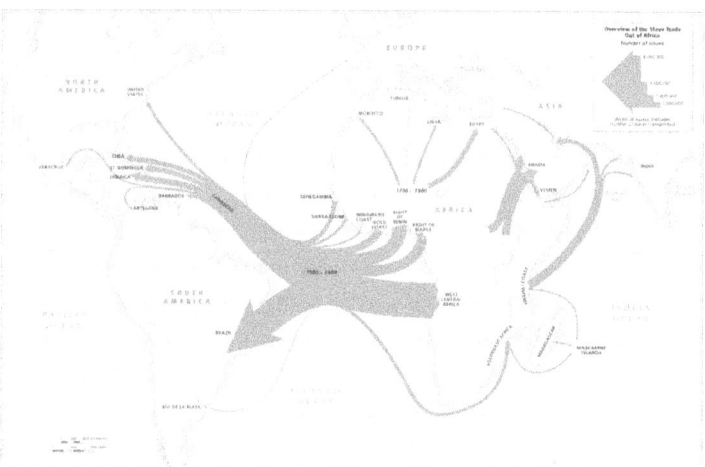

Figure 1.2 Map of trafficked Africans' routes, © Yale University Press, reprinted with permission.

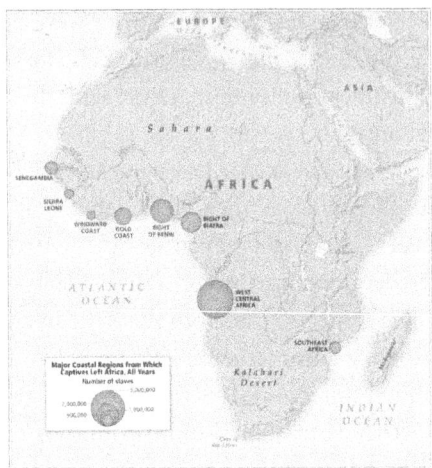

Figure 1.3 Major African coastal areas for the transportation of Africans, © Yale University Press, reprinted with permission.

On the Continent

> By the end of the fifteenth century, Portuguese merchants and soldiers had established outposts along four thousand miles of the West Coast of Africa, where they traded for slaves to be exported to sugar- and wine-producing lands off the coast. The Portuguese were shortly followed to Africa by the other imperial powers of Europe: the Spanish in the sixteenth century, the Dutch, Danes, French, and English in the seventeenth.[30]

The European countries that invaded and conquered most of Afrika imposed their own sociopolitical cultures on the people who were there. In the process of imposing European systems of living and thinking, all things that reflected Afrikan culture and thinking were dismissed as primitive or savage. These negative views, of course, included Afrikan religions. A form of benevolent patriarchalism became the whitewash for the brutality of colonization in an effort to make it seem as if all was done for the Africans' own good.

Complex political structures spanning multiple European nationalities and Afrikan states arose: "National boundaries were drawn arbitrarily, sometimes using a ruler rather than knowledge of ethnic national affinities on the ground. Not that that would have mattered much to the conquerors, whose sole aim was unfettered access to resources needed by the capitals of Europe."³¹ The processes of colonization were not easy and continued through the twentieth century.

Some people resisted colonization whenever they could. The stories of those who resisted are seldom told. The story of one effort to resist colonization helps bring such hidden histories of resistance into focus.

Born in 1830 to a religious family, Lalla Fatma N'Soumer led resistance against the French incursion into Algeria. In 1854, she and her brother, Tahar, enrolled fighters for *Imseblen*, a warrior group in the Algerian region of Kabylia. One French author described these fighters as heroic but demonstrated his own religious bias as he explained "that Tahar was in charge of enrolling these fighters, whereas Lalla Fatma knew how to exalt the Kabyles' religious bigotry and patriotism and make them determined to lead a desperate resistance."³²

Eventually, Tahar was captured, but Lalla and her troops fought on. While we know few of her actual words today, we have this brief excerpt as she was captured and questioned by the French commander:

> Randon had asked why her men shot the French troops, breaking the convention (i.e., the surrender) made by her brother. She answered: "*God wanted it. It is neither your fault, nor mine. Your soldiers went out of their ranks to penetrate my village. Mine defended themselves. I'm now your captive. I have no reproach to you. You shouldn't make any reproach to me. It was written this way!*"³³

Throughout the history of European and American colonialism, there has been resistance of one kind or another. This one instance in Algeria was not an outlier; there have been many attempts to resist and rebel against external control and oppression. The problem has been the jurists and historians who have written and silenced the stories that went against the European colonization processes. Only a few words of Lalla Fatma are known, which demonstrates how the narratives were controlled during the colonization of the continent.

Colonization continued across the African continent into the twentieth century. In the fifteenth century, Europeans sought resources, transporting people and raw goods to build their own countries. But the extraction process was just the beginning. The militaries of various countries established outposts at various strategic ports that provided water routes to their own countries as well as to the interior. These military posts were significant to begin establishing a given country's occupation of African lands.

By 1884, thirty years after Lalla N'Soumer and nearly 400 after the Treaty of Tordesillas, the Partitioning of Africa began with the Berlin Conference. There is a famous cartoon of that time with the German chancellor carving up a cake called Africa among the multiple countries that attended the conference. But partitioning was not as simple as cutting a cake. It took years for the actual carving to be completed.

Trading companies that were authorized by European countries began to control the gathering and importation of resources and people. These companies included: the Royal African Company; the Dutch East India Company; and the Royal Niger Company. These companies were not limited to importation and exportation; the extent of the Royal Niger Company's power provides an example. Working in northern Nigeria, the company was granted a royal charter in 1886.

> The British government in essence shifted the expenses and responsibility for the area to the company. In other words, the company was now placed in a position to exercise sovereignty on behalf of the British government. Thus the company at once established the usual government service courts of justice and an armed constabulary; customs duties and trade licenses were imposed to provide the funds necessary for administration.[34]

With the involvement of multiple European countries, there is no single story about the colonization of the continent. European countries began to withdraw after World War II as their own interrelationships shifted, even as they signed treaties with the new African countries that guaranteed the Europeans' continued control. The first African president of an independent Ghana was Kwame Nkrumah, who assumed office in 1957. His writings shine a harsh light on the impact of colonization.

President Nkrumah was a scholar and politician who gave testimony to the devastation of colonization on the continent. It did not matter, he said, if the colonizers were the French, British, or from another country, as if one country provides better "masters . . . as though there is virtue in the degree to which slavery is enforced." Only those who had never experienced "the miseries and degradation of colonialist suppression and exploitation"[35] could be "apologists for the colonialism of their own county, anxious out of jingoistic patriotism to make a case for it."[36]

Instead, the colonizers took everything and left nothing. As the president of a newly "liberated" country, Nkrumah outlined what was left in Ghana:

> It was when they had gone and we were faced with stark realities, that the destitution of our land after long years of colonial rule was brought sharply home to us. There were slums and squalor in our towns, superstitions and ancient rites in our villages. All over the country, great tracts of open land lay untilled and uninhabited, while nutritional diseases were rife among our people. Our roads were meagre, our railways short. . . . over eighty percent of our people were illiterate, and *our existing schools were fed on imperialist pap, completely unrelated to our background and our needs. Trade and commerce were controlled, directed, and run almost entirely by Europeans.* (emphasis mine)[37]

As this excerpt indicates, the withdrawal of Europeans was not a true departure. Representatives from these countries might have left, but they still retained significant control. The Europeans often controlled the extraction of a region's cocoa, minerals, or oil, and because there are few refineries on the continent, they controlled the exportation of raw materials. European companies owned the rights for extraction and exportation, aided by exclusive rights agreements signed by leaders of the old and new countries.

These acts and agreements set the stage for the postcolonial or neocolonial period, which is currently unfolding. While the old colonizers have retained their hold, new national players entered the race for African riches: Russia, China, and Saudi Arabia. What have colonization and neocolonization meant for traditional African spiritualities and religions? Religion, specifically Christianity, has been an integral component of Western colonization.

Papal decrees granted Europeans authority to claim any non-Christian lands, peoples, and resources, beginning in the fifteenth century. From the seventeenth century, Protestant countries continued to claim Christian superiority. Christianity was tied, in various degrees, to the governance and politics of each European nation. The political uses of Christianity for control and dominance were applied in various ways across all colonized lands, despite the good intentions of some clerics and missionaries. Christianity was used in myriad ways to establish colonial control, but I highlight only one here, and that is the impact of Christian missionaries.

African Mission Work

Christian missionaries were on board many of the exploration and enslavement vessels, often for the benefit of the sailors and sometimes for their own enrichment. A few of the extant records of the explorations and encounters with new populations were written by the first European missionaries. Some of the missionaries' reports on the brutalities of the human trade may have contributed to the slow growth of abolition movements.

The British Committee for the Abolition of the Slave Trade began in 1787.[38] The website of the Parliament of the United Kingdom states that "the Act of Parliament to abolish the British slave trade, passed on 25 March 1807, was the culmination of one of the first and most successful public campaigns in history."[39] The United States also ended the forced exportation of Africans that same year. Other nations slowly followed the legal abolition of the trade. African human trafficking from the continent began to slow, but it did not end. Illegal trading continued, especially for Portuguese and Spanish colonies. Britain, among other countries, had a fleet dedicated to enforcing the end of the human trade. Some decades later, arguing for extensive Christian evangelization throughout Africa, Sir Thomas Fowell Buxton wrote a book presented to Queen Victoria in 1840, which argued that human trafficking was a barrier to the spread of the gospel. If the trade ended, he contended, "Africa would present the finest field for the labors of the Christian Missionaries which the world has yet to see opened to them. I have no hesitation in stating my belief that there is in the negro race of capacity for receiving the truths of the Gospel beyond most other heathen nations."[40] Buxton's words represented a wider political push during his time to end any form of human trafficking from Africa and simultaneously and aggressively evangelize.

One of the Africans captured for illegal transport was thirteen-year-old Ajayi from Osogun in Nigeria. He was being transported by Portuguese traders when "his ship was intercepted by the British navy's anti-slave patrol and the slaves were liberated in Sierra Leone. There he became a Christian, taking at baptism the name of an eminent clergyman in England, Samuel Crowther." During this time, Crowther studied at an institution that trained Africans to serve as missionaries, eventually traveling to London to pursue ordination in the Anglican Church. He was also part of one Thomas Fowell Buxton's missions to Niger.[41]

Sierra Leone was an important outpost for British anti-trafficking efforts: the patrols would stop a transport, remove the captives, and drop them off in Freeport, Sierra Leone. Many liberated captives became Christians and had opportunities for Western education as the British had established schools. After being "saved" from enslavement, the attraction to Christianity and Western ideas was powerful. To clarify, however, Europeans did not introduce Christianity to the African continent. It had been in Ethiopia, among other locations, since the fourth century; this Christianity was very different from the religion of the colonizers.

In the colonized world, converted Africans such as Crowther became significant missionaries on behalf of various European countries, interpreting African cultures for the colonizers and representing new cultural ways to the indigenous communities. The missionaries' interpretations included translations to other languages while judging Afrikan religious concepts relative to European Christian beliefs. In 1845, Crowther was sent to Nigeria for mission work. With other African missionaries from Sierra Leone, they saw to "the construction of the Mission House, a sort of prefabricated house brought from Sierra Leone in bits . . . believed to be the first storey house in the Nigerian area."[42] That house is still standing in Badagry, Nigeria.

Crowther is notably known for translating the Bible into the Yoruba language, and in the process, misrepresenting aspects of traditional religion. For example, he claimed that the deity Èsù is often equated with the devil. However, the concept of Èsù is not translatable into English, and, like the house, Crowther's misrepresentation still holds validity for some. Eventually, Crowther himself was removed from that mission. Being Christian could not resolve racism.

Indeed, "[t]he racist treatment he [Crowther] was subjected to during his last days with the Niger Mission turned out to be counterproductive to the interests of the CMS. It radicalized young West African clerics toward the formation of independent congregations."[43] Buxton was part of a larger movement in Britain to evangelize the African continent, and Crowther was one of the native missionaries who made Buxton's dream become a reality. However, if these ideas had been in opposition to the colonization projects, they would not have been supported by the British government. Most of the colonizing countries found benefit in proselytizing among the African populations, or it would have been terminated. When the 1884 Berlin Conference concluded, the participating countries signed a document that outlined the extent of their cooperation with each other. Religion was given a role in Article 6: "Christian missionaries, scientists and explorers, with their followers, property and collections, shall likewise be objects for especial protection."[44] The Article identified mythical patriarchal religious benevolence to their colonizing efforts, promising religious freedom and agreeing to:

> watch over the preservation of the native tribes, and to care for the improvements of the conditions of their moral and material well-being, and to help suppressing slavery . . . [and] protect and favour all religious, scientific or charitable institutions and undertaking created and organized for the above ends, or which aim at instructing the natives and bring home to them the blessings of civilization.[45]

From Thomas Buxton to Samuel Crowther to the blessing of the Berlin Conference signers and many others, Christianity was incorporated as a method to establish the dominance of Western ways. This does not mean that any of these mission groups held sinister intentions; rather, the use of Christianity continued patterns of thinking that began in 711 CE as religions became politicized to promote the superiority of one culture over another culture and the purported blessings of Western civilization. Western cultures continue to influence African societies. The pursuit of European standards and lifestyles at all costs consumes many people. Some reject traditional healing or health practices as unsophisticated. Many women use hair straightening or skin lightening products to adopt European standards of beauty. While traditional African spiritualities might be rejected, aspects such as drumming have been integrated into African Christian practices.

Despite these strands of African societies, commitments to traditional cultures remain alive and active. They are not remnants. Traditional spiritualities still inform people's cultural perspectives. According to Thaddeus Mets and Motsamai Molefe, "some of the major philosophical tenets of Traditional African Religion. . . continue to be accepted by hundreds of millions of people in Africa."[46] Acceptance is not always a rejection of other religious ideas. Indigenous religions are culturally based and tied to family history and memory. However, they sometimes operate according to different definitions. When traditional spiritualities conflict with Western ideologies, it causes inner conflict in some people.

Malidoma Patrice Somé (1956–2021), for instance, gained insight into the tensions between two worlds when he adopted traditional spirituality.

As a child, Somé witnessed his community's spirituality in Burkina Faso. As a college student at a Western university, he wrote of the two worldviews: "I, a college student, continued to be more interested in what was going on in the minds of my elders than in the ideas propagated in the university classrooms. Was it because the more I grasped of the modern world, the more the traditional cried out to be known?"[47] Yet, he could also recognize that one world aided in comprehending the other. Somé recognized that he was "sealed off from my fellow students, who were all trying desperately to become nontraditional people. How often I grieved to hear unjust and ignorant comments aimed at village life! . . . most of the young men and women were confused: they were neither Westernized nor traditionalized."[48]

Somé chose to pursue the grueling process of initiation into the traditional spirituality but still experienced the split between worlds. "My enduring passion for magic, rituals, and ceremonies reassured me that the traditional world has swallowed me and that I was resisting the White world—or maybe I had grown to be a man trapped between the White and the traditional worlds."[49]

Whether Somé's personal experiences balancing his Afrikan spirituality with his Western education or President Nkrumah's analysis of the European controls on a continent, the impacts of colonization on the children of Afrika continue.

Then, the Diaspora . . .

In Everlasting Memory
Of the anguish of our ancestors.
May those who died rest in peace.
May those who return find their roots.
May humanity never again perpetrate such injustice against humanity.
We, the living, vow to uphold this.
        (Plaque at the Slave Castle, Elmina, Ghana)

Certain sites along the West African coast mark places of no return. These were ports where ships collected Africans who would be enslaved in European or American colonies, creating sites that have been called "The Door of No Return." For instance, on one island off the coast of Badagry, Nigeria, a sign marks the place where the Spirit Attenuation Well stood. Captured Africans were forced to drink from this well before being loaded

Figure 1.4 Site of Spirit Attenuation Well, Badgary, Nigeria, photo courtesy of Stephanie Mitchem.

onto ships. They were told that the water from this well would erase their memories of who they had been.

Many history books include details about the trafficking of Africans, such as the number and types of ethnic groups, the points of departure and arrival, and the cruel methods of transportation. Accordingly, that information does not need to be repeated here. Instead, this study addresses the long-term impact of enslavement on the people who were captured. People often equate the legal end of transportation or enslavement with the end of the "problem," but this view is misguided. The Spirit Attenuation Well is evidence that the aim of human trafficking was not simply a legalistic creation of a category, but a deeper attempt to construct groups of humans who accepted enslavement and dehumanization as their natural state. The Spirit Attenuation Well was symbolic of a much larger pattern of capturing Africans for forced labor.

African and New World lands and resources were claimed and renamed by Europe first and, later, by the United States, thus continuing Columbus's and the Doctrine of Discovery's patterns. Two other aspects of this colonizing template were employed to maintain power and profits. The first aspect involved claiming the importance of the role of Christians in "civilizing" Africans:

> The so-called master-race believed that an extension of their humanitarianism was to help the so-called barbarians grow up in their Eurocentric image, indoctrinating them in their worldview, texts, and languages. . . . People of African descent were forcibly alienated from the most basic norms of everyday life, owning nothing because they themselves were owned. Christian expansionists concluded that they not only had the right but a vocational responsibility to colonize the lands, bodies, labor, and minds of the rest of the world.[50]

Initially, there was resistance to bring Africans into Christianity because if they were baptized, it would be necessary to free them. To counter this risk, early in the development of American colonies, laws were written ensuring that Christian enslaved people were ineligible for manumission. A 1619 Virginia law clarified that enslavement did not end with "a conversion to Christianity."[51] Other colonies followed suit:

> By 1706 . . . legislation in at least six colonies declar[ed] that an enslaved person's baptism did not entail their freedom. In addition, many enslaved people who *did* become Christians had to deal with restrictions by masters who forbade them from attending church or prayer meetings. To get around these restrictions, and for alternatives to sermons by White clergy asking them to obey their owners, many Christian enslaved people held secret services with distinctive styles of praying, singing, and worship.[52]

These distinctive styles held remnants of Afrikan cultures, even as different ethnic groups were pressed together under enslavement. Sterling Stuckey defined the ring shout, a significant retention of African spiritual life: "Wherever in Africa the counterclockwise dance ceremony was performed—it is called the ring shout in North America—the dancing and singing were directed to the ancestors and gods, the tempo and revolution of the circle quickening during the course of movement."[53] Stuckey's classic work explains why the Spirit Attenuation Well did not work as intended. That is, dance and music forms that white people did not understand and viewed as exotic or sinful not only survived but also retained the underlying spiritualities that cut across different African ethnic groups.

The second aspect of the colonizing template was the retention of negative definitions that dehumanized one group of people while simultaneously defining Europeans as superior. Originally, Africans were deemed heathens, ignorant, even criminal, and thus qualified for capture and trafficking. Years ago, as my plane was landing in Ghana, Africa, I looked down and realized that the soil was red. Red dirt farming is different from black dirt farming—and most of the White European colonists in the United States South came from countries that had black dirt. For the sake of profit, they needed help to farm; the specific knowledge of the Africans was needed across the colonized world. The manifests of the human traffickers' ships listed where they picked the Africans with certain knowledge for transport to areas with indigo or rice or timber in the Americas and the Caribbean.[54] It was not simply brute strength needed; they needed the intelligence that the Africans held, countering the propaganda of Africans as ignorant heathens. There was a difference in each colony that held humans in bondage, and several of these differences will be seen in the coming chapters. For instance, in Brazil, enslavement was more brutal: working the Africans to death in mines or on farms was not seen as an issue because that colony was close to the African continent, so they could always just go get more humans to traffic and exploit.

There was other evidence that the Spirit Attenuation Well did not work, such as the many revolts against enslavement. There were also some Africans who escaped and created rebel communities. These rebel communities were easier to establish in rural areas with undeveloped land where the colonizing country depended heavily on managers to oversee the extraction of natural resources and control the laboring population. In Brazil, for example, escapees created *quilombos*. One leader of a *quilombo*, Zumbi, was captured and executed on November 20, 1695. Today, November 20 is celebrated as Black Awareness Day in Brazil, as Selenir Kronbauer of Grupo Identidade, Sao Paulo, Brazil, pointed out.

Queen Nanny of Jamaica was another famous rebel. At the beginning of the eighteenth century, communities of escaped Africans were called Maroons. According to the Jamaica Information Service, "Nanny was known by both the Maroons and the British settlers as an outstanding military leader who became, in her lifetime and after, a symbol of unity and strength for her people during times of crisis."[55] There were also multiple rebellions of enslaved people in the American colonies. Unlike Jamaica and Brazil, settler colonialism led to the United States becoming its own nation. Rebellion was often quickly squelched by the well-armed settlers. The Stono Rebellion, in 1739, was in the South Carolina colony. The enslaved Africans, many of whom were Catholic, wanted to escape from a Protestant colony to Catholic Florida, where they would have been considered free. "The Stono Revolt, like other rebellions, was not simply a conflict between masters and slaves; it should also be understood as a transatlantic imperial and religious conflict."[56]

However, the second aspect of the Columbus framework, promoting negative images of the indigenous people, was multiplied and hardened with the addition of race. Adding race to the list of negative representations shaped a "racial contract" for the ordering of society with sociopolitical and moral components. Charles W. Mills defined this Contract, established through colonization: "The Racial Contract establishes a racial polity, a racial state, and a racial juridical system, where the status of Whites and nonWhites is clearly demarcated, whether by law or custom. And the purpose of this state . . . is . . . specifically to maintain and reproduce this racial order."[57] In conjunction with enslavement, this racial order became known as the chattel principle, as Walter Johnson stated: "Bodies were shaped to their slavery. Their growth was tracked against their value . . . they were taught to view themselves as commodities."[58] These views cut across European and American colonies. Aimé Césaire expressed the effect as an equation: "Colonization = thingification."[59]

Enslavement was tied to race, with exoticized, exaggerated definitions tied to Black people that ultimately crafted a fiction of subhumans and justified the idea that other people could own them. Although international human trafficking ended, enslavement within national boundaries continued. Families were torn apart, and people were tortured as their labor was used to build countries as well as serve and build generational wealth for families other than their own.

The emancipation of Black people in any former colony could not erase the long-standing fictions of the "ignorant, lazy savage" intended by God to serve White people. Nor could emancipation eliminate the labor needs of the colonized countries. Like Somé, who discussed his sense of being split between two worlds, in 1903, W. E. B. Du Bois described what he called "double consciousness, this sense of always looking at one's self through the eyes of others."[60] Their perspectives describe one of the effects of segregating Black people from mainstream societies, wherein different cultural platforms grew into two distinct worlds. As Franz Fanon stated:

> Two centuries ago, a former European colony decided to catch up with Europe. It succeeded so well that the United States of America became a monster, in which the taints, the sickness, the inhumanity of Europe have grown to appalling dimensions, [61]

Indeed, Fanon noted, the United States had become remarkably efficient in its cruelty to Black people.

Violence against Black people was not abolished with the institution of slavery. On the contrary, it continued in myriad forms, sanctioned by law and through practices such as sharecropping, acts of vigilante justice, and racial terrorizing by the Ku Klux Klan, and Jim Crow laws in the United States. The bodies of Black people continued to be viewed as chattel, which is "the specter from slavery that perhaps has the greatest impact on Black people's current social-cultural realities. . . . The twenty-first-century version of this construct is the criminal Black body."[62]

This chapter focused on multiple strands of origin stories that make sense of the religions of the African Diaspora: Afrika/Africa, the continent and its Diaspora, empires and colonies, papal decrees and Christian missions, and the multiple effects of human trafficking. Each strand complicates generalizations about African religion described in the book's introduction and elaborates on the complex history that shaped the religious lives of those throughout the African Diaspora. Their religious lives were shaped by desires for freedom from oppression, politically or spiritually, with Afrika as the point of departure. In Chapter Two, I discuss two unique Diasporan religious groups shaped by Pan-Africanism.

Notes

1. John G. Jackson, "Introduction" to *The Story of the Moors in Spain*, by Stanley Lane-Poole (Black Classic Press, 1990; originally published 1886).
2. Arizona State University, "Lucy's Story," *Institute of Human Origins*, https://iho.asu.edu/about/lucys-story.
3. Arizona State University, "Celebrate 2024, A Year for Human Origins," *Institute of Human Origins*, https://iho.asu.edu/Lucy50.
4. Michael A. Gomez, *African Dominion: A New History of Empire in Early and Medieval West Africa* (Princeton University Press, 2018), 12, 13.

5 Isaac Samuel, "A Forgotten African Empire: The History of Medieval Kānem (ca. 800–1472)," April 20, 2025, https://www.africanhistoryextra.com/p/a-forgotten-african-empire-the-history?utm_campaign=comment&utm_medium=email&utm_source=substack&utm_content=post, accessed April 2015.
6 Ibid.
7 Gomez, *African Dominion*, 104–9.
8 Ibid., 371.
9 Ibid., 12.
10 Janina M. Safran, *Defining Boundaries in Al-Andalus: Muslims, Christians, and Jews in Islamic Iberia* (Cornell University Press, 2013), 1.
11 Stanley Lane-Poole, *The Story of the Moors in Spain* (Black Classic Press, 1990; originally published 1886), 24.
12 Safran, *Defining Boundaries*, 4.
13 Fèlix Retamero and Josep Torró, "One Conquest, Two Worlds: An Introduction," in *From Al-Andalus to the Americas (13th–17th Centuries): Destruction and Construction of Societies*, ed. Thomas F. Glick, Antonio Malpica, Fèlix Retamero, and Josep Torró (Brill, 2018), 3.
14 Bernard R. Goldstein, "Astronomy as a 'Neutral Zone': Interreligious Cooperation in Medieval Spain," in *Al-Andalus, Sepharad and Medieval Iberia: Cultural Contact and Diffusion*, ed. Ivy Corfis (Brill, 2010), 172.
15 Richard C. Taylor, "Ibn Rushd/Averroes and 'Islamic' Rationalism," in *Al-Andalus, Sepharad and Medieval Iberia: Cultural Contact and Diffusion*, ed. Ivy Corfis (Brill, 2010), 226.
16 https://www.alhambra.org/en/alhambra-history.html, accessed April 2025.
17 *Letter of Columbus to Luis de Sant Angel Announcing His Discovery, February 15, 1493*, https://www.ushistory.org/documents/columbus.htm, accessed April 2024.
18 Ibid.
19 Edmund S. Morgan, "Columbus' Confusion about the New World," *Smithsonian Magazine*, October 2009, https://www.smithsonianmag.com/travel/columbus-confusion-about-the-new-world-140132422/, accessed April 2024.
20 Ibid.
21 Nnimmo Bassey, *To Cook a Continent: Destructive Extraction and Climate Crisis in Africa* (Kraft Books Limited, 2013), 4.
22 Ibid., 5.
23 Morgan, "Columbus' Confusion about the New World."

24 Adekeye Adebajo, "Pan-Africanism: From the Twin Plagues of European Locusts to Africa's Triple Quest for Emancipation," in *The Pan-African Pantheon: Prophets, Poets, and Philosophers*, ed. Adekeye Adebajo (Manchester University Press, 2021), 11.
25 *Letter of Columbus to Luis de Sant Angel Announcing His Discovery*, February 15, 1493.
26 *Pope Alexander VI's Demarcation Bull, May 4, 1493*, The Gilder Lehrman Collection, GLC04093, https://www.gilderlehrman.org/sites/default/files/inline-pdfs/04093_FPS.pdf, accessed May 22, 2024.
27 Oyèrónké Oyèwùmi, *The Invention of Women: Making an African Sense of Western Gender Discourses* (University of Minnesota Press, 1997), 2.
28 Charles and Rah, *Unsettling Truths*, 75–6.
29 Bassey, *To Cook a Continent*, 5.
30 Walter Johnson, *Soul by Soul: Life Inside the Antebellum Slave Market* (Harvard University Press, 1999), 3.
31 Bassey, *To Cook a Continent*, 6.
32 Samia Touati, "Lalla Fatma N'Soumer (1830–1863): Spirituality, Resistance and Womanly Leadership in Colonial Algeria," *Societies* 8, no. 4 (2018): 126, https://doi.org/10.3390/soc8040126.
33 Ibid.
34 G. I. C. Eluwa, M. O. Ukagwu, J. U. N. Nwachukwu, and A. C. N. Nwaubani, *A History of Nigeria for Schools and Colleges* (Onitsha, Nigeria: Africana First Publishers, PLC, 1988, reprint, 2016), 205.
35 Kwame Nkrumah, *Africa Must Unite* (Frederick A. Praeger, 1963), xii.
36 Ibid.
37 Ibid., xiii.
38 Cf. Confidence W. Bansah, "Christian Colonialism, Slavery and the African Diaspora," *E-Journal of Religious and Theological Studies* 6, no. 2 (2020): 123–34, https://doi.org/10.32051/erats.2020.034.
39 "The Act of Parliament to Abolish the Slave Trade," *UK Parliament*, https://www.parliament.uk/slavetrade/#:~:text=The%20Act%20of%20Parliament%20to,successful%20public%20campaigns%20in%20history, accessed July 2024.
40 Thomas Fowell Buxton, *African Slave Trade* (originally published London: John Murray, Albermarle-Street; reprinted New York: American Anti-Slavery Society, 1840), xi.
41 "Crowther, Samuel Adjai (or Ajayi) (c. 1807–1891), African Missionary and Bishop," in *History of Missiology*, Boston University School of Theology, https://www.bu.edu/missiology/missionary-biography/c-d/crowther-samuel-adjai-or-ajayi-c-1807-1891/, accessed July 2024.

42 Eluwa et al., *A History of Nigeria*, 186.
43 Ibrahim B. Anoba, "Ethiopia Shall Stretch Her Hands Unto God: Ethiopianism as a Pan-African Religious Freedom Movement (1880–1940)," *Journal of Church and State* 64, no. 1 (2022): 57, https://doi.org/10.1093/jcs/csab001.
44 *General Act of the Berlin Conference on West Africa*, February 26, 1885, https://loveman.sdsu.edu/docs/1885GeneralActBerlinConference.pdf, accessed July 2024.
45 *General Act of the Berlin Conference on West Africa*, February 26, 1885.
46 Thaddeus Metz and Motsamai Molefe, "Traditional African Religion as a Neglected Form of Monotheism," *The Monist* 104, no. 3 (2021): 394, https://academic.oup.com/monist/article/104/3/393/6305009.
47 Malidoma Patrice Somé, *Of Water and the Spirit: Ritual, Magic, and Initiation in the Life of an African Shaman* (G. P. Putnam's Sons, 1994), 310.
48 Ibid., 310, 311.
49 Ibid., 311.
50 Katie Geneva Cannon, "Christian Imperialism and Transatlantic Slave Trade," *Journal of Feminist Studies in Religion* 24, no. 1 (2008): 132–3.
51 "In *Encyclopedia Virginia*, Hening's *Statutes at Large*, vol. 3," https://encyclopediavirginia.org/3433hpr-fe4b174ca5cf17e/, 447–8.
52 "A Brief Overview of Black Religious History in the U.S.," *Pew Research Center*, February 16, 2021, https://www.pewresearch.org/religion/2021/02/16/a-brief-overview-of-black-religious-history-in-the-u-s/, accessed July 2024.
53 Sterling Stuckey, *Slave Culture: Nationalist Theory and the Foundations of Black America* (Oxford University Press, 1987), 12.
54 Cf. Gwendolyn Mildo Hall, *Slavery and Ethnicities in the Americas: Restoring the Links* (Chapel Hill: University of North Carolina Press, 2005), 66–71.
55 "Nanny of the Maroons," *Jamaica Information Service*, https://jis.gov.jm/information/heroes/nanny-of-the-maroons/#:~:text=heroes,-PLACE%20OF%20BIRTH&text=Nanny%20was%20a%20leader%20of,people%20during%20times%20of%20crisis, accessed July 2024.
56 Katherine Gerbner, "Rebellion and Religion, Slavery and Empire in Early America," in *Religion and U.S. Empire: Critical New Histories*, ed. Tina Wegner and Sylvester A. Johnson (New York University Press, 2022), 24.
57 Charles W. Mills, *The Racial Contract* (Cornell University Press, 1997), 13–14.

58 Johnson, *Soul By Soul*, 20.
59 Aimé Césaire, *Discourse on Colonialism* (Monthly Review Press, 1972; 2000), 42.
60 W. E. B. Du Bois, *The Souls of Black Folk* (Bantam Books, 1989; originally published 1903), 3.
61 Frantz Fanon, *The Wretched of the Earth* (Grove Press, 1963), 313.
62 Kelly Brown Douglas, *Stand Your Ground: Black Bodies and the Justice of God* (Orbis Books, 2015), 76.

2

Growing African Diasporan Religions (ADR)

Chapter Outline

Adding to the Definition of African Religions and Spiritualities	53
African Diaspora and Religions	54
The Moorish Science Temple	60
The African Orthodox Church and the PAOCC	64
Kemet	69

Adding to the Definition of African Religions and Spiritualities

In the Introduction, I presented a general sketch of African religions and spiritualities. To recap:

- African religions are non-revealed and orally transmitted.
- All life is viewed cyclically and as interconnected with earth-based spirituality.
- There is often a primary source divinity that expresses specialized and fractionalized aspects of itself through other powerful and influential divinities.

- Blood relations/family are to be honored.
- Harmony and balance are keys to achieving holiness.

Additional similarities and distinctions allow comparisons of African Diasporan Religions and Afrikan Indigenous Religions.

Being earth-based, with a cyclical view of interconnected life, Afrikan and African Diasporan religions emphasize the spiritual as connected to the physical and are considered metaphysical. This perspective may seem to go against a scientific view, unsupportable to a Western-trained mind. However, African Indigenous religions, like many others, are not Western and draw from different cultural bases, drawing from different bases of logic. Beyond the cultural differences, the methods by which religions have been studied add to Western misperceptions about them.

When people study religions in a comparative religions framework, there are sections on Buddhism, Jainism, Islam, and Christianity. Each one is packaged neatly for easy consumption. Trying to easily package African Indigenous Religions reduces the complexities of the spiritualities, multiple cultures, and diverse histories, resulting in a lack of understanding or outright erroneous apprehensions. Attempting to do that with religions of the African Diaspora is not helpful because these are shaped by profound, traumatic experiences. As Sylvester Johnson stated:

> Colonialism and slavery are not merely discourse. They are historical realities, material practices, and political structures through which racial Blackness has been constituted and by which Black people have been dominated. It would be unthinkable, thus, for African Americans to demonstrate no special concern for realizing freedom as a political project. And it would be implausible to expect that the structures of African American religions would not be visibly and particularly marked by the coda of freedom.[1]

The "coda of freedom" is a critical marker, with governments, politics, and daily lives playing roles. This chapter focuses on African Diasporan Religions (ADR) and their meanings with two examples of early ADR.

African Diaspora and Religions

A colleague from Detroit, Michigan, led tours at the Charles H. Wright African American History Museum. He would invite visitors to consider the impact of the forced migration of enslavement by asking, "If an alien ship came here right now and captured all of us, took us to their planet, and told us that we were whoever they said we were, what would we have left?" Eventually, someone would say, "We'd have our memories." So, too, captured Africans had memories. However, over time and across generations, something happens. Memories shift and become bigger or smaller than reality; they will not be attuned to what is happening in the home country. Later generations "remember" their histories with shaded truths.

Captured Africans were spread out across the Diaspora and held their own memories. Those trafficked humans came from different ethnic groups across the continent, they shared ideas and blended their memories with others from the continent. They may have shared ideas and learned from the Native peoples they encountered, especially in terms of earth knowledge, such as the uses of local herbs and plants. Because Africans in the Diaspora were not integrated into White colonial societies, they built new cultures within the ones in which they were forced to live. W. E. B. Du Bois framed the image well, following his discussion of double consciousness: "To be a poor man is hard, but to be a poor race in a land of dollars is the very bottom of hardships. He felt the weight of his ignorance . . . Nor was his burden all poverty and ignorance . . . The Nation . . . [said to him]: Be content to be servants, and nothing more."[2] In this world, memories of Afrika gleamed with hope and, importantly, with affirmation of the humanity of Black melanated people.

Karl Marx famously referred to religion as an opiate for the oppressed. Perhaps this may be true for those comfortably steeped in Western culture. However, it is worth restating that religions carry cultures. For people of African descent with current or recessive memories, religions function differently: religions are not pledges of commitment to intellectualized creeds; they are a way of life.

The denial of the humanity of Black people began with European encounters on the continent of Africa and continued through trafficking and enslavement. (Forms of enslavement continue in other places in the world, a topic beyond the scope of this text.) Although legal enslavement ended in different countries throughout the nineteenth century, the function of denying humanity supported new forms of forced labor for Black people. In the US, persistent oppression was rewritten through the Ku Klux Klan, Jim Crow, anti-Black racial violence, and the establishment of legal boundaries of segregation. Each of these established separate and unequal social structures. Some Black Americans looked to the Afrikan continent to identify a place where they were important, where their very humanity was not questioned.

The idea of Afrika as a place of salvation had been integral to Black spirituality in the Diaspora, becoming a route to affirm Black humanity. As religion, specifically Christianity, had been used to deny Black people's humanity and to promote the European agendas for colonization, so Afrikan spirituality provided a critical platform for Black people to define themselves. These self-definitions were contrasted with and often fueled by their oppressive surroundings.

Various processes of retaining and affirming Black people's humanity arose during the time of enslavement. In the 1920s, Zora Neale Hurston captured the words of Black spirituality in her ethnographic work that included interviews of Black people in the South. Some of her interviews focused on various forms of Black religion and the concepts, practices, and humor that comprise them. She boldly stated: "The Negro has not been christianized as extensively as is generally believed. The great masses are still standing before their pagan altars and calling old gods by a new name."[3]

Christianity had not been able to provide a consistent religious home to heal the traumas of colonialisms and oppression. Consider that European art portrayed Jesus and his family as White people, sometimes clothed in medieval or Renaissance dress, and these works were hung on church walls and shown in stained glass windows. These images sent clear messages to Black people about the White-defined reality of God.

Here is another level of complexity: Black people are not a monolithic group. Some Black people embraced the White definitions of God. In 1933, Carter G. Woodson stated the internal conflict in terms of education: "The Negro's mind has been all but perfectly enslaved in that he has been trained to think what is desired of him."[4] I met an older African American woman some years ago who was upset with images of Black Jesus. She exclaimed: "My Jesus is *White*!"

Artistic representations were not the only ways to signal a White Christianity. Claims about the superiority of Whites and the inferiority of Black people, the legalization of chattel enslavement, the theft of land, and the stripping of human rights: these were built into myriad Western Christian theological constructions. Many of these constructions were not theologically sound, as exemplified by the argument for the righteousness of submissive enslavement: After Noah woke from a night of drunken sleep, he realized that one of his children had mocked him. In anger, he delivered a curse to dark-skinned "children of Ham" who would forever serve as slaves to their brothers.[5] As Gomez explained, "For the eighteenth and nineteenth century slave holder, it . . . meant that African slavery had been providentially decreed."[6]

Consequently, the Christianity preached throughout the African Diaspora "provided a 'sacred canopy' for certain inequitable power relations . . . explicitly and implicitly."[7] The explicit messages were theological constructions of social inequities; the implicit messages created a tradition that constructed "a certain collective theological consciousness that allows for, if not sanctions, unrelenting oppression of various human beings."[8] It is true that Black people found ways to Africanize Christianity in Africa and the Diaspora. However, their methods sometimes became sources of confusion in themselves, as in the case of the woman who declared that her Jesus was White.

Yet, despite Spirit Attenuation Wells or exclusive art, memories linger. Many people are intellectually capable of recognizing lies. Spirituality became a significant method for holding onto reality while surviving and sometimes thriving. The world made by colonization may have seemed settled—or at least controlled—to those who benefited from the governmental and social structures. But the paths of religions of the African Diaspora expose the ferment that flowed through the intellectual and spiritual lives of the people extracted from Afrika.

One evidence of the determination to use spirituality and memories for survival is found in Zora Neale Hurston's report of the mystical High John de Conquer who appeared for enslaved Black people in the US. "Distance and the impossible had no power over High John de Conquer. He had come from Africa. He came walking on the waves of sound. Then he took on flesh after he got here."[9] High John protected the enslaved Africans and befuddled the enslavers: "The sign of this man was a laugh. . . . It helped the slaves to endure. They knew that something better was coming. So they laughed in the face of things. . . . And the White people who heard them were struck dumb that they could laugh."[10] After enslavement ended, High John returned to Africa, but he left his spirit in the High John de Conquer root, which is still understood to have spiritual power in some Black communities.

While Hurston identified the power of Black religious life in the US, other scholars did not view religion as favorable. W. E. B. Du Bois was among those who saw things differently than Hurston. Du Bois believed that "deep religious fatalism" had been born "under the lax moral life of the plantation, where marriage was a farce, laziness a virtue and property a theft."[11] This 1903 statement by Du Bois represented the range of Black intellectual history as complex and dynamic even as Black people struggled to address the impact of colonization. As is often the case among scholars, Du Bois himself became one of the chief proponents of the idea of Pan-Africanism, eventually leaving the United States and relocating to Ghana in 1961. He stayed there until his death two years later. Du Bois is entombed at the W. E. B. Memorial Center for Panafrican Culture in Accra, Ghana.

Pan-Africanism and Religions

Real or imagined connections between Black communities in the Diaspora and Africa were operative across oppressed communities before it was given a name. For instance, High John is an example of an early image that connected trafficked Africans and their descendants via spiritual memory of a continent that gave them the power to laugh in terrible situations. Pan-Africanism, named so at the beginning of the twentieth century, provided one line of thought that has been integral to Black intellectual life.[12]

Beginning in 1900, Pan-African conferences were held, even as topics and those attending changed.[13] Certainly, the people attending at the beginning were mostly men and mostly from the educated classes, and so Pan-Africanism was often considered an activity for elites. Yet, in 1920, Marcus Garvey collaborated to develop the Pan-African flag—of red, black, and green—which became a symbol that the masses could appreciate. Garvey's role in popularizing Pan-Africanism was invaluable. For the purposes of this study, Pan-Africanism can serve as a platform to inform African and Diasporan religions and spiritualities. In this chapter, I will focus on Pan-Africanism in the United States in order to trace certain ADR.

The Harlem Renaissance (approx. 1917–1937) fed Black sociocultural life in New York City and beyond, especially as Black people migrated from Southern poverty and sharecropping in search of better opportunities. The era also fueled the development of Pan-Africanism. Countee Cullen was a poet of the Harlem Renaissance. His poem, "Heritage," begins with the question, "What is Africa to me?" By the close of the poem, Cullen focuses on his deepest pain, that Jesus is not Black: "Must my heart grow sick and falter, Wishing He I served were black. . . . Lord, I fashion dark gods too. . . ."[14] Cullen's poem captures a very particular spiritual pain, looking for "dark gods" to define self. Cullen's question, "What is Africa to me?" is both personal and communal, reflecting a motivation to discover personal identity and community heritage. His question itself functions as a subtext, running through African Diasporan religious life.

There was no place for Black "forgetting" living under segregated societies, while viewed as subhuman, violently and legally excluded from enfranchisement. "Forgetting" would have been akin to accepting White colonial definitions of inferiority. The recognition of Black humanity could not wait for or rely on a White belief that it was true. In contrast, Pan-Africanism invites people in Africa and its Diaspora to reaffirm their humanity using several intellectual strands that can be defined in multiple ways.

Pan-Africanism is a somewhat conflicted term, its history connected to colonialism in all its forms. Capturing the levels of complexity in a definition of the term, Adekeye Adebajo stated:

> Pan-Africanism can be defined as the efforts to promote the political, socioeconomic and cultural unity, emancipation and self-reliance of Africa and its diaspora. The ideology argues that Africans on the cntinent and around the globe share a common history and destiny... The concept of Pan-Africanism developed amid the sweltering oppression of slavery in the Caribbean and the Americas, and was transported back to Africa by its students who went to study in the US and Europe.[15]

As noted, Black people in Africa and its Diaspora made many attempts to establish connections among themselves as they sought paths away from oppression. By necessity, these efforts went beyond a single period of time, as the termination of human trafficking and legal enslavement evolved into efforts to secure voting and other civil rights even as there were struggles for liberation in African nations—none of these could alone resolve the traumas exacted by centuries of colonialism. "Africans and their descendants are still on a painful quest for three magic kingdoms:

peace and democratic governance; socio-economic transformation; and cultural equality."[16] Religions and spiritualities run through each of these three "kingdoms," aiming to provide a road map for liberation. Different religions and spiritualities can emphasize different aspects of the three.

Several forms of African-derived religions in the United States identified connections to the African continent and traditions of Black cultures and identities. I discuss two uniquely African-identified religions that began in the twentieth century. These were not the only Black religions crafted during the twentieth century that drew strength and imagery from an African focus. But the stories of these two religions demonstrate the influence of Afrika and the longing to connect with personal and communal truths, answering for themselves "what is Africa to me?" Importantly, these two demonstrate that such religious constructions are not simply exotic or emotional opiates for oppressed people. The Moorish Science Temple and the African Orthodox Church/Pan-African Orthodox Christian Church are examples of religions that are "typically taken from the fabrics of Islamic-Judeo-Christian traditions and woven into entirely novel patterns, informed by a vision of Africa as a historical power and, in some instances, a future destination."[17]

Following these two, I discuss Kemetic principles that were drawn from ancient Egyptian religion. The growth of Egyptology aided these principles and influenced Black American intellectual, spiritual, and cultural life through greater incorporation of Afrikan religious thought. The Moorish Science Temple, African Orthodox Church, and Kemetic principles offer insight into African Diasporan religious thought.

The Moorish Science Temple

Islam has had a significant presence throughout northern and western Africa, as was seen earlier in this text from Mansa Musa on a pilgrimage to Egypt to the Amazigh who swept through most of the Iberian Peninsula. When the European human trafficking of Afrikans began in the sixteenth century and lasted for another three centuries, Muslim captives were included. As Silviane A. Diouf wrote, "Islam prohibited the selling of free believers, [but] the practice did not always follow the principle." Many Muslims who were sold had been on the losing sides in various wars. The scheme to sell them despite the prohibition was "to declare that the other Muslims were lax in their practices and beliefs."[18] The actual number of African Muslims transported, the religious historian C. Eric Lincoln said, we may never know.

> How many thousands (or perhaps tens of thousands) we shall never know, for the slave masters had no interest in recording the cultural and spiritual achievements of their chattels. What is more, the slave trade required and maintained a determined myopia regarding the religious interests of its hapless human commodities: first to avoid the embarrassment of knowingly selling an occasional Black Christian, but more often in support of the fiction that the religious depravity of the Africans made them legitimate targets for spiritual rehabilitation through the dubious ministrations of chattel slavery.[19]

Islam had been in the Diaspora, although its presence was generally unrecognized. Today, researchers are collecting the histories of captured, practicing Muslims.[20]

Without solid data on the extent of the Muslim presence among the captured Africans and their descendants, it might seem unusual that Timothy Drew (1886–1929) became Noble Drew Ali and began the Moorish Science Temple (MST). There are multiple versions of Drew's history, but the one known by his followers is this:

> [Drew] was born in North Carolina in 1886, possibly to a Cherokee woman and a Moroccan Muslim father, or maybe to freed slaves… he left home at 16 and joined a band of Gypsies who took him overseas to Egypt, Morocco, and the Middle East. In Morocco, he was approached by the high priest of a mystical Egyptian cult who recognized him as the latest reincarnation in a line of prophets including Buddha, Confucius, Jesus, and Muhammad. The priest gave Drew a book that he said was a lost section of the Koran, and when Drew returned to the States, he called it the Holy Koran of the MST of America.[21]

This version of the founder's story leaves out considerable detail and while adding some questionable portions. Nonetheless, this account burnishes Noble Drew's authority to establish a new religion. MST is sometimes considered the formal arrival of Islam in the US.

The 1920s were fewer than sixty years past Emancipation. Many Black people moved to Northern cities during the Great Migration, which began in 1910, to escape the South's lynchings, terrorism, sharecropping, and the establishment of Jim Crow laws. Most of the migrants moved to urban centers, which changed the demographics of the US. However, the North and Midwest did not necessarily provide better or expanded opportunities for education or work. As C. Eric Lincoln wrote:

> Timothy Drew was not an educated man, but he had somehow learned enough about Islam to consider it the key to what would fifty years later be called "Black liberation." Islam was the religion of the Moors, the Black conquerors from Africa who once ruled much of Europe. . . . Drew had no training in the social sciences but he did have the perception to realize that there is a very definite relationship between what you are called and how you are perceived, and between how you are perceived and how you are treated.[22]

The founding story of Noble Drew Ali takes him beyond the shores of the United States. Drew said he had received wisdom from his African and Middle Eastern travels. While traveling, a Moroccan mystic saw in Ali a prophet and gifted him with sacred teachings, which Drew named *The Holy Koran of the Moorish Science Temple of America*. This text is most often called the *Circle 7 Koran* because of a number 7 in a circle on the cover of each text. This is *not* the same text as the accepted Qurʻan. Instead, Drew specified in the *Circle 7 Koran* that he had received secret teachings:

> The reason these lessons have not been known is because the Moslems (sic) of India, Egypt, and Palestine had these secrets and kept them back from the outside world, and when the time appointed by Allah they loosened the keys and freed these secrets, and for the first time in ages have these secrets been delivered in the hands of the Moslems of America.[23]

Prophet Drew Ali founded the first Temple in 1913 in Newark, New Jersey,[24] but the publishing date of the foundational text was 1927, as MST was incorporated in Cook County, Illinois.

Prophet Drew Ali established a unique religion to address other issues. The text itself has been critiqued for drawing from too many other religious sources. Edward E. Curtis IV provided a thorough analysis of multiple texts that were used but emphasized:

> All of these metaphysical texts offered the idea that human beings, through effort, might liberate themselves from their various forms of slavery, especially to a negative state of mind. Salvation was defined not as the otherworldly resting place of good souls, but as a this-worldly state of being . . . Noble Drew Ali appropriated various trains of American and

African American religious, political, and social thought to create his own understanding of what it meant to be a Moor. His religious identity was a hybrid; it was bricolage. But that did not make it any less authentic than any other religious identity.[25]

MST provided an early expression of a religion that was not an opiate to put Black people to sleep but one that required members to be alert.

As a religion of the African Diaspora, MST embodied Pan-Africanism. Ali's theology focused on a people's mental decolonization through spirituality, countering the impacts of colonization. One of the MST's pamphlets states: "The object of our Organization is to help in the great program of uplifting fallen humanity and teaching those things necessary to make our members better citizens."[26] The members define themselves as follows:

> We are Moorish American . . . because we are descendants of Morrocans [sic] and born in America . . . and know they are not Negroes, Colored Folks, Black People or Ethiopians, because these names were given to slaves by slave holders in 1779 and lasted until 1865 during the time of slavery, but this is a new era of time now, and all men now proclaim their free national name to be recognized by the government in which they live and the nations of this earth.[27]

Noble Drew Ali took MST members beyond what they viewed as the limits of Christianity and US society for improving Black people's lives. Gayraud Wilmore pointed out that "The movement spread to Detroit, New York City, Philadelphia, Chicago, and numerous southern cities. . . . At the height of its popularity, the membership may have risen to as many as twenty or thirty thousand persons."[28] The *Circle 7 Koran* discourages intermarriage with "the pale skin nations of Europe," stating further: "We are returning the Church and Christianity back to the European nations, as it was prepared by their forefathers for their earthly salvation. While we, the Moorish Americans are returning to Islam, which was founded by our forefathers for our earthly and divine salvation."[29]

MST members re-identified their nationality as Moorish Americans. Members renamed themselves with El or Bey to claim that identity. Wilmore emphasized the importance of their new identities: "The new faith, with its lapel buttons, red fezzes, and identification cards, opened up a whole unexplored and fascinating perspective . . . new books to read . . . and a new lifestyle in the drab existence of the great industrial centers of the nation."[30]

Following violent fractures among the leadership of the organization, Noble Drew Ali died mysteriously in 1929. The MST split into different factions, with one branch eventually becoming the Nation of Islam.

Being a member of MST was not a panacea for all problems faced by Black people in any section of the US. Segregation was by law and practice throughout the country. White fears and stereotypes of people of color were the impetus for multiple forms of violence and social exclusion. Of note, under J. Edgar Hoover's direction, FBI agents were directed to surveil Black populations. "Every agent had to have at least one informer who reported to him regularly on the activities of black people. In Washington, DC, every agent was required to assign six informers to spy on black people."[31] The MST did not escape their unpleasant scrutiny. The surveillance added to paranoia with agents" cultural and religious misunderstandings. The following is an excerpt from a September 1931 FBI report, now available through the Freedom of Information Act:

> According to Bey [the informant] the organization [MST] stands for equality of all races and the agent has advised that Bey, in his conversation concerning the organization and purposes of the Moorish Science Temple, indicated a very radical attitude in that he condemned by inference, at least, all capitalistic forms of government and seemed to favor a revolution of some type.[32]

Yet, MST continues today, with temples in different cities, including Huntsville, AL, Washington, D.C., Newark, NJ, and Chicago, IL. There are several MST sects that have different understandings. Some may celebrate Moorish American Christmas on January 8, the birthday of Noble Drew Ali, as mentioned in a 1969 report from Pittsburgh, PA: "Although the day is celebrated in much the same manner as the Christian feast, the Moors substitute stars and crescents, streamers, pyramids, and the camel—the sacred Moorish animal."[33]

The African Orthodox Church and the PAOCC

During the period that Noble Drew Ali developed his ideas regarding Moorish connections to Islam, the African Orthodox Church grew from the aims of Marcus Garvey (1887–1940) and the United Negro Improvement Association (UNIA). The core ideas from Garvey and the African Orthodox were claimed three decades later with the establishment of the Pan-African Orthodox Christian Church (PAOCC). Pan-Africanism, a concept for which Garvey is given much credit, was the through line that helped birth the PAOCC and the Shrine of the Black Madonna.

Marcus Mosiah Garvey, born in Jamaica, was steeped in the complex situations of the Diaspora. His analytical and leadership abilities could be discerned in his early twenties when, as Sylvester Johnson writes, Garvey began his own newspaper, *Garvey's Watchman*. According to Johnson, three things shaped Garvey's "analysis of race and empire and his strategies of activism. . . . first was labor activism in the Caribbean . . . Second was racial Blackness as a diasporic formation. . . . Third was anticolonial nationalism rooted in the pursuit of a Black self-governing state."[34]

Leaving Jamaica in 1910 for work in Costa Rica, Venezuela, and Colombia, Garvey's travels mirrored thousands of other Caribbean migrants who became traveling laborers available to replace the free labor of the enslaved. Garvey traveled to London in 1912, where he was influenced by the Pan-Africanist ideas of Dusé Muhammad, an Egyptian writer.[35] Garvey returned to Jamaica and founded the UNIA in 1914, eventually leaving for the United States and New York City in 1916.

While Garvey was not the first proponent of Pan-Africanism, the UNIA carried the idea throughout the African Diaspora. "Centered in Harlem, the UNIA was the literal embodiment of pan-Africanism, and in time, established 996 branches in forty-three countries, including Cuba, South Africa, Europe and even Australia. Its membership is difficult to calculate, but it conceivably numbered in the hundreds of thousands at its apex."[36] After some exchanges with other Black leaders in the Diaspora, the UNIA focused on efforts to reconstruct Black countries, preferably on the African continent. Garvey, through the UNIA, actively promoted the idea of "Africa for Africans."

Garvey's Pan-Africanism was primarily political and economic. His influence cut across the Diaspora and into the continent of Africa. One of his most ardent supporters was US-educated Kwame Nkrumah, who would become President of Ghana.[37] Garvey's economic efforts aimed to support Black self-sufficiency. For instance, the Black Star Line of cargo ships was intended to deliver goods between Black countries. "The UNIA was now taking shape . . . as an ingenious economic conduit to create corporate infrastructure, market networks, and economic and political sovereignty in the Black Diaspora."[38] Garvey's drive to achieve Black self-sufficiency indirectly led to his downfall when, in 1923, he was convicted of fraud regarding the Black Star Line. After serving three years in prison, he was deported back to Jamaica. His followers believed the conviction was rigged and unjust. In 2025, President Joe Biden posthumously pardoned Marcus Garvey, which had been sought by followers and family since the original conviction. "While the conviction did not define Garvey's legacy... the posthumous pardoning will help restore the dignity of his global movement."[39] Marcus Garvey's legacy includes the development of Black religious thought.

Garvey did not want to promote a single religion for the UNIA's membership but wanted to remain open to all Black people of any faith. He remained a Christian and admired the Catholic Church, which had been an early influence in his life. However, Garvey promoted the idea of God as Black, canonizing Jesus as the "Black Man of Sorrows" and Mary as the "Black Madonna."[40] These statements were not meant merely to colorize God. "Instilling confidence that a supreme god was allied with the politics of Black liberation became a necessary element of an anticolonial agenda," influencing "a broad array of Black religious communities by virtue of the fact that numerous members of those communities were devoted affiliates of the UNIA."[41]

Marcus Garvey had clear ideas about the importance of religion and its role in building Black communities. His influence on Black religious life went beyond the fact that many members of different faiths were involved with the UNIA. Garvey operated meetings of the organization with a religious ethos, as detailed by Randall K. Burkett. With liberal use of Hebrew and Christian scriptures, religious terminology such as "missionaries," and ritualized meetings, Garvey was an inspiring speaker. Burkett cited one of Garvey's speeches to emphasize this ethos: "Let the world know that this is the hour; this is the time for our salvation. Prayer alone will not save us; sentiment alone will not save us. We have to work and work and work if we are to be saved ... the time is now to preach the beatitude of bread and butter. I have contributed my bit to preaching this doctrine."[42]

In 1920, Episcopal Rev. George Alexander McGuire (1866–1934) was elected the first chaplain of the UNIA. In 1921, he compiled the "Universal Negro Ritual," which was "modeled after the Book of Common Prayer."

He developed the training for other chaplains. "McGuire hoped that the chaplains would function as spiritual leaders to members, inculcators of racial and moral values."[43]

McGuire was also the initiator of the African Orthodox Church, a new denomination that was modeled on the Episcopal Church. Both McGuire and Garvey wanted the church to be in line with Apostolic succession, meaning it would have a link to Jesus's apostles. Bishops of Roman Catholic and Episcopalian traditions claim this authority. Therefore, McGuire was "consecrated bishop of the new denomination by the exarch and metropolitan of the American Catholic Church, Most Reverend Jospeh Rene Vilatte."[44] The African Orthodox Church continues today with its Cathedral in New York City.[45]

While the African Orthodox Church is deliberately independent of White leadership with Black images of Jesus and Mary, it is basically a Christian denomination. In 1953, Albert B. Cleage Jr. (1911–2000) took Garvey's and McGuire's ideas to the next level, a distinction that Cardinal Aswad Walker made:

> Not only were Jesus and Mary Black, but Christianity was an African religion, with a God who chose a group of Black people to be His people . . . Cleage and the PAOCC not only questioned and rejected Eurocentric beliefs and ideas in all areas but worked to build a theology, church and other institutions that reflect beliefs and ideas coming from an African (Black) worldview.[46]

The PAOCC is the Pan-African Orthodox Christian Church, with individual churches referred to as the Shrines of the Black Madonna.

If the Harlem Renaissance asked, "What is Africa to me?" and Pan-Africanism sought the "three magic kingdoms" of self-governance, economic expansion, and cultural equality, by the mid-twentieth century, the focus in the United States had expanded again. Civil rights movements expanded into Black Power movements, and in the 1960s, Black theology added new questions. There was no unanimity in Black communities or the wider American society about any of these social or religious shifts. Albert Cleage was trained in theological schools, ordained in a Christian tradition, and was an established minister. He stepped in with a theological answer that built on Garvey's teachings—Black Christian Nationalism—"Though separated by several decades in terms of the height of their ministries, their positions and beliefs are incredibly similar. Yet each had strongly different opinions on the positioning of the church in their respective movements."[47]

Cleage was opposed to efforts for integration, as the Civil Rights Movement sought, challenging that "integration is asking Black people to become a nonpeople.[48] In contrast, Cleage claimed that Black Christian Nationalism is designed to address the real conditions of Black people in the United States and throughout the Diaspora. "Believing nothing is more sacred than the liberation of Black people, we are a revolutionary Pan-African movement dedicated to the building of a heaven on earth in the here and now for all Black people everywhere.... We are pragmatic realists."[49]

The first Shrine of the Black Madonna that Cleage established was in Detroit, Michigan. There are also Shrines in Atlanta, Georgia, and Houston, Texas. Each shrine also has a cultural center and bookstore, with education and resources from Afrikan perspectives.

The Christianity of the Shrine of the Black Madonna is distinctive: every Black man is a Jesus; every Black mother is a Madonna. Each Shrine has a prominently placed artwork of the Black Madonna holding a Black child. Jesus becomes the model of the heroic journey to liberation to which every Black person is called. There are sacraments in the PAOCC, but these are different as well. Cleage wrote: "For Black Christian Nationalists, baptism symbolizes dying to the old Uncle Tom ways and coming into a new birth of understanding and commitment.... We rise in the newness of life committed to a revolutionary struggle for the liberation of Black people."[50]

Sin, in Black Christian Nationalist theology, is acting on Western individualism "because it separates a man from his Black brothers and sisters, who constitute his only channel of communication with God.... African communalism is not a socioeconomic system but a theological statement that emerges from the total Black experience."[51] In this view, salvation is to be found separated from Western individualism, grounded in the PAOCC, and working for the liberation of all Black people.

In 1972, Albert Cleage changed his name to Jaramogi Abebe Agyeman, which means "liberator, holy man, savior of the nation" in Swahili.[52] The emphasis on Black African roots was a central component of the PAOCC/Black Christian National religious instruction for all members. The cultural centers and bookstores remain open; they have expanded with a farm and retreat center called Beulah Land. Part of their educational program was to bring in speakers who could engage the community on different aspects of their Black religious identity. Like Garvey, the PAOCC educational efforts influence the wider African American communities. Even as they developed Black Christian Nationalism, other strands of African spiritual thought developed.

Kemet

The MST held Moorish Africa as a central component in its spiritual development; the PAOCC/BCN drew on African communalism and culture as central to its theological development. In the approximately forty years from the beginning of the MST to the PAOCC, multiple social shifts impacted Black Americans, such as the Civil Rights and Black Power Movements. These US movements also had an impact across the Diaspora as people in one nation watched and learned from other nations" struggles for liberation. In this period, Black scholars expanded their scholarship on Afrika and its religions. One strand had grown slowly during the Harlem Renaissance and, by the 1950s, it gained vigor and traction among Black communities: Egypt and its relations to Black cultures and religions, with Kemetic studies. Kemet is the ancient name for Egypt, the word meaning "Black land."

European and, by extension, American scholarship had long pushed the idea of Greece and Rome as cradles of civilization; this view supported colonization and justified racist structures. By the early 1800s, with the translation of the Rosetta Stone, it became clear to European scholars that Egypt, as Dr. Charles S. Finch III noted, was the progenitor of "mathematics, medicine, astronomy, metallurgy, philosophy, religion, and the arts," and all was tied to Africa. "Cherished Greece, not the father but the child? Not the master but the pupil? Of an African race? It just wouldn't do."[53] The new information at the beginning of the 1800s created an intellectual crisis, so scholars went out of their way to identify Egyptians as NOT Black African but as Asiatic. The field of Egyptology was born.

One of the most significant Egyptologists was the British scholar E. A. Wallis Budge (1857–1934). From 1883, Budge worked in increasingly higher positions in the Egyptian section at the British Museum, was knighted in 1920 for his research, and retired in 1924. His name is attached to many of the contemporary versions of *The Egyptian Book of the Dead*.

The Book of the Dead is not a single book but a collection of many Egyptian papyri that Budge and others had located and translated. The translations include voluminous information on Egyptian religion, history, and culture. As stated at the beginning of one volume: "'Book of the Dead' is the title now commonly given to the great collection of funerary texts which the ancient Egyptian scribes composed for the benefit of the dead. These consist of spells and incantations, hymns and litanies, magical formulae and names, words of power and prayers, and they are found cut or painted on walls of pyramids and tombs and painted on coffins and sarcophagi and rolls of papyri."[54] The collection is believed to have been in use from approximately 3700 BCE.[55]

Here, the divinities of Egypt were defined: Osiris, Isis, Ra, Thoth, and Horus, among others. The common Western names of these divinities are different from Kemetic names. In Figure 2-1, the common, Kemetic, and hieroglyphic names are given. The divinities' instructions on the creation of arts, science, or math were translated. The stories of the divinities were told. In one of the stories, Osiris was murdered by another divinity. His wife, Isis, found him, resurrected his body, and impregnated herself; their son was Horus. Osiris ruled Tuat, the land of the dead, the opposite of Ra, the Sun Divinity, who ruled the sky.[56] These stories were important because they informed how humans should live justly. The journey of a moral life was thought to point the way to the afterlife and thus served as the basis of the final judgment. It was outlined as follows in the text:

> The divinity Osiris will sit in judgment, in the Hall of Maat, flanked by the divinities Law and Truth. The soul will plead: "Behold, I have come to thee and I have brought maat to thee. I have destroyed sin for thee. I have not sinned against men. I have not oppressed (my) kinsfolk. I have done no wrong in the place of truth. I have not known worthless folk. I have not wrought evil. I have not defrauded the oppressed one of his goods..."[57]

There are forty-two measures of an individual's life, known as the 42 Laws of Ma'at. I will discuss these in more detail in the next chapter. Following these Laws, the ultimate measure of a just life is that the heart should be as light as a feather; it is weighed during divine judgment to determine where the soul will go after death.

While these were the works of scholars, the information flowed from other channels into intellectual streams. "Several... Harlem Renaissance artists studied or traveled to European cities and met and shared ideas

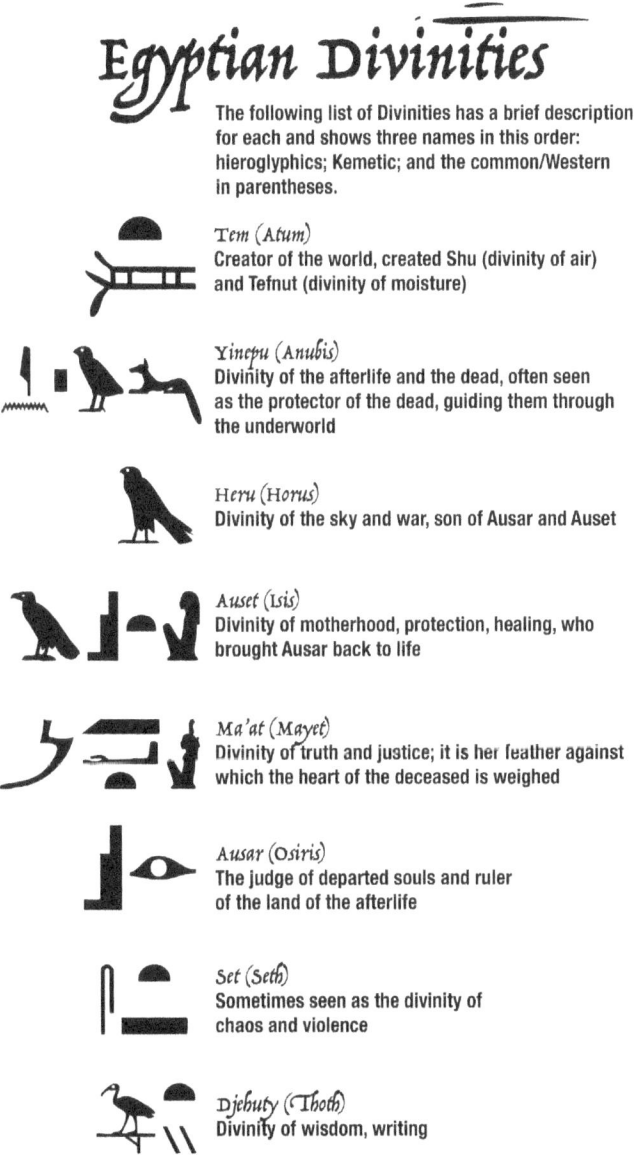

Figure 2.1 Egyptian Divinities, artwork courtesy of The Noble Esthetic, LLC.

with artists of various cultural backgrounds, including those from the Caribbean and Africa."[58] Poets and playwrights began to mention Egypt, and artists such as Aaron Douglas "used symbols and visual representations of ancient Egypt in various ways."[59]

Matching the rigor of any European scholar, Cheikh Anta Diop (1923–1986) was Senegalese and published in *Présence Africaine* in 1955 while a student at the University of Paris. Drawn from the 1955 work and later writings, Diop's book, *The African Origin of Civilization: Myth or Reality*, was published in the United States in the 1970s,[60] but his work had become known among Black scholars who traveled to Europe or Pan-African conferences. Among the first things Diop pushed back on were limited interpretations of Kemet: "We know that the Egyptians called their country *Kemit*, which means 'black' in their language. The interpretation [that] *Kemit* designates the black soil of Egypt, rather than the black man, and by extension, the black race of the country of the Blacks, stems from a gratuitous distortion by minds aware of what . . . this word would imply."[61] Diop stated in the Preface that he began his research in response to the effects of colonization.

He used extensive research to reposition Egypt within the Afrikan continent, in dialogue with Nubians, Ethiopians, Syrians, the Bornu, and Mansa Musa from Mali. Further, he was able to demonstrate that Egypt influenced Greece instead of the other way around. Diop stated: "It is impossible to stress all that the world, particularly the Hellenistic world, owed to the Egyptians." He proceeded to distinguish between Greek and Egyptian characters:

> By virtue of their materialistic tendencies, the Greeks stripped those inventions of the religious, idealistic shell in which the Egyptians had enveloped them. . . . To the extent that the Egyptians were horrified by theft, nomadism, and war, to the same extent these practices were deemed highly moral on the Eurasian plains. Only a warrior killed on the battlefield could enter Valhalla, the Germanic paradise. Among the Egyptians, no felicity was possible except for the deceased who could prove, at the Tribunal of Osiris, that he had been charitable to the poor and had never sinned. This was the antithesis of the spirit of rapine and conquest.[62]

Among Black communities in the US, as well as in other places across the Diaspora, an embrace of Egypt through Kemetic principles began to inform Black religious and spiritual life. Kemetic principles are spiritual components drawn from Egyptian thought and religion. These Kemetic principles were clearly from Afrika and did not sound or feel like Western ideas. The musical and literary arts of the Harlem Renaissance were just the beginning of defining Black concepts and voices. Pan-Africanism, especially through the spread of the UNIA, continued to shape Black Diasporan social understandings. The infusion of these ideas continued as the Black Power and Civil Rights movements pointed communities toward defining themselves—and their religions—again.

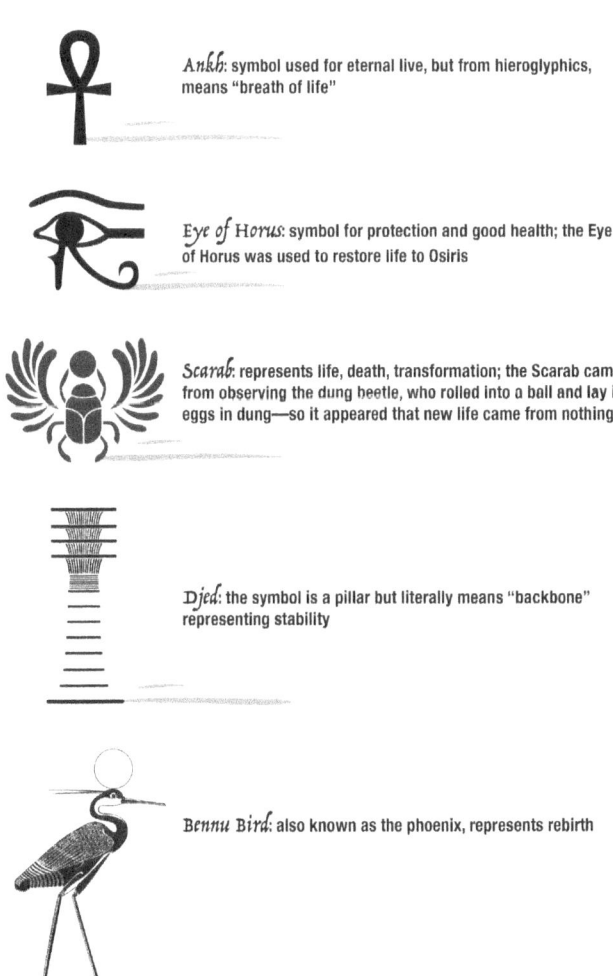

Figure 2.2 Kemetic symbols, artwork courtesy of The Noble Esthetic, LLC.

Egyptian religious symbolism began to show up on posters in college dorms or on t-shirts. The musician who changed his name to Sun Ra (1914–1993) wore Egyptian-styled clothing and defined his avant-garde jazz as drawing from the past and pointing toward the future in space. Sun Ra is sometimes credited with influencing what we know today as Afrofuturism. Sun Ra was a primary influence for another young musician, known as Pharoah Sanders, who aimed to create spiritual jazz. If the question from Countee Cullen was "What is Africa to me?" the answer was given in another poem by Nikki Giovanni (1943–2024). In "Ego Tripping," Giovanni defines herself in the opening line as tied to the Afrikan past: "I was born in the Congo, I walked to the fertile crescent and built the sphinx."[63] Symbols that had been on the walls of Pharaoh tombs could be found in Black bookstores and, sometimes, in Black Christian churches. Such symbols indicate spiritual content that was felt and celebrated by Black communities. (See Figure 2.2.)

Diop also pointed to possibilities in connecting Egyptian and Black Diasporan cultures:

> Because of this essential identity of genius, culture, and race, today all Negroes can legitimately trace their culture to ancient Egypt and build a modern culture on that foundation. A dynamic, modern contact with Egyptian Antiquity would enable Blacks to discover . . .... that these temples, these forest of columns, these pyramids, these colossi, these bas-reliefs, mathematics, medicine, and all this science, are indeed the work of his ancestors and that he has a right and a duty to claim this heritage.[64]

The religion of Ausar Auset stepped up to accept this challenge.

Notes

1 Sylvester A. Johnson, *African American Religions, 1500–2000: Colonialism, Democracy, and Freedom* (Cambridge University Press, 2015), 404.
2 Du Bois, *The Souls of Black Folk*, 6–7.
3 Zora Neale Hurston, *The Sanctified Church* (Berkeley: Turtle Island 1981), 103.
4 Woodson, *The Mis-Education of the Negro*, 24.
5 Genesis 9:25, *The New Jerusalem Bible* (Doubleday, 1985), 28.

6   Michael A. Gomez, *Reversing Sail: A History of the African Diaspora*, 2nd ed. (Cambridge University Press, 2020), 25.
7   Kelly Brown Douglas, *What's Faith Got to Do with It? Black Bodies/Christian Souls* (Maryknoll: Orbis Books, 2005), 9.
8   Ibid.
9   Hurston, *The Sanctified Church*, 70.
10 Ibid., 69.
11 Du Bois, *The Souls of Black Folk*, 138.
12 Other names were used throughout the Diaspora other than Pan-Africanism, such as Negritude. (Cf. Aimé Césaire, *Discourse on Colonialism* (Monthly Review Press, 1972; 2000); Ibrahim B. Anoba, "Africa Shall Stretch Her Hands unto God: Ethiopianism as a Pan-African Religious Freedom Movement," *Journal of Church and State* 64, no. 1 (2022).
13 Cf. https://www.blackpast.org/global-african-history-pan-african-congresses-1900-1945/, accessed August 2024.
14 Countee Cullen, "Heritage," https://allpoetry.com/poem/8497383-Heritage-by-Countee-Cullen, accessed August 2024.
15 Adebajo, "Pan-Africanism: From the Twin Plagues of European Locusts to Africa's Trible Quest for Emancipation," 4.
16 Ibid., 3.
17 Gomez, *Reversing Sail: A History of the African Diaspora*, 195.
18 Silviane A. Diouf, *Servants of Allah: African Muslims Enslaved in the Americas*, 15th anniversary ed. (New York University Press, 1998; 2013), 30.
19 C. Eric Lincoln, "The Muslim Mission in the Context of American Social History," in *African American Religious Studies: An Interdisciplinary Anthology*, ed. Gayraud S. Wilmore (Duke University Press, 1989), 342.
20 Cf. National Museum of African American History and Culture, https://nmaahc.si.edu/explore/stories/african-muslims-early-america.
21 Tasneem Paghdiwadwala, "The Aging of the Moors," *The Reader*, November 15, 2007, https://chicagoreader.com/news-politics/the-aging-of-the-moors/, accessed August 2024.
22 Lincoln, "The Muslim Mission," 344.
23 *The Holy Koran of the Moorish Science Temple of America*, Divinely Prepared by the Noble Prophet Drew Ali, 3.
24 *The Holy Koran of the Moorish Science Temple of America*.
25 Edward E. Curtis IV, "Debating the Origins of the Moorish Science Temple," in *The New Black Gods: Arthur Huff Fauset and the Study of*

African American Religions, ed. Edward E. Curtis and Danielle Brune Sigler (Indiana University Press, 2009), 77.
26 *Moorish Literature*, Moorish Science Temple of America, Inc. (n.d.), 19.
27 *Koran Questions for Moorish Americans*, Moorish Science Temple of America, Mt. Clemens, MI (n.d.), 1, 8.
28 Gayraud Wilmore, *Black Religion and Black Radicalism: An Interpretation of the Religious History of Afro-American People*, 2nd ed. (Orbis Books, 1983), 159.
29 *The Holy Koran of the Moorish Science Temple*, 59.
30 Wilmore, *Black Religion and Black Radicalism*, 160.
31 Betty Medsger, "Just Being Black Was Enough to Get Yourself Spied on by J. Edgar Hoover's FBI," *The Nation*, January 22, 2014, https://www.thenation.com/article/archive/just-being-black-was-enough-get-yourself-spied-j-edgar-hoovers-fbi/, accessed August 2024.
32 Federal Bureau of Investigation, *Moorish Science Temple of America*, BU File 62-25889, https://vault.fbi.gov/Moorish%20Science%20Temple%20of%20America/Moorish%20Science%20Temple%20of%20America%20Part%201%20of%2031/view#bypass-fullscreen, accessed August 2024, 34.
33 Dolores Frederick, "Moors Observe 'Yule' Wednesday," *The Pittsburgh Press*, January 5, 1969, https://www.newspapers.com/article/the-pittsburgh-press-moorish-science-tem/32292474/, 2.
34 Johnson, *African American Religions*, 275.
35 Gomez, *Reversing Sail*, 202.
36 Ibid.
37 Wilmore, *Black Religion and Black Radicalism*, 151.
38 Johnson, *African American Religions*, 282.
39 Melissa Hellmann, "Inside the 100-Year Fight to Get a Black Revolutionary Pardoned," *The Guardian*, Januray 26, 2025, https://www/theguardian.com/culture/2025/jan/26/marcus-garvey-pardon-campaign, accessed April 2025.
40 Cardinal Aswad Walker, "Princes Shall Come Out of Egypt: A Theological Comparison of Marcus Garvey and Rev. Albert B. Cleage Jr.," *Journal of Black Studies* 39, no. 2 (2008): 215.
41 Johnson, *African American Religions*, 293.
42 Randall K. Burkett, "Religious Ethos of the Universal Negro Improvement Association," in *African American Religious Studies: An Interdisciplinary Reader*, ed. Gayraud S. Wilmore (Duke University Press, 1989; 2nd printing 1992), 67.
43 Ibid., 73–4.

44 Wilmore, *Black Religion and Black Radicalism*, 150.
45 A listing can be found at https://www.netministries.org/see/churches.exe/ch26904, accessed August 2024.
46 Walker, "Princes Shall Come Out of Egypt," 195.
47 Ibid., 197.
48 Albert B. Cleage, *Black Christian Nationalism: New Directions for the Black Church* (Detroit: Luxor Publishers of the Pan-African Orthodox Christian Church, 1987; 1972), 13–14.
49 Ibid., 9.
50 Ibid., 58.
51 Ibid., 69.
52 *This Far by Faith* series, Public Broadcasting Service, https://www.pbs.org/thisfarbyfaith/people/albert_cleage.html, accessed September 2024.
53 Charles S. Finch III, "The Black Roots of Egypt's Glory," *The Washington Post*, October 10, 1987, https://www.washingtonpost.com/archive/opinions/1987/10/11/the-black-roots-of-egypts-glory/1c3faf74-331c-4cc1-a6a0-3535fa3e098a/, accessed September 2024.
54 E. A. Wallis Budge, *The Book of the Dead*, 1920 ed. (Auckland, New Zealand, 2008), 4.
55 Ibid., 8.
56 Ibid., 26.
57 Ibid., 31.
58 "The Harlem Renaissance: Art, Politics and Ancient Egypt," The Equiano Center, https://www.ucl.ac.uk/equiano-centre/educational-resources/fusion-worlds/context/harlem-renaissance-art-politics-and-ancient-egypt, accessed September 2024. (Note: The Equiano Center, located in the UK, ceased to operate in 2017 but has left the website as a resource.)
59 "The Harlem Renaissance: Art, Politics and Ancient Egypt."
60 Cheikh Anta Diop, *The African Origin of Civilization: Myth or Reality* (Lawrence Hill Books, 1974).
61 Ibid., 7.
62 Ibid., 230.
63 Nikki Giovanni, "Ego Tripping (There May Be a Reason Why)," 1968, https://poets.org/poem/ego-tripping-there-may-be-reason-why, accessed September 2024.
64 Diop, *The African Origin of Civilization*, 140.

3

Evolving African Diasporan Religions (ADR)

Chapter Outline

Connections and Distinctions	79
AIR, General Features	82
Ausar Auset	91

There was no holy book or sacred churchyard left behind in Africa. All that the traditional African needed for the creation of holy ground and sacred places, he found on the plantations and in the cities of the South. Initiated Africans who landed in the New World were thus fully equipped to continue time-honored traditions which connected them to the dead, the living, and the yet unborn.[1]

Connections and Distinctions

The journey through earlier chapters presented wider contexts for studying African and Diasporan religions. The first two African Diasporan Religions discussed—MST and PAOCC—demonstrated the deeper yearnings that many Black people experienced. With the Harlem Renaissance and UNIA, Pan-Africanisms advanced the hunger for a sense of home.

Black religious scholarship grew from Pan-African concepts to Egyptology. Then, the embrace of Egyptian religion threw the primacy of

Greek and Roman religions into a different timeline. Egyptian religion was proven to be much older than Judaism, Christianity, or Islam. Comparisons began, and the contents of Abrahamic religions were challenged. For instance, the 42 Laws of Ma'at were seen as the template for the Ten Commandments, noting that Moses lived for years in Egypt.

Abrahamic religions' leaders resist such connections because their theologies claim the singular truth of their faiths. The ideas of orthodoxy (right belief) and orthopraxy (right practice) were held in contrast to heterodoxy (straying from the right path) and heresy (completely opposed to accepted belief). From such theological bases, something like the Inquisition, discussed in chapter 1, had its own logic. But, before the hardening of historical lines between religions, before a belief in religious intellectual property, there were easy exchanges of religious concepts among different groups. The exchanges might have occurred because of a clan's movement to a different region, marriages between communities, or the capture of other villages. When people moved, they brought their beliefs with them, even as they encountered new ones. The idea of a religious conversion that demands the denial and exclusion of all others is a newer concept of religious belief, informed by ideas of orthodoxy and heresy. Religious history did not have such sharp lines of demarcation.

I encountered evidence of such religious fluidity during a trip to Morocco that included a visit to Volubilis. Volubilis is a Roman ruin that has been designated a UNESCO World Heritage site. It is a small site, but it shows the importance of the Romans' establishment of ports related to their trade routes. The site dates to the third century BCE. Over time, several cultures and peoples came together to create and build the town. The Roman portions were the most preserved, a testament to their engineering skill. I expected to see the aqueducts, mosaics, baths, triumphal arches, and amphitheater. There was a temple for Jupiter. Then, there was also a plaque at the location where the temple of Isis had been. Logically, I know that ancient people exchanged religious beliefs. But I did not expect to find Egyptian Isis at a Roman site in Morocco. A plaque dedicated to the goddess states: "In Egyptian mythology, Isis was the wife of Osiris and the vanquisher of nocturnal forces. In the classical world, she came to be regarded as the Universal Feminine Principle." Isis's temple was in a prime location within the city, as the plaque noted, "a sign of great devotion . . . once rendered to her." Ideas, divinities, practices, and beliefs were substituted for one another in ways that our contemporary minds may not easily embrace.

Sylvester A. Johnson outlined the importance of these interreligious exchanges:

> [W]ere it not for the practice among religious authors of borrowing wholesale or piecemeal from pre-existing textual traditions (our contemporary term for this is *plagiarism*), mainstream Jews, Muslims, Christians, and Buddhists would have little to show for scriptures. All religions are invented—scriptures are richly dependent upon pre-existing material—the Bible, Qur'an, Book of Mormon, Bhagavad Gita. Practices are always eclectic—ritual ablutions, sacrifice, music, etc., in the "great world religions." All derive from intersubjective responses to and participation in political, economic, social, and ideological realms. However, *none* of the data functions to undermine the authentic status of established religions, nor should they. *New* religions, however, are most frequently held to an impossible standard of historicity.[2]

A religion or spirituality is not weakened or invalidated because some of its life is derived from that of another.

From colonization through Pan-Africanism, as Black scholarship grew, there were shifts in how scholars studied the religions and spiritualities of Africa and its Diaspora. Ugandan scholar, Okot P'Bitek (1931–1982), defined the challenges, refusing to use Christianity as the primary contrast with Afrikan religions: "The first duty of an African scholar is to remove these rusty Greek metaphysical dressings as quickly as possible before African deities suffocate and die inside them. . . . The study of African religions should aim to understand the religious beliefs and practices of African people, rather than to discover the Christian God in Africa."[3]

We see such a redirection with the introduction of ancient Egyptian religion and Kemetic principles. There is a shift here: a religion grounded in Kemetic principles begins to lose its Western shaping. A new perspective on African Diaspora religions begins, one drawn directly from Afrika. Therefore, a distinction can now be made between African Diasporan Religions (ADR) that grow in the Diaspora and Afrikan Indigenous Religions (AIR) that are sometimes called African Traditional Religions. There are connections between these categories; ADR can and will draw from AIR. I presented some general characteristics of these traditions in the Introduction. The focus of this chapter on AIR takes a deeper dive into these features, thereby providing more substance to our discussion.

AIR are the origins of the following general features, some form will surface in each ADR. These general features also bring the sharpest contrast with Abrahamic religions. Western Abrahamic religions, especially Christianity, operate from systematic theologies. Systematic theologies set up outlines where both orthodoxy and heresy can be fitted into defined slots. Because AIR are not Western, there needs to be another lens, not a system, with which to view them. The following general features add to the general characteristics presented earlier and provide a lens to view the structures and concepts of both AIR and ADR. These general features are: cosmology, community, divinity, ancestors, divination, orality, and social pragmatism.

AIR, General Features

COSMOLOGY, in an Afrikan spiritual frame, is the consideration of the origin of the universe, earth, humans, and all life. If cosmology is referenced in a strictly scientific frame, the discussion would be limited to astrophysics, math, galaxies, the age and origin of the earth, and perhaps evolution. But in a spiritual framework, cosmology includes all those but steps into the metaphysical, not merely the origins of the universe but issues of design and purpose. Those issues relate to divine and human beings, the spiritual components of all life, and the interconnections between them. In this spiritual cosmology, the living, the ancestors and spirits, the divinities, nature, and the universe, are all interwoven.

The Ghanaian philosopher Kwasi Wiredu (1931–2022), often credited with bringing new life to African philosophy, brought to light sharp contrasts between African and Western philosophies, including religion. With a focus on material realities, he used the results of colonization as a basis for comparison. His work provides several key notes in outlining AIRs' general features.

Wiredu wrote:

> African categories of thought are in many cases fundamentally empirical. They contrast profoundly with the transcendental way of thought that one finds in much Western philosophy. It leads . . . to differences in the conception of God. In much African thought, God is a kind of cosmic architect, while in most Western thought, God is a transcendent creator of the universe out of nothing.[4]

In Afrikan thought, God is not divorced or distant from the cosmos. Thus, cosmology is a holistic study of interdependent parts. It follows, then, that the sacred can be found in many places on earth and in the heavens.

E. Bolaji Idowu (1913–1995), a Nigerian scholar, was also a Methodist leader whose scholarship focused on African Traditional Religion. Idowu wrote of the importance of these earthly sacred spaces and the connections that can be found, "All over Africa, there are places each of which is considered to be the sacred city, the sacred grove, or the sacred spot, especially because it is believed, according to the people's cosmology, that the place is the center of the world, the place where creation began, where the human race hid its cradle, and from where the race dispersed all over the earth."[5]

So, how do these ideas connect to the Black Diaspora? Throughout the Diaspora, Black people were never incorporated into the White societies in which they were laborers and caretakers; we know that the Spirit Attenuation Well did not work. However, as Alice Eley Jones asserts, "There was no holy book or sacred churchyard left behind in Africa. . . . [T]he traditional African [had all that was needed] for the creation of holy ground . . . on the plantations."[6] Components of the African cosmology are more evident in religions that align closely with AIR, but other aspects will still have resonance, such as the following general feature, community.

COMMUNITY is connected to this cosmological view. Community refers not only to families or neighborhoods but also to entire towns or regions. Many African people can state who their family and community members are, going back generations.

> African society is widely known to be communalistic. . . . In such a social formation, an individual is brought up right from the beginning with a strong sense of solidarity with large kinship groups. This orientation entails a sense of obligation to those groups. In case one might suspect that an individual in such a society must be borne down with a multitude of obligations, it must be understood that all members of the groups in question bear corresponding obligations to the given individual.[7]

That sense of community continues in Africa, even as Western concepts of individualism seep into society. But for those Black people whose families were forcibly transported to new lands, given new identities, and criticized for not matching White standards of beauty and culture, even as their humanity was questioned, community took on different meanings.

Race played starring roles before and after some civil rights were granted. In 1995, bell hooks wrote: "Racial integration altered the face of blackness. The separate and distinct culture of blackness that had been constructed in the midst of racial apartheid was disrupted by profound changes in economic opportunity, geographical shifts, and access to White institutions that had once been segregated."[8] These social changes did not resolve the practices of racism. Black people continued to feel what Joy De Gruy called "post-traumatic slavery syndrome,"[9] or the long-lasting impact of racism. De Gruy's term is applicable not only to the United States but also in many situations across the Diaspora. Hence, De Gruy's emphasis on the need for Black people to build strong communities as a way to heal: "To continue on the road to health, we need our communities to regain their vibrancy and relevancy. We need to begin to instill in ourselves and our children a sense of responsibility to others to reinvent rites of passage that get beyond what is merely ceremonial."[10] The need for healing helps drive some Black people to church—and sometimes, ADR is attractive to those seeking healing through healthy community ties.

There is one important facet within AIR that applies to the Diaspora that serves to build community. Training about the spirituality in AIR is not text-based but community-based. Knowledge of songs, signs, practices, and rituals has been communicated among members from birth. Those who seek membership must learn the traditions and the rites, with graduations to higher levels including priesthood as more knowledge is gained. Teachers are those who have advanced in different aspects: one teacher may have knowledge of history, another of healing, another of the rituals. This process of transmission might shift today with the use of social media. But the religious community connection is still necessary. When ADR develops, this method of transmission of knowledge builds new practices of community in Western societies.

DIVINITY is often misrepresented as "polytheism" or "animism" by those who view African religions as primitive; both misrepresentations need to be corrected. Multiple divinities are part of the structure in most African spiritualities. E. Bolaji Idowu defined the importance of "Deity":

> With regard to the creation, control, and maintenance of the universe, only Deity is in absolute origin of all things, only he has absolute power and authority. In African thought, Deity is absolutely essential and cannot be disregarded; the notion of a god as so transcendent that he is not immanent

is alien to African belief.... Africans are explicit about the divine rulership and absolute control of the universe.[11]

This concept of the Divinity is integral to African cosmology. Divinity taps into humanity and connects with the universe. There are multiple names for Deity across the continent, and Idowu names some to emphasize the superiority of this Divinity: "The Akan say that God is 'of all the earth, the King and Elder.' The Edo name for God, Osanobwa, means 'The Source-Being who carries and sustains the universe.' The Lugbara concept . . . 'God is not outside society, but rather above it completely . . . behind all people and all things, as their creator.'"[12] Such views of a supreme Divinity flow throughout Africa's indigenous religions.

Confusion can occur in Western discussions of African religion with the inclusion of other divinities. The supreme Divinity might not have a dedicated shrine; the array of divinities might function as lieutenants on that Divinity's behalf. Groups of African divinities invite comparison with Greek and Roman pantheons, but this is misleading. Further, it is easy to lose oneself in stories of these divinities; the glamour or mystery might tempt a student to let these become the full focus primarily while studying African religions. However, there are other contexts to consider, especially since African cosmologies tie all life together. Therefore, the divinities may have different purposes for humans' lives and for planet Earth. Different groups of divinities will be discussed under their respective AIR or ADR later in the book.

The notion that African religions are "animist" also surfaces in a derogatory way. This perspective is also misleading. The idea of a spirit-filled universe ties back to the core concept of Cosmology. Wiredu addresses the negative view by offering clarity: "I ought, perhaps, to dispose quickly of the allegation, often heard, that Africans believe that everything has life. The Akans, at least, are a counterexample. Some objects, such as particular rocks or rivers, may be thought to house an extra-human force, but it is not supposed that every rock or stone has life. Among the Akans, a piece of dead wood, for example, is regarded as notoriously dead."[13]

ANCESTORS are an integral part of an African cosmology. For Africans, "The ancestors are regarded still as heads and parts of the families or communities to which they belonged while they were living human beings: for what happened in consequence of the phenomenon called death was only that the family life of this earth has been extended into the afterlife of the super sensible world."[14] The ancestors were and remain central in the lives of Africans, inextricably tied to a spirituality that understands everything in life and the universe as connected. Those who are deceased continue to interact with their families, and sometimes they return by being reincarnated into another generation. As such, ancestors must be venerated.

Anthony Ephirim-Donkor wrote of the processes of becoming and venerating ancestors as a member of a Ghanaian Akan community. From a cosmological perspective, he stated, "Although ethical existence and generativity is thought of as an individual quest, it is incumbent upon the community to safeguard its content."[15] To live well in the universe, each person must work for balance and harmony as an individual within a community. The ancestors are those who

> Achieved eternal existence after first achieving perfection as elders. . . . Eternity . . . is a dynamically active state due to the phenomenon of reincarnation. It is believed that the ancestors may reincarnate as many times as possible to help people. Those who die without fulfilling their purpose of being also reincarnate to accomplish their God-given existential purpose."[16]

There are multiple ways ideas of ancestral interaction and veneration flowed into the Diaspora, not always in religious contexts. Family members sometimes wonder at a child who is "just like" a deceased relative. Honoring those who have fought for justice and liberation becomes a shared ancestral legacy among many in the Diaspora. Their contributions are celebrated on formal or informal holidays. In Brazil, I traveled to places where the images of those who fought for freedom, including Martin Luther King, Sojourner Truth, and Che Guevara, appear on t-shirts or are spray-painted on walls. Ancestors and reincarnation have demonstrated to their descendants that they are a reality, infused in their DNA. These ancestors have now been infused into Black literature. Marvel's *Black Panther* movies and Beyoncé Knowles's *Black is King* music video are twenty-first-century depictions that include Black ancestral images; the ancestor also figures in Julie Dash's 1991 *Daughters of the Dust*.

However, ideas of ancestor veneration and reincarnation are not exclusive to Afrikan spiritual or religious thought. They are found in many ancient indigenous spiritualities and are undergoing a renaissance in some New Age religions.

DIVINATION is not exclusive to the African Continent. The practice is found in many indigenous religions, among many people. It is a spiritual science, among other rituals. From a Western framework, however, the idea of the spiritual is in opposition to the physical, or that which is not scientifically provable. Spirit/soul becomes a private matter, and, in this view, spiritual science might refer to using positive affirmations to soothe one's mind, contemporary zeitgeist trends, and other evidence-based psycho-emotional interventions designed to uplift one's spirit. Such forms are often limited to psychology and self-help books. At the same time, the person who admits to psychic experiences in certain settings would be considered mentally unstable. From a science-based, Western mindset, only nature and other humans might be considered real; intuition and psychic abilities are invalid as proofs of reality. From this Western frame, truth fits in a very narrow box.

In general, divination "ranges from simple beliefs about and the interpretation of omens, dreams, and the flipping of a coin, to complicated methods such as graphology, gambling, horoscopes, tarot cards, *I Ching*, and a game of cards. . . . It is through such systems that human beings communicate with spiritual agents and vice versa."[17] For AIR and ADR, divination is a normal part of the cosmological view, where all of life is understood to begin in the spiritual before becoming part of the physical; therefore, communication and contact with divinities or ancestors to discover the best path forward in day-to-day living makes sense. As Tracey E. Hucks notes, "Divination as a "diagnostic process" has remained fundamental across African and diasporic geographical and cultural contexts."[18]

Philip Peek, who has long studied divination, offers a more extensive definition of the nature and function of divination: "A divination system is a standardized process deriving from a learned discipline based on an extensive body of knowledge. . . . Divining processes are diverse, but all follow set routines by which otherwise inaccessible information is obtained. . . . The final diagnosis and plan for action are rendered collectively by the diviner and the client."[19]

Divination connects the diviner to the appropriate location of the spirit world on behalf of the client, seeking answers from a supreme source, including divinities, ancestors, or other spiritual forces. The questions could be about physical health, family problems, a child's future, gaining wealth, avoiding legal problems, or any other problem. Any life issue could be broached through divination. The diviner is trained to receive and interpret answers that are drawn from multiple sources, many of which are orally transmitted. Some of these methods were lost because Africans were forcibly transported to the colonies. However, Hucks' research on divination suggested that, such loss notwithstanding, the "spiritual grammar of healing, restoration, and curative practices" continued, sometimes blending with the ideas of other cultures.[20] Consequently, new forms of contacting the spirit world and Afrika were developed to improve lives across the Diaspora, as High John de Conquer's walk across the waters, mentioned in the last chapter, demonstrated.

ORALITY AND SOCIAL PRAGMATISM: In our times, the written word is prized, especially in the West. The educational system, starting at the preschool level, emphasizes text-based literacy. A verbal agreement, without a written contract, has little value. So, when a community's history, traditions, and religions are remembered through oral transmission, they become invisible to people whose knowledge base is valued only when presented in written form.

There are drawbacks to textual traditions. The text can become theoretical in such a way that it is separated from daily life. For instance, a Western philosopher can argue that there is no such thing as social justice, there is only justice, that is, the theory. The text can become dogmatic and authoritarian. There are, within many local states, laws that are known as "zombie" laws, with no meaning for the current age, and if enforced, would require contemporary humans to live as people did 150 years ago. Text-based traditions require a certain reading level for members of a community to fully participate in their governments. A different kind of creativity is needed for textual communities, as Zora Neale Hurston pointed out: "Now the people with highly developed languages have words for detached ideas. That is legal tender. 'That-which-we-squat-on' has become 'chair.'"[21]

The oral tradition has certain advantages, and Laura Jarmon points out several in defining Black folk narrative. Tradition can retain its authority because it remains relevant to the contemporary community. Oral traditions can facilitate communication as the speaker can adapt language to fit the audience. These traditions can speak truths that are tied to the lives of the community and, when needed, adapt to fit current circumstances.[22] The "truth" becomes real in the present moment for the community with deeper understandings of meanings for their individual and communal lives.

It is possible for an AIR/ADR tradition to evolve with the times, including blending other cultures' ideas. Tradition becomes pragmatic and represents how the trafficked Africans could adjust and retain their cultures; the processes of blending are sometimes referred to as hybridization. Hucks wrote of her research: "I have found that Africana populations accommodate multiple habitations of the sacred, blurring religious boundaries and traversing multiple sacred cosmologies in ways that are self-authorizing."[23]

These general features—cosmology, community, divinity, ancestors, divination, orality, and social pragmatism—will show differently for various AIR and ADR. Social pragmatism and the fluidity necessary for the evolution of religions increase the possible variations. In 1973, E. Bolaji Idowu wrote:

> We notice that the new interest in African Traditional Religion is not a phenomenon restricted to Africa. It has become global . . . finding its way into the curriculum of every higher institution of learning throughout the world; there are European and American professors and lecturers in the field, even though they may never have visited Africa. . . . This interest is not only academic . . . There is also the deeper interest of those who have come to believe more and more that the religion has satisfying spiritual values to offer.[74]

On one hand, it is not easy for members of the Diaspora to step into any AIR. Such a shift requires moving away from a Western way of thinking and into unfamiliar cultural norms: social structures, foodways, family and community relationships, and educational and economic values.

On the other hand, it remains true that some Black people in the Diaspora feel separate from Western cultural norms, despite being grounded in a value system that has become part of their lives. Therefore, ADR may be a more comfortable fit, especially since it was developed in a specific Diasporic location.

Through these aspects of AIR/ADR, one inheritance from colonialism continues today: race and racism. In 2016, a United Nations working group reported on its study of Black human rights violations in the United States. The group toured several cities across the United States. Black human rights violations did not end with emancipation at the end of the Civil War. Their research disclosed ongoing police violence, criminalization, and disparities in access to health care, education, and housing. They also cited the climate, namely "the dangerous ideology of White supremacy [that] inhibits social cohesion among the United States population."[25] The UN group noted several positive steps that the government had taken and offered some recommendations framed by the following caution: "The legacy of colonial history, enslavement, racial subordination and segregation, racial terrorism, and racial inequality in the United States remains a serious challenge, as there has been no real commitment to reparations and to truth and reconciliation for people of African descent."[26]

Racism necessitates affirmation of humanity as integral to healing. The need for healing persists as race and racism continue to feed colonialism, neocolonialism, and toxic capitalism.

Pan-Africanism sought to counter many aspects of racial hatred and oppression in Africa and throughout the Diaspora.

These issues can become catalysts for some in the Diaspora to seek spiritual experiences that affirm their humanity, bringing forms of healing for current or inherited experiences of oppression. Marcus Garvey, W. E. B. Du Bois, and Cheikh Anta Diop seeded the spiritual hunger for greater connection with African spirituality. Race, as a dehumanizing force, acted as a catalyst for MST, PAOCC, and other ADR. However, AIR did not build its ancient spiritualities with the intent to focus on race. A White person who wants to become a member of an AIR or an ADR will find a community that will accept them. Dr. Wándé Abímbọ́lá had the title "spokesperson for Ifá in the world." Ifá is one of the AIR that will be discussed in the next chapter. Dr. Abímbọ́lá directly addressed racial wounds and spirituality: "We would like to see this religion as a tool to heal all those wounds. This religion should not be part of the racial problems of the Americas or the world. This religion should be used as a bridge, as something to cure and heal those wounds, so that the future of the world will be one where there is no hate."[27] The flexibility and social pragmatism of these spiritualities' general features can bring the issue of race into focus in other ways. One example comes to mind.

When the Moorish Science Temple splintered after the death of Noble Drew Ali, one of those groups named itself the Nation of Islam. The Nation has specifically focused on identification as Black Muslims. After Malcolm X made pilgrimages to the holy site, Mecca, he became concerned about the authority and authenticity of the Nation of Islam's approach to the religion. Specifically, Malcolm X noted the presence of White people on his trips to Mecca. In 1985, one Nation of Islam group shifted to embrace

Sunni Muslim traditions, an orthodox branch. The focus on race became secondary to the focus on the faith. However, the Nation of Islam continued with a focus on Black liberation tied into its faith life. Each development of faith—from MST to Nation of Islam to Sunni Islam—aimed to heal the effects of racism on its Black members through religion. Each of these can be considered ADR. If these groups sought to find healing through one path, others sought life-affirming spirituality through a Kemetic passage.

Ausar Auset is an ADR that identifies as Pan-African. Ausar Auset represents an evolution from the Moorish Science Temple and the Pan-African Orthodox Christian Church in that it takes a sharper turn to an Afrikan heritage, having access to the trove of materials from ancient Egyptian religion. Using these as a base, updating the material for current times, Ausar Auset aims to participate in spiritually healing Black people.

Ausar Auset

In 1973, Ausar Auset began, under the leadership of Ra Un Nefer Amen. His title is Shekhem Ur Shekhem (King of Kings) and Ashem Ur Ashem (Chief Priest).[28] Ausar Auset is based in Brooklyn, New York. Ausar Auset drew from Egyptian religion, utilizing the information available through the translated papyri. The basic beliefs existed but were updated for contemporary times. Ausar Auset seeks "dynamic, modern contact with Egyptian Antiquity," as Diop stated. Since they are based in Brooklyn, Ausar Auset or any Kemetic-focused group can take advantage of the materials that are available in the city of New York, as I experienced.

I have a love/hate relationship with museums as they are conceived in European frameworks. I love the artwork, even though the idea of "art for art's sake" is stiffly Western. I am glad to study African historical artifacts and documents, but I feel queasy about the provenance of the objects. Some years ago, I visited the Metropolitan Museum of Art in New York City with the same mix of joy and misgiving. While I was wandering through the Egyptian exhibits, I saw a group of Black people in African garb, clearly a class, with their teacher explaining the statuary and reading the hieroglyphics. I requested permission to walk with the class; it was granted with the understanding that I would leave whenever instructed to do so. For the next hour, I trailed the group, as the teacher not only read the hieroglyphics but also corrected the translations posted by the museum. The teacher's corrections reflected the perspectives of the class's faith and religion. Through such exhibits, Kemetic principles are no longer locked in antiquity, having become a lived religion. Here was a group taking advantage of stateside resources: Afrika is available for those who seek it.

Spiritual science understood within an African or Diasporan religious framework is detailed and expansive. The practices of spiritual science are part of the Moorish Science Temple and the Pan-African Orthodox Christian Church, but they become full-blown in Ausar Auset. Spiritual sciences in this Afrikan frame are processes wherein an individual learns to develop their spiritual capabilities based on Egyptian scripture. Divine beings, other humans, ancestors, other spirits, and nature are all part of the learning process.

The Laws of Ma'at are of prime importance for Ausar Auset and the basis of the spiritual science of religion. As Muata Ashby wrote:

> There is a process of responsibility wherein the *spiritual aspirant* recognizes that he or she has the obligation to act righteously and, in doing so, purify their own heart. . . . True spiritual strength comes from leaning upon the *Self* within for spiritual support and being, rather than upon external situations. . . . Thus, within the teachings of Maat can be found all of the important injunctions for *living a life* which promotes purity, harmony, and sanctity. While these may be found in other spiritual traditions from around the world, seldom is the emphasis on non-violence and balance to be found.[29] (italics mine)

The study guide written by Ashby is for both the practitioner and the curious and aims to focus a life on a higher calling. Ma'at is observed as part of a spiritual science that connects the individual with the universe. This individual-universe connection is central to a basic understanding of the perspective that informs the relationality of human beings to the universe, which is so divergent from that of the West. The author stressed: "Anubis (god of discernment between reality and illusion) and Djehuti (god of reason and truth) oversee the scale of Maat. They judge the condition of the Heart (Ab) and determine its level of spiritual achievement."[30]

Modern imaginations have been fascinated with the various Egyptian divinities and symbols. The tombs in the Pyramids draw attention,

42 Laws of MAAT

1. I have not committed sin.
2. I have not committed robbery with violence.
3. I have not stolen.
4. I have not slain men and women.
5. I have not stolen food.
6. I have not swindled offerings.
7. I have not stolen from God/Goddess.
8. I have not told lies.
9. I have not carried away food.
10. I have not cursed.
11. I have not closed my ears to truth.
12. I have not committed adultery.
13. I have not made anyone cry.
14. I have not felt sorrow without reason.
15. I have not assaulted anyone.
16. I am not deceitful.
17. I have not stolen anyone's land.
18. I have not been an eavesdropper.
19. I have not falsely accused anyone.
20. I have not been angry without reason.
21. I have not seduced anyone's wife.
22. I have not polluted myself.
23. I have not terrorized anyone.
24. I have not disobeyed the law.
25. I have not been exclusively angry.
26. I have not cursed God/Goddess.
27. I have not behaved with violence.
28. I have not caused disruption of peace.
29. I have not acted hastily or without thought.
30. I have not overstepped my boundaries of concern.
31. I have not exaggerated my words when speaking.
32. I have not worked evil.
33. I have not used evil thoughts, words or deeds.
34. I have not polluted the water.
35. I have not spoken angrily or arrogantly.
36. I have not cursed anyone in thought, word or deeds.
37. I have not placed myself on a pedestal.
38. I have not stolen what belongs to God/Goddess.
39. I have not stolen from or disrespected the deceased.
40. I have not taken food from a child.
41. I have not acted with insolence.
42. I have not destroyed property belonging to God/Goddess.

Figure 3.1 42 Laws of Ma'at, artwork courtesy of The Noble Esthetic, LLC.

including tools, jewelry, or food; the process of embalming; or the hieroglyphics. These artifacts become the lure for some students. However, for this introductory text, the focus on Ma'at and its connection to the Pan-African religion, Ausar Auset, is central to understanding something deeper about its meaning: the process of the soul's journey and connection to the universe.

An essay by Sekhmet Ra Em Kht Maat (Cher Love McAllister) provided one of the clearest presentations of the "Kemetic model of the cosmological interactive self," to present the interdependency of creation, which includes humans. She cited Ra Un Nefer Amen's definition of cosmology, which emphasized that it "provides a framework that guides thinking and action through the vast array of seemingly unrelated life situations . . . showing how all events in a person's life are integrally related to his/her destiny."[31] Maat/McAllister drew from ancient hieroglyphic writings. Another Kemetic priest stated:

> "We do know that the Nuk Au Neter was chiselled on the wall of the pyramids more than 4,000 years ago," said Kemetic priest Ser Maa Keru Men Metu. He has been a priest at the Philadelphia chapter for more than eight years. "These are very highly spiritual and moral teachings on the walls of those pyramids. It is important to study those laws to improve the quality of our lives. Through those writings, we come to learn how divine we really are," Metu said.[32]

Maat/McAllister drew from this work and the works of Ra Un Nefer Amen and Muata Ashby to define Kemetic cosmology. A very condensed version of the cosmological process follows.

NU is the beginning, before anything is made. NU is Primeval Waters. NU is all-encompassing, with infinite potential. Creating itself out of NU is NTR, and here reside the qualities and conceptualizations of all spiritual and physical realities. From NTR, NTRU comes forth to bring all into existence, and the basis for all is Ma'at. "Maat, then, is the spiritual force that is a direct extension of Nus' potential to reflect itself as existence. . . . Maat, then, is the spiritual force governing, if you will . . . unification of the Ntru, Ntr, and Nu, and . . . the continuous connectivity and relationship between the Ntru."[33] Therefore, when a human or community breaks one of the 42 Laws of Maat, there is a violation of the universe itself.

The aim for practitioners of Ausar Auset is to evolve spiritually. The first steps in Maat are to assist the initiate in moving beyond a level of survival, eventually bringing them to enlightenment. Ashby cited an Egyptian proverb: "Those who live today will die tomorrow, those who die tomorrow will be born again; those who live MAAT will not die." This logic is different from Western science, which aims to be quantitative and uses a series of proofs to demonstrate facts.

Like all mystery religions, spiritual aspirants to Ausar Auset enter classes where they learn that "its spiritual view is that man (*sic*) is a divine being because man is made in the likeness of God and shares the spiritual wisdom and power of the Creator." [34] They learn chants and other affirmations taken from the Egyptian papyri that will "change his/her consciousness from body consciousness ('I am a body') to Cosmic Consciousness ('I am God')."[35] This is not a solitary journey; it is one in which community life is important, as is stated on one of the organization's websites: "For a people to grow spiritually, and hence come harmoniously and productively together, they must encounter the spiritualizing forces not in the halls of education or between the pages of books, but at every turn of their day-to-day interaction with life and with each other." [36]

So how is Ausar Auset Black? I return to Cheikh Anta Diop's words: "A dynamic, modern contact with Egyptian Antiquity would enable Blacks to discover . . . that these temples, these . . . are indeed the work of his ancestors and that he has a right and a duty to claim this heritage."[37] For members of Ausar Auset, there is reclamation of an Afrikan heritage, adapted for the current age. At the same time, Ausar Auset identifies itself as a Pan-African religion, a concept that did not exist for the ancients, but here, it is open to all Black people to claim a heritage. The members conduct themselves separately from Western ethical bases in favor of one that is more resonant with African identities.

Adoption of Kemetic principles or practicing some form of Egyptian religion is not limited to Black people. Kemetic studies are attractive to others in this age of new religions, with some of those forms referred to as neo-paganism. That there may be forms that are designated paganism upsets their Afrikan flavor: paganism is often more free- and independent-acting, with nature as the primary focus.

The next chapter turns to three African Indigenous Religions that originated in West African areas: Ifá, BaKongo or BuKongo, and Vodun. These are not the only indigenous religions from the continent. However, each of these has an outsized influence on the development of different ADR, which will be discussed in later chapters.

Notes

1. Alice Eley Jones, "Sacred Places and Holy Ground: West African Spiritualism at Stagville Plantation," in *Keep Your Head to the Sky: Interpreting African American Home Ground*, ed. Grey Gundaker (Charlottesville: University Press of Virginia, 1998), 104.
2. Sylvester A. Johnson, "The Rise of Black Ethnics: The Ethnic Turn in African American Religions, 1916–1945," *Religion and American Culture: A Journal of Interpretation* 20, no. 2 (2010): 139.
3. Okot P'Bitek, *Decolonizing African Religions: A Short History of African Religions in Western Scholarship* (New York: Diasporic Africa Press, 2011 reprint; originally published 1971), 51–2.
4. Kwasi Wiredu, "Reflections on Cultural Diversity," *Diogenes* 52, no. 1 (London: Sage Publications, 2005), 125.
5. E. Bolaji Idowu, *African Traditional Religion: A Definition* (Maryknoll, NY: Orbis Books, 1973), 161.
6. Jones, "Sacred Places and Holy Ground," 104.
7. Wiredu, "Reflections on Cultural Diversity," 123.
8. bell hooks, *Killing Rage: Ending Racism* (New York: Henry Holt and Company, 1995), 242.
9. Joy DeGruy, *Post Traumatic Slave Syndrome: America's Legacy of Enduring Injury and Healing*, 2nd ed. (Joy DeGruy Publishing Inc., 2017).
10. Ibid., 189.
11. Idowu, *African Traditional Religion*, 160.
12. Ibid., 160–1.
13. Kwasi Wiredu, introduction to P'Bitek, *Decolonizing African Religions*, xxiv.
14. Idowu, *African Traditional Religion*, 184.
15. Anthony Ephirim-Donkor, *African Spirituality: On Becoming Ancestors* (Trenton: Africa World Press, Inc., 1997), 5.
16. Ibid., 140.
17. Umar Habila Dadem Denfulani, "Pa Divination: Ritual Performance and Symbolism among the Ngas, Mupun, and the Mwaghavul of the Jos Plateau, Nigeria," in *African Spirituality*, ed. Jacob K. Olupona (New York: The Crossroad Publishing Company, 2000), 87.
18. Tracey E. Hucks, "Habitations of the Sacred," *Harvard Divinity Bulletin* 41, nos. 3–4 (Summer/Autumn 2013): 44.
19. Philip M. Peek, "The Silent Voices of African Divination," *Harvard Divinity Bulletin* 41, nos. 3–4 (Summer/Autumn 2013): 34–5.

20 Hucks, "Habitations of the Sacred," 45.
21 Hurston, *The Sanctified Church*, 49.
22 Laura C. Jarmon, *Wishbone: Reference and Interpretation in Black Folk Narrative* (Knoxville: The University of Tennessee Press 2003), xxvi–xxvii.
23 Hucks, "Habitations of the Sacred," 44.
24 Idowu, *African Traditional Religion*, 207.
25 Report of the Working Group of Experts on People of African Descent on its mission to the United States of America, United Nations Working Group of Experts on People of African Descent, no. 41, https://digitallibrary.un.org/record/848570?ln=en&v=pdf (Geneva: United Nations, 2016), 12.
26 Report of the Working Group of Experts on People of African Descent, no. 68, 16.
27 Wándé Abímbólá, *Ifá Will Mend Our Broken World* (Roxbury: Aim Books, 1997), 29.
28 Ausar Auset Atlanta, GA website: https://ausarausetatl.com/ra-un-nefer-amen-i.
29 Muata Ashby, *The 42 Precepts of Maat and Their Foundation in the Philosophy of Righteous Action of the Wisdom Text Sages of Ancient Egypt Study Guide* (Miami: Sema Institute of Yoga, 1998), 20.
30 Ibid., 19.
31 Sekhmet Ra Em Kht (Cher Love McAllister), "Towards an African-centered Sociological Approach to Africana Lesbian, Gay, Bisexual, Transgender, Queer, and Intersexed Identities and Performances: The Kemetic Model of the Cosmological Interactive Self," *Critical Sociology* 40, no. 2 (March 2014): 245.
32 Arlene Edmonds, "Kemetic Priest Claims Nuk Au Neter Are World's Oldest Scriptures," *Philadelphia Tribune*, August 26, 2016, https://www.proquest.com/newspapers/kemetic-priest-claims-nuk-au-neter-areworlds/, accessed September 2024.
33 Sekhmet Ra Em Kht (Cher Love McAllister), "Towards an African-centered Sociological Approach to Africana Lesbian, Gay, Bisexual, Transgender, Queer, and Intersexed Identities and Performance," 245.
34 Ausar Auset Atlanta, GA website: https://ausarausetatl.com.
35 Ashby, *The 42 Precepts of Maat*, 19.
36 Ausar Auset International, Ausar Auset Atlanta, GA website: https://ausarausetatl.com/aasintl.
37 Diop, *The African Origin of Civilization: Myth or Reality*, 140.

4

Afrikan Indigenous Religions (AIR)

Chapter Outline

Ba'Kongo	100
Ifá	106
Vodún	109
Themes and Questions	113
Moving On . . .	116

There are multiple religious and spiritual groupings on the continent of Africa. The first map of Africa (Figure 1.2) shows the routes by which groups were brought to the Americas and the Caribbean. The second map (Figure 1.3) highlights that the bulk of the captives came from the West Central region of Africa. The contemporary areas in Africa are roughly the Republic of Congo, Nigeria, Togo, Ghana, and Benin. The three traditions defined in this chapter are selected because of their relationships to ADR: BaKongo, Ifá, and Vodún. Various religious and spiritual traditions have roots in these three.

 The captives could not carry their own religious traditions whole cloth, as in their homes, into the new lands. Instead, they adjusted, utilized what they had and what they remembered, and blended when it was necessary. The ethnic and regional mixtures of trafficked Africans resulted in new combinations of religious and spiritual thought. The term often used for this mixture by religion scholars is "syncretism." This term emphasizes that something new is formed, but its parts are unrecognizable or negligible. For this volume, the term hybridization will be used to demonstrate the history and development, and to show that some sections of what was created can be traced back to their sources. It is important to emphasize that these traditions could survive for two reasons.

First, while there has been enslavement in other lands throughout history, to turn humans into chattel under colonization was distinct and devastating. As a result, separate societies developed where Black people often understood the world of White people, which was necessary for their survival. The reverse, for White people to understand Black concepts, was not true. This separation did not end in the late 1800s or the early 1900s but continued in some ways for the next one hundred years. Consider that *Brown v. Board of Education* and the Civil Rights Movement occurred in the mid-twentieth century. Yet, Black people are still villainized, and questions of who Black people are and what "they" might do fuel White people's fears and justification of mistreatment. Sociocultural gaps continue, and the lives of Black people across the globe are still in jeopardy. Religion and spirituality that reckon with Black lives while affirming Black humanity will continue to draw members.

The second reason for the survival of these religions in the colonies will be shown in detail below, in the discussion of the practice of adaptation among African religions. In other words, the captured Africans had skills to pragmatically shape religious traditions as needed.

Turning to the three African traditions, some aspects will be highlighted here, not exhaustively. The studies of these Afrikan traditions have also developed over time, moving away from the definitions of the colonizers and finding their own voice. The processes of recovering Afrikan spiritual thought reflect an unspooling of the bindings of colonial structures while able to introduce other conversations with the African Diaspora.

Ba'Kongo

The spirituality of the BaKongo is, in some ways, the most philosophical and, simultaneously, the most difficult for Westerners to grasp. An example is the symbol of the circle. When I began these studies, I oversimplified the meaning of the circle, seeing it as representative of the cyclical birth-life-death-rebirth. However, it is much more. The forms of this spirituality will underlie various versions of Diasporan spiritual thought.

Kia Bunseki Fu-Kiau (1934–2013) was a leading scholar of BaKongo thought. He recovered and re-centered ways of thinking about Afrikan spirituality and filled in what had been missing in earlier Pan-African scholarship. Marimba Ani noted the significance of Fu-Kiau's work from her perspective as an African Studies scholar. Fragments from Kemetic texts, common sense, "distorted anthropological descriptions of Europeans . . . along with glimpses into a painfully disrupted past made possible by our own broken Ancestral memories" provided the basis for "Afrikan-centered reconceptualization."[1] She stressed that Fu-Kiau presented a fuller picture with

> Afrikan conceptions of energy as they related to human beingness. Mûntu (the human being) is perceived of as sacred in birth and is venerated throughout the life process... which connects the visible and invisible world. . . . Fu-Kiau's discussion is a medium through which we can come to understand Afrikan metaphysics as a foundation for the explanation of physical and biological sciences . . . based on teachings of Elders, themselves trained in the indigenous initiation schools of Afrikan civilization.[2]

The scholarship on African traditions has been connected to and fueled by Afrikan scholars whose works reached into Diasporan communities. The possibilities of making these connections have already been discussed in previous chapters, including with Cheikh Anta Diop and Kwame Nkrumah, among others.

Fu-Kiau, from Kinshasa, Congo, told of his journey to understand Kongo cosmology after the colonizing Belgians were expelled:

> I finished [teacher education] in 1958, and I taught school for two years. Then I moved to the capital city, Kinshasa, and took classes at the university while teaching. I decided I had to do research myself . . . and decided to open a small school in 1963. I built a center, and then an elder came one Sunday and said, "Fu Kiau, you cannot succeed unless you are initiated." I began new training, and it led to my discovery of Kongo cosmology.[3]

Initiation into an AIR or ADR should be a critical change in the perspectives of individuals and their spiritual communities; it is not guaranteed and depends on the person and the community. The paths to initiation are different for various traditions and across regions. However, within each tradition, initiation is vital.

Fu-Kiau identified initiation's signal importance in his tradition:

> To be initiated is to be ready to accept responsibility, both as a mature human being and as a powerful spiritual being. . . . It is to enter into the process of learning *mu kula*, to grow, to the full understanding of *N'kîngu mianzîngila* ("principles of life/living"), principles that could assist one to keep that potential power and to pass it on safely to one's offspring.[4]

Such understanding cuts across all ADR and AIR. Initiation, however, is not an end in itself. Instead, it allows the initiate to continue spiritual growth in a specific tradition. As one author stated, "Initiation does not end in fact until the moment when one breathes one's last breath."[5]

Echoing the experiences of Malidoma Patrice Somé, discussed in Chapter 1, Fu-Kiau's focus as a teacher shifted when he was initiated and learned the Kongo cosmology. His resulting books and lectures had an international impact, bringing new appreciation for Afrikan spirituality. One European anthropologist stated the bald truth: "The concept [of the human moving in space and time between this world and the other] itself is so abstract as to have eluded several generations of European ethnographers, themselves inclined to empiricism and convinced that the African mind is incapable of abstract thought [which] generated an apparent puzzle, that of the persistence of beliefs in magic and witchcraft despite the intensive educational efforts of foreigners."[6] Outside of literary fiction, that which is not provable in a Western scientific frame is not significant or of value, adding to the layers of misinterpretation.

The BaKongo Deity is *Nzambi Mpungu*, who has granted humans a system of *minkisi*, or sacred medicines. Healing is central to the belief system, especially self-healing power. Such power comes from being balanced, "through what we are taught, what we see, and through what we eat."[7] *Nzambi Mpungu's* "illuminating spirit and healing powers are carefully controlled by the king (*mfumu*), the ritual expert (*nganga*), and the sorcerer (*ndoki*)."[8] When necessary, therapy can occur. In an Afrikan context, Fu-Kiau stated that therapy "can take the form of debate, conversation, play, ritual, cooking party, dance, war game, trip, weaving, running, bathing or washing hands ceremony, working with clay (pottery), massage, meditation, singing, drumming, storytelling, laughter play, touching, iconographical writing, inhalation, or hypnotism."[9] This view of therapy stands in contrast to a Western view, where people do not work in community and are divided, set up to constantly compete against one another, and any failure demonstrates unfitness.[10]

Afrikan Indigenous Religions (AIR) 103

The Bakongo Cosmogram
Yowa/Dikenga Cross

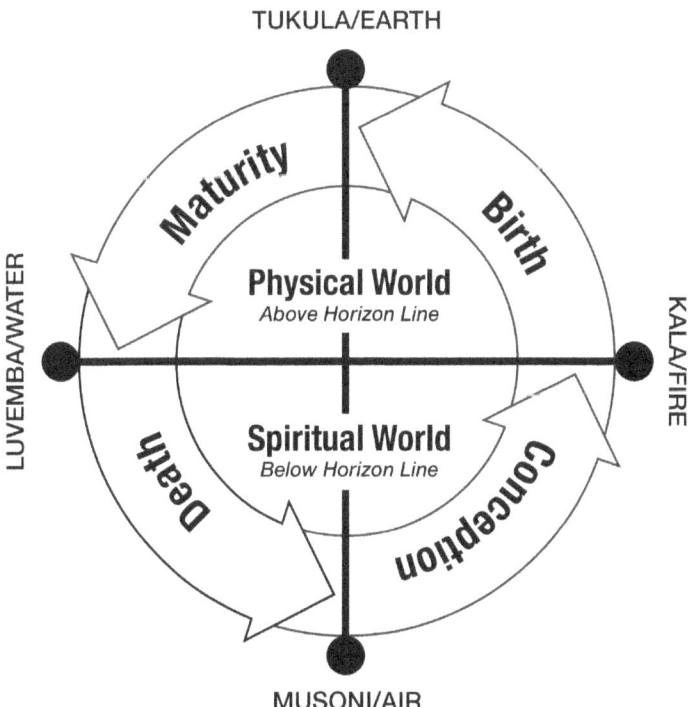

Figure 4.1 BaKongo Cosmogram, artwork courtesy of The Noble Esthetic, LLC.

The circle as a symbol shows up throughout Africa, and its meaning is shaded from one group to another. The concept I mentioned at first—life-death-rebirth-life—is one aspect. For Kongo cosmology, the circle becomes more complex. A line with an empty circle at its center, *mbûngu*, is "a symbol of emptiness, a world without life,"[11] Fu-Kiau explained. From this, a fire-force erupted, kalûnga, "and became the source of life . . . the symbol for force, vitality and more, a process and principle of change, all changes on earth."[12] Kalûnga, as life force, divides the physical world (*Ku Nseke*) from the spiritual world (*Ku Mpémba*). Kalûnga is referred to as a river or ocean separating the two worlds. The resulting symbol is called the *yowa* or *dikenga* cross, a circle divided into four quadrants. The sun itself follows the path around the circle, rising and setting in the physical and the spiritual worlds.

> Coded as a cross, a quartered circle or diamond, a seashell's spiral, or a special cross with solar emblems at each ending—the sign of the four moments of the sun is the Kongo emblem of spiritual continuity and renaissance. . . . In certain rites, it is written upon the earth, and a person stands upon it to take an oath or to signify that he or she understands the meaning of life as a process shared with the dead below the river.[13]

Mûntu (the human) "is a second sun rising and setting around the earth."[14] Human life proceeds in four stages, moving around the circle with the four moments of the sun: "1) rising, beginning, birth or regrowth 2) ascendancy, maturity, responsibility 3) setting, handing on, death, transformation 4) midnight, existence in the other world, eventual rebirth."[15] A human's life is continuous.

The appearance of a cross at the center, to demarcate the quadrants, led some missionaries to suppose that the people in Congo learned from their Christian belief in Jesus's crucifix. Fu-Kiau countered such an idea: "Contrary to what many students have said, the sign of the cross was not introduced into this country and into the minds of its people by foreigners. The cross was known to the BaKongo before the arrival of Europeans, and corresponds to the understanding in their minds of their relationship to their world."[16] Conversely, it may have been this idea of the cross and water baptism reflecting the separation of worlds that made Christianity more acceptable to the captive Africans.

The cosmogram of Kongo is embodied and drawn on the ground during ceremonies, with singing and having a designated person stand on the point of the cross or in the center of the circle. Robert Farris Thompson explained that

> Drawing a "point," invoking God and the ancestors, formed only a part of this most important ritual of mediation. The ritual included "singing the point." . . . They believe the combined force of singing Ki-Kongo words and tracing in appropriate media the ritually designated "point" or "mark" of

contact between the worlds will result in the descent of God's power upon that very point.[17]

Ritual is central to daily life, providing healing and building community: "Nothing in the daily life of Kôngo society is outside its cosmological practices."[18] All life experiences flow around this circle in counterclockwise movements, including parenting, family life, and community leadership. Fu-Kiau highlighted marriage, *lôngo*, as "one of the most important social institutions . . . a physically living symbol of the alliance(s) between, at least, two communities."[19] Love is not the catalyst for marriage but the creation of alliances. Children, then, do not "belong to parents, it is a collective, and societal relationship . . . the society accepts automatically the responsibility to raise all offspring of such a lôngo."[20]

BaKongo spiritualities show up in different ways in the Diaspora and will surface in the next chapters' discussions of some ADR, such as ground drawings. More importantly, the circle remains an influence. Western thinking is described as linear, and the myth of progress through time, forgetting the past, might drive a conversation. Under the influence of the circle, return becomes expected. A young child in a family may be remarked as being "just like" a deceased family member.

A circle is fluid, and the pragmatic approach to life found in AIR/ADR does not depend on clear starting and stopping lines, also known as a linear approach. Circular thinking can be creative, finding new ways and paths. Remnants of this Kongo circle may have been influences in Black culture developments. For instance, a saying in Black communities when encountering life's obstacles is to "go over, under, around, or through" the obstacle, which could be a reflection of a circular pattern of thinking. Another historic remnant of the BaKongo traditions can be found in the ring shout. Sterling Stuckey identified dance as a place where the circle can be seen: "Whenever in Africa the counterclockwise dance ceremony was performed—it is called the ring shout in North America—the dancing and singing were directed to the ancestors and gods, the tempo and revolution of the circle quickening in the course of movement. The ring in which Africans danced and sang is the key to understanding the means by which they achieved oneness in America."[21] This circular dance movement could be found in many communities of enslaved Africans. The dancers were not to lift their feet from the ground, moving in rhythmic steps in the circle. Such reflections of BaKongo spirituality are subtle, but they will surface in consideration of African Diasporan life and within ADR.

Ifá

Ifá also has complex layers that might challenge the Western reader. It is sometimes seen as a simpler tradition, so this section presents a brief overview of its layers.

Ifá practitioners claim that it is over 300,000 years old, older than Egyptian religion and one of its influences. Ifá does have literature on which divination and communal or individual prayers are drawn. The literature is often communicated orally; therefore, it is not comparable to written sacred literatures. As a result, the depth is easily overlooked. "Ifá does . . . represent the greatest unwritten Book on Earth, a perennial fountain of esoteric knowledge, from which all Prophets; Messengers; Messiahs; and Apostles, past, present, and future, sip."[22] The Yorùbá perspective seeks balance and harmony at the heart of its life ethic as part of a "cosmology [that] imparts a complex religious philosophy," defining the city of Ile-Ife as the center of the world.[23]

"To the Yorubas and other Africans, Ifa has always been an essential part of life. It forms the foundations of the all-governing principles of life for them. They consult Ifa for guidance and assurance on life situations, such as before a betrothal; before a marriage; before a child is born"[24] and all life events. This description of Ifá and the traditional religion of the Yorùbá people, who populated portions of modern-day Nigeria, Benin, and Togo, is not what is usually considered first. Instead, multiple divinities, the Òrìṣà, often lead scholars to refer to the religion as Ifá/Òrìṣà. This tends to reduce the tradition to something parallel with Greek divinities, but it is much more complex. Ifá "can simply be defined as 'the esoteric word of Olódùmarè which was used to create the universe and its fullness in the beginning, which is still binding.' The word consists of sacred elements that are forever constant and eternal."[25]

The chief deity is Olódùmarè, neither male nor female, who breathed life into the world and humans. "As the essence and symbol of Supreme Creative Power, Olódùmarè influences every particle of life and dust with life force (Àṣẹ), eternally binding all life together. It is this common telepathic thread, Àṣẹ, through which spirit, humanity, and nature communicate."[26] Here is the heart of the spiritual technology—the cosmology of Ifá.

Olódùmarè is the Supreme Being. That Olódùmarè is supreme and not the Òrìṣà is told by E. Bọlaji Idowu. One thousand seven hundred divinities decided that they, rather than Olódùmarè, should hold the greater power. They met and suggested to Olódùmarè that they hold power for sixteen years. "Olódùmarè . . . suggested it might be wise for them to experiment for sixteen days in the first instance. This suggestion was joyfully accepted. They set about their task. But after only eight days . . . the universe was, in fact at a standstill. . . . The heavens withheld its rains; rivers ceased to flow; rivulets became gutted with fallen leaves; the ears of corn filled but did not ripen. . . ."[27] They returned to Olódùmarè, embarrassed and pleading for mercy, and he laughed and forgave them. Olódùmarè returned the world to its normal running. The Òrìṣà left singing Olódùmarè's praises.

The structure of Ifá, then, has Olódùmarè at the top of the divinity hierarchy, followed by the Òrìṣà. With this hierarchy, Ifá is sometimes referred to as a qualified monotheism. The monotheistic character is often obscured because the Òrìṣà are the most visible representations of Ifá since they have shrines; Olódùmarè does not. This or a similar divinity hierarchy is followed in related ADR, but the Supreme Being remains in charge.

While there are many Òrìṣà, numbered in the hundreds or thousands depending on who is counting, several were specifically tasked with aiding the earth and its inhabitants. Some Òrìṣà may be identified by their energies, such as fire, water, or wind, or by a particular power, such as healing. Some Òrìṣà have special leadership roles, such as Èṣù, Ọrúnmìlà, and Ọbàtálá. The Òrìṣà traveled with captive Africans and became part of Diasporan religious traditions: Orixás in Brazil; Orishas in Cuba; Lwa in Haiti; Orishas in the United States. "The orishas are beheld not outside the individual but deep within; and the individual, through ritual address, possesses the gods and goddesses as a way of repossessing those essential, divine aspects of one's self."[28]

Humans are sacred, woven into the fabric of the universe. The relationships between Olódùmarè, the Òrìṣà, humans, all life, the earth, and the universe, as was pointed out in the last chapter, draw from a cosmology that centers community, with each person's ancestors having a central role. Before birth, each spirit-to-become-human chooses a destiny, a path that may be interwoven with problems and challenges.

Divinities

(The following list of a few divinities' names give examples of some relationships between AIR and ADR. Please note that the names may be similar, but characteristics may differ to meet new situations!)

Ifá	Vodún	Candomblé	Lucúmi/Santería	Vodou (Ayiti) and Voodoo (U.S.)
Olódùmarè	MawuLisa	Olorum	Olorun	Bondye/Olodumare
Èṣù	Legba	Exu	Elegua	Eleggua/Papa Legba
Ogún	Gu	Ogum	Ogun	Papa Ogún/Papa Ogún
Ọbàtálá	Orishánla	Oxum	Ochun	Erzulie/Erzulie
Ọṣùn	Oshun/Aziri	Oxalá	Obatala	Orula/Obatala
Ṣàngóó	Xevioso	Xangô	Chango	Chango/Chango
Yemọja	Oboto	Iemanjá	Yemaya	N/A/Yemaya

Figure 4.2 Chart of Orisa/Orixas/Orishas, artwork courtesy of The Noble Esthetic, LLC.

Each human is responsible for working to fulfill the destiny that was received before birth. This is the task of a lifetime. Deidre Badejo defines the focus: "Morality in Yorùbá cosmology creates harmony in the cosmos. Immorality, on the other hand, creates disharmony which ruptures the individual and/or communal psyche."[29] There is Heaven in this cosmology, but it should never be equated with a Christian version. For Christians, death is terminal with a possible reward of Heaven; for Ifá practitioners, there is life as an ancestor, with a possible return. The Òrìṣà and Ifá work with humans, aiming to assist in fulfilling or correcting that destiny. In this, divination is important.

While àṣẹ, mentioned above, may be available, divination, prayer, human-to-spirit intimate relationship development, balanced morality, and inner peace, amongst other things, make àṣẹ more accessible. The spiritual life of the Yorùbá and the Ifá practitioner requires personal and communal responsibility. Robert Farris Thompson pointed out that individual good character is required. How can good character be determined? By learning coolness or gentle generosity of spirit, Thompson reported. "Coolness, then, is part of character, and character objectifies proper custom. To the degree that we live generously and discreetly, exhibiting grace under pressure, our appearance and our acts gradually assume royal power. As we become noble, fully realizing the spark of creative goodness God endowed us with. . . we find the confidence to cope with all kinds of situations."[30]

So, the lived spirituality of the Yorùbá—Ifá—creates a philosophical bedrock that reflects the general characteristic of social pragmatism. This is a metaphysical spirituality that is embodied. Ifá parallels the BaKongo focus on healing the whole life of the person, who is grounded in community. To achieve wholeness, the components of life in Ifá, as noted, include balanced character, divination, prayer, and ritual to achieve àṣẹ and fulfill destiny. Therefore, Thompson could state: "The Yorùbá remain the Yorùbá precisely because their culture provides them with ample philosophic means for comprehending, and ultimately transcending, the powers that periodically threaten to dissolve them."[31]

These divinities and concepts flowed with the captives into their new lives: they expressed and shaped the ideas in multiple ways. But Vodou blended religious concepts starting on the African continent and, when transported to the colonies, established other lineages of ADR.

Vodún

The tradition known as Vodún is perhaps the most misrepresented of the three AIR discussed in this chapter. BaKongo is dense and philosophical, which has led many of my students' eyes to glaze over as we wrestle with the concepts. As Ifá moved into the Diaspora, it became somewhat glamorous in its art, various performances, and presence. However, Vodún came to hold a special negative space. None of these misunderstandings were about the realities of the traditions but were bound up in Western imaginaries. As Vodún encountered the West and colonization, its poor reputation developed and was cemented with racism, as Danielle Boaz covered in *Voodoo: The History of a Racial Slur*.[32] Those larger stories may come up in the next chapters. The focus here is on the source, the beginning of Vodún and its meanings, and perhaps on some of the reasons for the early distrust of the tradition.

"Vodou, Vodu, Voodoo, etc is distinct from other indigenous religions from the interiors of Western and Central Africa."[33] These names are interchangeable, including the designation, Fa. The use of multiple names probably added to the West's confusion about the tradition.

Those reasons may include the myths that surrounded the tradition and its people. One is the legend of Prince Agasu's conception.

> Around the fifteenth century, according to tradition, Aligbonon, [who was the daughter of the King] while seeking water in a forest, met and was made love to be a leopard spirit; the mystic union resulted in the birth of Prince Agasu, legendary ancestor of all the Fon of Dahomey, whose name is remembered in Haiti. . . . Around 1600, the youngest [of Agasu's descendants] trekked north and founded Abomey, capital of Dahomey.[34]

Another reason for misunderstandings may be the historic existence of the only documented female army in history, referred to as the Amazons of Dahomey. A fighting phalanx of women counters everything that the West, by the 1700s, had constructed about who women should be. "How they came to be or what their original purpose was is an unresolved quandary. . . . The Dahomey Amazons were recruited and trained from a young age, making them ruthless and more efficient warriors than men."[35]

Vodún developed in the area that cuts across several contemporary nations in the Gulf of Benin, including Benin, Togo, Nigeria, and Ghana. "In this region, society is organized around ethnic groups, the village, the family, and kinship. Each of these groups has its own vodu or vodun, ancestral and guardian deities."[36] Vodún is believed to be at least 10,000 years old. The kingdom of Dahomey, founded from Prince Agasu's lineage (1625–1894), is sometimes considered of central importance to Vodún, although there is no central religious center; as stated above, each group or family has its own vodu.

Koffi Kôkô is a performance artist based in France, from Ouidah, Benin. He is also an ordained Vodún priest, the Dah. For the Dah, performance and spirituality are connected, as is all life. One author defined these connections: "The Vodún cosmology believes that everything is connected, of divine essence, governed by spirits and forces of nature, including the sacred sites, streams, trees, and rocks inhabited by various spirits and deified ancestors."[37] The Dah presented a more metaphysical description of Vodún.

> Vodun can also be described as a culture, a heritage, a philosophy, an art, as dance, a language, medicine, a style of music, as justice, power, an oral tradition of tales or myths and rites. Vodun offers the answers that our ancestors have found to philosophical questions that all people are asking ... Vodun represents much more than a belief system: it is an entire way of life, an art of living.[38]

As the fighting force of women in Dahomey demonstrated, Vodún can be a source of political resistance, or as stated by Eric Montgomery, "The Vodún ... spirits are all about justice, and they demand to be regularly fed and remembered."[39]

Sarah M. Reynolds has studied Vodún in depth and provided this description:

> Common practices within Vodun include: the use of Fa divination (also called Ifá divination by the Yoruba people who created the system); the use of praise songs specific to each vodun; the use of ritual dances specific to each vodun; the creation of shrines to different vodun; regular offerings of items and possible animal sacrifices—also specific to each vodun; possession by the different divinities; and the traditional healing of both spiritual and physical ills.[40]

Reynolds also noted distinctions among Vodún priests, which is reminiscent of the Dahomey warriors: "In Vodun, women priestesses are generally equal to their male counterparts. Moreover, women, more generally, are considered to be spiritually powerful in certain ways that men are not."[41]

There are several similarities with the deities of Ifá (see Figure 4.2), attesting to the blending of traditions. However, Vodún is distinctive as well. For instance, the supreme Deity is Mawu Lisa. "Benin holds to the existence of a supreme being, a female, called Mawu. She has a twin brother, Lisa, from whom she is inseparable. The pair, Mawu-Lisa, while not the object of a cult, are considered the masters of all the vodun, whom they have assigned to the earth to serve humans."[42] The most important divinity is Fa, who "rules over divination, revealing to the individual the vodun to honor as well as the proper rites to follow in order to gain its protection or appease its anger."[43] The Dah stated: "These spirits form a hierarchy, which assigns the forces of nature and human society to powerful deities but also to individual spirits of rivers, trees, and stones."[44] The purpose, he emphasized, is to make connections among the already interconnected universe: divinities, humans, nature, and within ourselves. In this recognizing and reconnecting process, humans are able to resolve conflicts, "without falling into dogmatism and ambitiously trying to win over followers happy to adhere."[45]

That there are similarities between Vodún and Ifá may have Westerners thinking one is simply the knock-off of the other. However, AIR and ADR did not establish sharp lines of demarcation; instead, they used aspects of other traditions that "fit" their own needs. It is helpful to repeat Tracey Hucks' words here: "I have found that Africana populations accommodate multiple habitations of the sacred, blurring religious boundaries and traversing multiple sacred cosmologies in ways that are self-authorizing."[46] Such accommodation was not newly invented in the colonies, but had been part of the practice in Afrika. Combining traditions in Vodún also became a way to consolidate control over certain captured populations, "through the capturing of neighboring people's drummers and vòdún priests to assimilate their religious practices into those already practiced in the kingdom."[47] The processes of spiritual exchanges went both ways: "Supported both by intergroup marriages and by war, new spirits, new cults, new secrets, and ultimately new beliefs were introduced to each group from the other."[48]

All these concepts of Vodún are very different from the negative portrayals that were carried by the colonizers. Seeking peace and balance while simultaneously being willing to use spirituality in a fight for freedom remains consistent with discussions in the next chapters. But the Dah's words, in closing this section, show Vodún in a different light: "Living Vodun consciously and in practice means the individual is totally subordinated to universal law. Knowledge and practice together constitute a complete programme, a philosophy that has endured over the centuries."[49]

Themes and Questions

With the history presented in the first two chapters, these brief sketches of three AIR inform understandings of the ADR that will be discussed in the next chapters, which have direct relationships with each other. Without these contexts, ADR indeed seems like exotic misadventures of the captive Africans. Instead, the captives and their children drew from the philosophical, cultural, and social structures that they knew in order to build alternative spaces that would be self-healing. This was possible because of their spiritualities. Some of these spiritualities remained, some were built into something new, and some were lost or unnecessary.

In my teaching, I have found that there are certain areas that often become confusing about AIR/ADR: ritual which links to questions about sacrifice; gender, which is different in an Afrikan framework; and orality, which links to questions about initiation. None of these can be reduced to Christian equivalences, even though we may see in the next chapters that ADR might hybridize some aspects of Christianity.

Ritual aims to achieve life balance or coolness. Divination is one such ritual, but there are more. Ritual is earth-based and can be specific to a spiritual practice, such as healing, in which case there may be some precise requirements to be fulfilled for the work to be effective. But ritual also can be drawn upon based on a given need. As an example, on one visit to the Spirit Attenuation Well in Badgary, Nigeria, where African captives were boarded onto the ships, the Black Americans in the group experienced a range of unsettled emotions. The Yorùbá priest leading the group performed a libation, which involved prayers and pouring out water in honor of the ancestors who were taken through that Point of No Return.

One component of ritual is sacrifice. This has been part of the AIR/ADR. There are many kinds of sacrifice, from fruits to specific actions. But students get caught in discussions of animal sacrifice. Deidre Badejo described sacrifice from a Yorùbá perspective that can extend across the AIR: "Sacrifice seals the covenant between [the people] and binds human beings to communal and personal fulfillment. Personal fulfillment is both communal and spiritual when it seeks health, wealth, cleansing, safe and healthy childbearing, health, individual female health, personal and communal achievement."[50] She also cited the celebrated author Wole

Ṣóyínká, who referred to sacrifice as an act of "cosmic adjustment."[51] Despite this tradition, there are initiates in AIR and ADR who believe it is time to end animal sacrifice.

The second area surrounds the roles of women in AIR and ADR. There are multiple ways to look at this topic. Depending on the community, women can be initiated and priesthood is possible. But this changes according to the traditions of different communities. One community in Lagos forbids women from the work of animal sacrifice, reasoning that women produce children. I asked why the restriction was in place when men also contribute to the production of children. One of the women in the group cut in and quipped that men's part in producing a child is only about two minutes, bringing the group to laughter.

It is important to remember that gender and gender roles are not understood in a Western framework. The Amazons of Dahomey clearly show that African men and women had other understandings of gender roles. As Beninese economist Leonard Wantchekon stated: "The French made sure this history wasn't known. . . they said we were backward, that they needed to 'civilize us', but they destroyed opportunities for women that existed nowhere else in the world."[52] Oyèrónkẹ́ Oyěwùmí wrote that the imposition of Western ideologies about gender were processes to further the success of colonization. The first process, she stated, was the use of race to signal a Black and lower human form. "The second process . . . was the inferiorization of females."[53]

Instead, the gender role assignments in many Afrikan communities were not enforcement of a lower form of society but an indication of difference. For instance, there are separate men's and women's societies that have defined duties. Separate roles for women and men were not designed to inhibit women but to define the work to be done by each. Social power was assigned to each group. The evidence of these gendered separations can still be seen across Africa and the Caribbean, where women are often the vendors. Cheryl Townsend Gilkes also pointed out how such separate gendered structures flowed from the African continent to the United States, highlighting how Black women have worked throughout their communities and churches: "The colonial model suggests that the history of black people as *Africans* is as relevant as their history in the United States for interpreting the black experience. . . . Why not incorporate such references into histories and analyses of black womanhood within *relatively* autonomous social worlds?"[54]

Another aspect of gender and sexuality is LGBTQ. Some African countries today outlaw any form of same-sex love. Notably, Uganda and Ghana have laws that restrict, brutalize, imprison, or, in Uganda, impose death. Returning to Oyèwùmí's contrast between the West and her own Yorùbá society: "Since in Western constructions, physical bodies are always social bodies, there is really no distinction between sex and gender. In Yorùbá society, in. contrast, social relations derive their legitimacy from social facts, not from biology. . . . Biological facts do not determine who can become the monarch or who can trade in the market."[55] She continues with her analysis, focusing on the cultural limits of Western feminism: "The splitting of hairs over the relationship between gender and sex, the debate on essentialism, the debates about differences among women, and the preoccupation with gender bending/blending that have characterized feminism are," she contends, built into Western thought and its social hierarchies.[56]

One area related to discussions of gender is female genital mutilation or FGM. This practice occurs in some areas of the African continent. FGM is serious and raises important social and ethical health questions. It is outlawed in various African countries, from Egypt to South Africa. Yet it is sometimes still practiced in violation of the laws. For instance, Tonny Abet reported in November 2021 that Ugandans cross "to Kenya to undergo female genital mutilation as a way to escape tough penalties against the practice in Uganda."[57] What is important for these discussions of AIR and ADR: FGM is NOT a religious tradition, although many of the people who support the practice believe that it is religious.

None of this is meant to deny or cover up the existence of patriarchy, sexism, or sex role enforcement across the African continent. But the question must be asked: how much is based on indigenous beliefs and how much has been imported from the West?

Third, knowledge is passed on verbally, travels with a priest, and is not book- or building-bound. Sacred knowledge is transmitted orally, from the adept in one area of the tradition to the apprentice. This process of communicating knowledge or, as the Dah stated, an entire way of life and art of living, also reinforces the bonds of community, one of the key aspects of AIR which will be seen in ADR. Koffi Kôkô added another dimension in thinking about orality: "The sacred potential of oral transmission is much more intense than that of the knowledge one receives through written words, which are tamed and limited by grammatical rules. The magic of orally transmitted words cannot be analyzed intellectually. Their rhythm and sound are in sync with their message and mysterious content."[58]

Some questions may surface about students' or researchers' levels of involvement or response to AIR/ADR. There can be a draw to the mysticism and sense of wholeness of spirituality. Students of any religion may come to appreciate that religion, but appreciation does not indicate that they should pursue membership. Further, those who are researchers do not have to be initiated, as Eziaku Atuama Nwokocha explained in her writing. She talked about her own non-initiate status as she researched Haitian Vodou: "As a non-initiate, the border between outsider and insider is a boundary to interrogate and respect. I vehemently reject the idea that to meaningfully study African and African Diasporic religions I have to become initiated in the faith. To become initiated purely for the sake of my work would be disingenuous and disrespectful to the communities I engage with."[59]

However, some may pursue a deeper connection that requires another level of commitment and responsibility. As we have seen with MST, PAOCC, and Ausar Auset, the willingness to change one's name and adopt different living patterns becomes part of the spirituality. If that is the choice, apprenticeship and re-learning are required. Some experiences of initiates will be seen in the coming chapters.

Moving On . . .

Social and political constructions occurred because of the human trafficking of Africans, but the Spirit Attenuation Well or other trickery did not destroy the memories of the captives. These meanings from home became part of ADR, even if the source was lost to memory over time. As was seen in the Moorish Science Temple (MST), Pan-African Orthodox Christian Church (PAOCC), and Ausar Auset, Black people in the Diaspora often seek these religious traditions to heal from the past and move into their futures. Each of them, which will be true of ADR, involves being renamed within that tradition. Fu-Kiau's words capture the significance of the act of renaming to reclaim what had been lost:

> Names from Africa, their mother land, are reappearing among blacks in the New World *mu nîngisa n' sing'a dikûnda* (to strengthen the bio-

genetico-cultural rope of the black community) worldwide. And this upward spiral nomenclature victory among black people in the New World will incontestably show physical manifestations of improvement in all aspects of their life.[60]

The next chapters move into the histories and growth of several African Diasporan spiritualities and religions.

Notes

1. Marimba Ani, *Introduction to Kimbwandende Kia Bunseki Fu-Kiau, Self-Healing Power and Therapy, Old Teachings From Africa* (Clifton, NJ: African Tree Press, 2001 reprint), xi.
2. Ibid., xii–xiii.
3. From exhibit notes, "Art from Africa: Long Steps Never Broke a Back," Seattle Art Museum, 2002, https://www1.seattleartmuseum.org/Exhibit/Archive/longsteps/fukiau.htm#.
4. Kimbwandende Kia Bunseki Fu-Kiau, *Self-Healing Power and Therapy, Old Teachings From Africa*, 17.
5. Dominique Zahan, "Some Reflections on African Spirituality," in *African Spirituality*: Forms, Meanings, and Expressions, ed. Jacob K. Olupona (New York: Crossroad 2000), 22.
6. John M. Jantzen and Wyatt MacGaffey, *An Anthology of Kongo Religion: Primary Texts from Lower Zaire* (Lawrence: University of Kansas, 1974), 31.
7. Fu-Kiau, *African Cosmology of the Bantu-Kongo*, 19–20.
8. Robert Farris Thompson, *Flash of the Spirit: African and Afro-American Art and Philosophy* (New York: Vintage Books, 1984), 107.
9. Fu-Kiau, *Self-Healing Power and Therapy*, 47–8.
10. Ibid., 46–7.
11. Kimbwandende Kia Bunseki Fu-Kiau, *African Cosmology of the Bantu-Kongo: Principles of Life and Living* (Clifton, NJ: African Tree Press, 2001 reprint), 17.
12. Ibid., 19–20.
13. Robert Farris Thompson, cited in Sterling Stuckey, *Slave Culture: Nationalist Theory and the Foundations of Black America* (New York: Oxford University Press, 1987), 12.
14. Fu-Kiau, *African Cosmology of the Bantu-Kongo*, 25.

15 Fukiau kia Bunseki, *n'Kongo ye Nza Yakun'zungidila*, 1969, cited in John M. Jantzen and Wyatt MacGaffey, *An Anthology of Kongo Religion*, 34.
16 Ibid., 34.
17 Thompson, *Flash of the Spirit*, 110.
18 Fu-Kiau, *African Cosmology of the Bantu-Kongo*, 38.
19 Ibid., 39.
20 Ibid., 40.
21 Stuckey, *Slave Culture*, 12.
22 Ṣọlágbadé Pópóọlá Fákúnlé Oyèsànyà Gbolahan Okemuyiwa, *Ifa: Its Core Values, Vol. 1: What is Ifa?* (Phoenix: Ifaworks, LLC, 2016), 7.
23 Deidre Badejo, *Òṣun Ṣèègèsí: The Elegant Deity of Wealth, Power and Femininity* (Trenton, NJ: Africa World Press, 1996), 47.
24 Okemuyiwa, *Ifa: Its Core Values*, 6.
25 Ibid.
26 Badejo, *Òṣun Ṣèègèsí*, 50.
27 Idowu, *African Traditional Religion*, 159.
28 Clyde W. Ford, *The Hero with an African Face, Mythic Wisdom of Traditional Africa* (NY: Bantam Books, 1999), 145.
29 Badejo, *Òṣun Ṣèègèsí*, 68.
30 Thompson, *Flash of the Spirit*, 16.
31 Ibid.
32 Danielle Boaz, *Voodoo: History of a Racial Slur* (New York: Oxford University Press, 2023).
33 Eric James Montgomery, "Vodún/Vodu, Resistance, and North/South Relations in Undemocratic Togo," *Journal of Religion in Africa* 50, #3–4 (Leiden: Brill 2020), 226.
34 Thompson, *Flash of the Spirit*, 165.
35 Kylie Kiunguyu, "Benin's 30m 'Amazon' Statue Honours the Women Warriors of Dahomey" (Washington: https://AllAfrica.com/stories/202208040019.html), August 3, 2022.
36 Laënnec Hurbon, *Voodoo, Search for the Spirit* (New York: Harry N. Abrams, Inc. Publishers, 1993), 14.
37 Montgomery, "Vodún/Vodu, Resistance, and North/South Relations in Undemocratic Togo," 226.
38 Koffi Kôkô, "What is Vodun?" in *Performance Research*, 25, 6/7, 163, https://doi.org/10.1080/13528165.2020.1909956.
39 Montgomery, "Vodún/Vodu, Resistance, and North/South Relations in Undemocratic Togo," 227.
40 Sarah M. Reynolds, *Vodun: Race, Identity, and the Politics of Representation*, 2024 Dissertation, Tulane University, 6.

41 Ibid., 14.
42 Laënnec Hurbon, *Voodoo, Search for the Spirit* (New York: Harry N. Abrams, Inc. Publishers ,1993), 17–18.
43 Ibid., 16.
44 Kôkô, "What is Vodun?" 163.
45 Ibid.
46 Hucks, "Habitations of the Sacred," 44.
47 Sarah Politz, *Transforming Vòdún: Musical Change and Postcolonial Healing in Benin's Jazz and Brass Band Music* (Ann Arbor: University of Michigan Press, 2023), 4.
48 Timothy R. Landry, "Vodún, Globalization, and the Creative Layering of Belief in Southern Bénin," *Journal of Religion in Africa* 45 (Leiden: Brill, 2015): 186.
49 Kôkô, "What is Vodun?" 164.
50 Badejo, *Òṣun Ṣẹ̀ẹ̀gẹ̀sí*, 63.
51 Ibid., 69.
52 Cited in Kiunguyu, "Benin's 30m 'Amazon' Statue Honours the Women Warriors of Dahomey."
53 Oyèrónkẹ́ Oyěwùmí, *The Invention of Women: Making an African Sense of Western Gender Discourses* (Minneapolis: University of Minnesota Press, 1997), 152.
54 Cheryl Townsend Gilkes, *If It Wasn't for the Women: Black Women's Experience and Womanist Culture in Church and Community* (Maryknoll, New York: Orbis Books, 2001), 62.
55 Oyěwùmí, *The Invention of Women*, 12.
56 Ibid., 13.
57 Tonny Abet, "Ugandans Cross to Kenya for Female Genital Mutilation," November 25, 2021, https://allafrica.com/stories/202111260098.html, accessed December 2024.
58 Kôkô, "What is Vodun?" 164.
59 Eziaku Atuama Nwokocha, *Vodou en Vogue: Fashioning Black Divinities in Haiti and the United States* (Durham: University of North Carolina Press, 2023), 21.
60 Fu-Kiau, *Self-Healing Power and Therapy*, 16.

5
Candomblé

Chapter Outline

Introduction	121
Brazil	122
Creating Candomblé	124
Salvador, Bahia	127
Aspects of Candomblé	128
Establishing Candomblé	133
Conclusion	135

Introduction

"Why do you want to take students to Brazil? They speak French there. There aren't any Black people there, it's a Catholic country. What does Brazil have to do with Black studies?" The dean at the school where I was employed years ago challenged my proposed study abroad trip for undergraduate students. I was then the director of African American Studies, and I had an appointment in Religious Studies. After I brought the dean information about Brazil and its Black populations, cultures, religions (including Candomblé), and language (Portuguese), he cleared our travel.

The trip's objective was to broaden students' views beyond the narrow window of the United States in terms of Black spiritualities and cultures.

And it was successful. Yet, in that dean's response, the ongoing ignorance about Brazil is highlighted. As one author stated, even as "Brazil operates as a center for economically weaker countries in Latin America, the African continent, and elsewhere in the so-called developing world.... Brazil remains peripheral when it comes to the global dissemination of culture and knowledge."[1] Despite the appearance of being on the fringe of global culture and knowledge, African-Brazilians have developed significant ADR, with Candomblé as one of the most important.

Brazil

More captured Africans were taken to Brazilian colonies by human traffickers than were taken to the United States' colonies. While the captives were from various regions of the continent, the majority were from Nigeria, Ghana, and Benin, bringing AIR with them. The majority were Yorùbá, called Nagô in Brazil. Therefore, Ifá had a significant, but not exclusive, influence on the ongoing development of the ADR of Brazil.

To get a sense of the scope of these trafficked Africans, Zeca Ligiéro noted: "By 1538, the first African captives were brought to Brazil by European ships.... it initiated nearly four centuries of slave importation.... Originally, the trafficking went in the direction of Salvador, the old capital of Brazil, and then to the cities of Recife, Salvador, and Sâo Luis."[2] While the trafficking began in the mid-1500s, Ligiéro emphasized that it was the last cycle, from 1770 to 1850, that brought the "mass transport of Yorùbá to Salvador.... This mass arrival of the Jeje people (Fon, Ewe, and Aja) and the Yorùbá, called Nagô in Brazil, was a reason for their strong influence on Bahia's cultural life."[3] It was primarily to Bahia that my study abroad group was headed. I will return to the importance of Bahia shortly.

With distinctive colonization policies, Portugal was more interested in stripping the rich lands of resources than in establishing colonies, although huge swaths of land were granted by the crown to individual nobility. Additionally, the mountainous topography of some areas limited the establishment of landed colonies. Therefore, because Brazil is so close to Africa, the Portuguese colonizers deemed it economically justified to work the captives to death and then return to the continent to capture more.

The Portuguese used the enslaved Africans for mining, farming, and all manual labor. Africans were not scooped up haphazardly by the traffickers; those with certain skills were targeted for capture. Mining provides an example of the traffickers' deliberations.

Brazil is rich in minerals, particularly gold and silver. Enslaved Africans were engaged in the labor of working the mines. But some of the Africans brought skills from the African continent beyond brute labor that were valued. "Some groups of African origin are recurrently associated with mastery over the mining and metallurgy techniques found in Minas Gerais (*a state of Brazil, meaning "many mines"*) in the eighteenth century. The relevance of African iron production knowledge in Brazil is found in the works of travelers . . . and . . . researchers . . . The local techniques largely stemmed from African knowledge."[4]

The importance of such skill levels cannot be understated, as the enslaved were able to leverage status or freedom. Even from the communities of the escaped Africans, *quilombos*, which were often seen by the authorities as hotbeds of resistance, any skilled metalworkers' services were still sought. Gwendolyn Midlo Hall wrote that "Mina" might have meant coming through the trafficking site of Elmina, Ghana, but later may have been understood as "miner." Hall gave this example of the importance of Mina: "In 1726, the governor of Rio de Janeiro wrote that Africa slaves exported from Whydah (Ouidah, Benin) were reputed to have a special gift for discovering new gold deposits. 'For this reason there is not a Mineiro who can live without a negress from Mina, saying that only with them do they have any luck.'"[5]

It was possible for enslaved people to be granted freedom. This happened most often with manumission being granted as part of the last will and testament of the enslaver. These freed people found ways to earn money, with women predominant in markets and others in skilled trades, such as goldsmiths and smelters. However, freedpeople had no path to acceptance in Brazilian society. In fact, skin color—darker-hued skin was reviled—and origin—Brazilian-born was more likely to be of a lighter skin color—created other social class perceptions and structures.

In 1822, Brazil declared its independence from Portugal. Enslavement was losing its luster internationally as Brazil sought to join the community of nations. Brazilian abolition movements expanded even as landowners fought to hold on to their free labor pool. Brazil, the last country to do so, ended enslavement by law in May 1888. The "Golden Law" was signed by

Princess Isabel of Bragança. However, the law had a loophole so that new forms of enslavement continued: "After abolition was implemented, the formerly enslaved were still at the mercy of landowners who would grant them permission to live on their property in exchange for free labor, leaving them indebted to their former employers and without much more freedom than what they'd had before."[6] Those freed people who were not in servitude found themselves excluded from their former oppressive positions ("You're free!") but had nowhere to go.

This was the world where Candomblé was formed. Its development shows another way, quite different from Ausar Auset, PAOCC, and MST, that Afrikan religious thoughts were reestablished on new grounds with new situations.

Creating Candomblé

As Africans were brought to the Brazilian colonies, they carried their religions with them, and over time, these began to be re-crafted into Candomblé. "The word *Candomblé* translates to the veneration of selected deities (orixás) through dance and music."[7] There are longer discussions of the word's meaning, such as connecting it with *calundus*, tied to the establishment of religious societies as approved by Brazil's rulers and the Catholic Church. These societies were approved as places for the enslaved to gather for healing and prayer.[8] In that process, "the enslaved Africans were able to devise a strategy to conceal their Candomblé religious practices by pretending to worship Catholic saints while actually venerating African deities with similar sacred symbols and characteristics."[9]

While syncretism is a term that I usually avoid, here I follow Niyi Afolabi's perspective. He states that the term syncretism is problematic. That is, Afolabi claims, "all religions are syncretic because they represent a huge synthesis that integrates several elements to form a new whole."[10] Despite this difficulty, he contends, the African and Brazilian synthesis became a device to "retain the African culture that the enslaved struggled to sustain through many strategic negotiations with the oppressing colonizer."[11] The fusion of African deities with Catholic saints represented a truer version of syncretism with its tight, almost seamless blending. (Some anti-syncretism Candomblé movements today are trying to separate the African from the European, since it is no longer necessary to hide.) These processes of blending did not happen overnight. The flexibility of AIR also characterized the development of Candomblé. As cited in the last chapter, "Adaptability, flexibility, tolerance, and openness are distinguishing characteristics of African cultures and their religions and spiritualities."[12]

Candomblé, like other ADR, is not held together by an institution; there is no central controlling office. Instead, "practitioners organize in autonomous worship places known as *terreiros*."[13] These worship spaces are unique. Zeca Ligiéro gave a general description of the space arrangement of *terreiros*. There are several rooms that are shrines to different Orixás. Upon entering, the first room is for Exu, the divinity of change and the crossroads. The doors to this and each shrine are closed unless there is a ceremony. There may be a patio with sacred plants needed for specific rituals connected with the Orixás of the *terreiro*. "The largest constructed part is generally a large covered area, which must be high with good ventilation where most of the rituals and public ceremonies happen.... The kitchen is another space that is extremely important... [where] the devotees prepare foods" for the community and for the Orixás.[14]

The growth of African-derived religions in Brazil did not start or stop with Candomblé. Other ADR include Babassuê, Batuque, Jarê, Macumba, Omolocô, Pajelança de Negro, Quimbanda, and Umbanda, among others. However, "Candomblé takes precedence due to its historical, cultural, and demographic significance."[15]

There are accounts of Candomblé's existence in the mid-1700s, but its origins are shrouded in legend. One Candomblé *terreiro* is mentioned in 1785 court records, where arrested participants were from Jeje or Dahomey communities and were practicing Vodun. "The spiritual leader of the house, a freedman named Sebastião, appears to have established a reputation as a *curandeiro* (healer) and magician."[16]

Legend names three freed women—Iyá Dêtá, Iyá Kalá, and Iyá Nassô[17]—as the founders of one of the most important *terreiros*. (Iyá means mother.) It's believed that they were originally from Ketu, between Dahomey and Yorùbá. One legend says they walked back to Africa, to Ketu, to study. How the travel happened, they and possibly others, spent several years studying. When they returned, they "established the Candomblé house... initially called Iyá Omi Asé Airá Intilé in Salvador,

Bahia ... [and renamed] Ilê Axé Iyá Nassô Oká after its transportation to Engenho Velho, where it stands to this day."[18] That legend provides a neat and simplistic understanding of the beginnings of Candomblé. A much more complex view is offered by Rachel Harding.

Harding stressed the multiple layers of different ethnicities that can be found within Candomblé that reflect Brazilian ethnicities. For instance, she noted multiple Jeje elements in Candomblé's structures. "The three sacred drums of Candomblé are known as the *rum*, *rumpi*, and *lê*. . . . [Portions of the] initiation process are described in Jeje terms. . . . [Other Jeje language terms include] the *peji* (sanctuary, the sacred space of the deity), *runco* (retreat space for initiating devotees), and *ajuntó* (personal guardian spirit.)"[19] Harding also explored the connections with African Muslims who were part of the Brazilian communities and were known for their wisdom. "Most of Bahia's Nagô Muslims had recently converted, either in Africa or in Brazil; and because Islam in West Africa was strongly permeated with traditional beliefs, there was likely in Bahia an openness between the two religions similar to what had existed in Africa."[20] Additionally, Brazilian Indians, or *caboclos*, provided information on native plants and animals.[21]

Harding identified the *libertos* of Salvador, that is, the free Black people, as leaders of religious communities throughout the nineteenth century, despite governmental surveillance, harassment, and restrictions.

> They nonetheless used whatever means were at their disposal to create a life of relative autonomy for themselves. African freedpeople used the money they earned from their trades, transport services, and petty commerce to contribute to black institutions such as the *irmandades* (lay Catholic associations) and *juntas de alforria* (manumission clubs) and were often able to buy or build small houses or to rent rooms in which to live ... often [sharing] living spaces.[22]

Harding refers to these associations and to Candomblé as alternative spaces of Blackness, cutting through ethnic lines and creating communities around religious and African identities.

To develop Candomblé with an African identity, some adjustments had to be made. For example, sacred plants were critical components in ritual and healing ceremonies, but what was available in Brazil was different from what was available in Africa. The extensive research of geographer Robert Voeks provided a window into the botanical connections between

Candomblé and Yorùbá. He stated: "The most fundamental religious secret of a babalorixá [priest] is the knowledge of how to collect, prepare, and administer consecrated plants. Among Candomblé followers, a highly esteemed babalorixá is a person who 'knows all the leaves.' To surrender this knowledge to anyone except an initiate is to invite severe spiritual punishment."[23] Because of the importance of these plants, it is believed that those who traveled to Africa to study returned with some. Voeks noted that a clear indicator of the transportation of sacred plants from Africa to Brazil is the Obi or kola nut shrub. The Obi were regularly objects of trade to Brazil in the mid-1800s. "The African shrub is now cultivated throughout Bahia specifically for Candomblé worship."[24]

Salvador, Bahia

Salvador is a city where tourists and scholars look for experiences of Candomblé or signs of "Africanness" in the state of Bahia. Samba classes, street musicians, exhibitions of Capoeira (a martial art), or shopping in Pelourinho all seem to confirm Bahia's cultural designation as the "Black Mecca." There are problems with such travel brochure language.

The history of Brazil and its racial structures did not magically go away, as one author pointed out. "Salvador . . . is fundamentally anti-black, as evidenced in state mandated violence against blacks, and economic and political inequality between Afro-descendants and Whites."[25] Race itself is defined differently in Brazil, with skin color, mentioned above, becoming a marker—the lighter the skin, the better perceived socially. Even facets celebrated today as signs of African culture, as Rabelo and Duccini point out, "up to the first half of the twentieth century, these 'ethnic' cultural features were called '*colsas de preto*' (black people's things) or 'African,' and this was meant as no compliment."[26]

The later change in perception was, in part, fueled by increasing tourism. Some tourists seek the "exotic," and Salvador can provide that experience. But tourism to Brazil must include the perspectives of those from the Diaspora, who bring a different analytical gaze to their visits. That gaze can begin with relief at being in a space where most of the people are of color, which can be felt very differently from work and travel experiences in primarily White countries.

Since the 1980s, some Salvadorans have developed a defined Black consciousness that looks to the struggles for justice that others in the Diaspora have experienced. It is not unusual to find a spray-painted graffiti of Martin Luther King Jr. or Harriet Tubman on the walls within a favela (poor neighborhood). I was on a crowded beach in Rio de Janeiro, and a vendor walked by, selling t-shirts with the image of Che Guevara. "Che!" I exclaimed. An unknown White American man was nearby and angrily snarled at me, "He was a communist!" Here, "communist" is language that locks in racial misunderstandings. Black people look to someone who fights for freedom beyond an ideological label; people in power view such fights as a threat to their dominance. The branding of "communism" misrepresents the effects of oppression or the fight against them, while simultaneously serving to shut down conversation.

Black, Brown, and Indigenous Salvadorans have established structures to address multiple social inequities, from a domestic workers' union to Black Brazilian cultural centers, to environmental justice programs, to farm worker land reclamation projects. Samba schools, capoeira exhibitions, and especially Candomblé make more sense when presented in this true context of the "Black Mecca." When I have taken students to Brazil, time is spent in all these settings; otherwise, Candomblé is presented without context, an exotic spot for tourists' gazes.

Aspects of Candomblé

Candomblé and Ifá are often compared since there seem to be so many similarities. But Candomblé is distinct, developing through the layers mentioned in the previous section. There is one concept in particular that has deep similarities in both Yorùbá and Candomblé traditions: *axé* or in Yorùbá, *aṣẹ*.

One author refers to *axé* as "the core aspect . . . the divine energy that pervades the universe and ensures creation. . . . Axé connects everyone in the universe and is therefore not restricted to human beings but is part of every being, living as well as supernatural. Without *axé*, nothing would exist."[27] *Axé* pervades the universe and identifies the healing properties of various flora, returning to Voeks' analyses of different sacred plants and the importance of a babalorixá's knowledge. Harding takes the analysis further, stressing that axé provides more than healing: "The mutual process of healing and cultivation of axé in Candomblé (as in traditional African religion) not only involves pharmacopoeia applications and ritual adjustments of imbalance, but also signals the need for initiation and its labored, communal realization."[28]

The orixás themselves were given different parts of axé that correspond with the natural world. (For names of Orisa/Orixá/Orishas, see Fig. 4–2) As Ligiéro stated: "Every Orixá represents a different force of nature, and through refining our sensitivity, we can ascertain that the presence of an Orixá is alive in the natural environments to which they correspond."[29] It is more than Orixás relating to natural elements; specific Orixás govern each human "whose identities are revealed through divinatory rites."[30] This statement uncovers several components of Candomblé belief.

The Orixás, fewer in number than those in Ifá, are all connected with Olorum, the Lord of Orum or heaven, and with certain aspects of nature. As examples, Ogum is a divinity of war and iron is his element; Oxum is spring water; Xango is fire and lightning; Oxala is associated with air. Exu is different; he is considered the Messenger between heaven and earth and is integral to every Candomblé ritual. Most importantly, the Orixás want to be involved with humans.

There is a story recounted by José Porcher that Orum and Earth were once joined, and Orixás and humans could travel freely between the two. But a human touched dirty hands to Orum, fouling it. "Olorum, the Lord of Heaven, the Supreme God, angered by the filth, waste, and carelessness of mortals, blew with divine wrath and forever separated Heaven from Earth." The divinities were unhappy and sad; they missed interactions with humans. "They walked around in sadness and sulked. They went to complain to Olodumare, who eventually consented that the orixás could occasionally return to earth" but they would have to "take on the material bodies of their devotees." Oxum was given the task of preparing the devotees for visits of the Orixás, thereby cleansing and beautifying human bodies for possession: "Finally the little brides were made . . . they were ready for the gods . . . [who could] safely return to Aiê [earth], they could ride the bodies of their devotees. . . . The orixás were happy."[31]

This story highlights a few points about Candomblé. Heaven and Earth were separated because of human disrespect, and the Orixás were not happy about the separation. Here, the divinities are humanized, given feelings of sadness, while they complained to Olodumare. Olodumare did not reconnect heaven and earth. Instead, Oxum was tasked with finding a solution to the Orixas' discontent. Her solution: the invention of initiation. The initiates, the "brides," were ready for possession by the Orixás for whom they were initiated, allowing the divinities to return to Earth. This kind of origin story answers questions about why initiation is needed and why possession occurs. It also demonstrates how *Axé* is the activating and underlying force among all beings, including divinities.

Possession, in connection with initiation, is not what is portrayed in Western movies or television—something demonic takes a person's body and mind to commit evil acts mindlessly. Instead, Ligiéro explained its meaning, sometimes referring to it as a "trance." Initiation is a long process that acquaints and connects a specific Orixá with a certain person. That initiate's life is "governed by the same philosophy that orientates the Orixá.... In this intimate contact between the initiated and the divinity, the person receives, alongside the energetic aura of the Orixá, revelations of their own unconscious energy, which can blossom aspects of their life in a harmonious and rejuvenating way."[32]

The fusion of Orixás with Catholic saints may have begun initially to hide the worship of African deities. But the practices of Candomblé find such an established cross-identification of the two, which often made the connection seamless. The Orixá/Catholic saint connection can be seen clearly during public rituals. Ayodeji Ogunnaike attended one such ritual: "Every year in Salvador, Brazil, thousands of people take part in an almost ten-kilometer procession on foot to follow an image of the crucified Christ called *Nosso Senhor do Bonfim* and to witness or participate in the ritual cleansing on the steps and interior of the cathedral."[33]

The ritual is *Lavagem do Bonfim* or *Lavagem* (Washing) and has a Catholic origin. However, Ogunnaike continued:

> The overwhelming majority of its participants and most important figures are practitioners of ... Candomblé.... In fact, the cultural symbol of the *Lavagem* is not the image of the crucified Christ, but rather the ... Afro-Brazilian priestesses and devotees of Candomblé who follow the image, wash the stairs of the church with their own secret combination of special leaves and water, and then use that same water to cleanse the faithful.[34]

While there, he asked several of the participants about the identification between Orixás and Catholic saints. One respondent, Dona Iraci, said that

Jesus and Oxalá are the same since "Oxalá is the 'father of all orixás and all of humanity'" and that the whole world, according to the Gospel of John, "was created by Jesus."[35] Therefore, she concludes, they are one. Ogunnaike spoke with another woman, Maria da Conceção Carvalho, who informed him that the first Africans who were brought to Brazil "absolutely believed that [the saints and orixás] were the same and that it was not merely a survival strategy.... Her grandmother taught her that 'the Father is God, the Son is God, and the Holy Spirit is the same God ... The Three are the same Person' and the saints and orixás operate in a similar way."[36]

Women's names have surfaced several times in this discussion of Candomblé, from the three women who founded one of the first terreiros to the divinity Oxum's invention of initiation to those interviewed at the *Lavagem*. Women have had strong leadership roles from the past to the present in Candomblé. "In addition to their leadership, women have been the foundational roots for the formation and sustenance of Afro-Brazilian identity over the many centuries of struggle."[37] The leadership of the terreiro includes "veneration of Orixás, festivities, initiations, sacrifices and healing rituals ... [Mãe Valnizia Bianch] states: 'Candomblé is an example of a welcoming, caring religion without prejudices; and I speak based on my experience of 29 years at the Terreiro do Cobre.'"[38] How initiation and priesthood happen are distinct in some ways for Candomblé. Priests are called *Pai de santo* or *Mãe de santo*, that is, Father or Mother of saints.

One important facet holds true across AIR and ADR: initiation is a lifelong process and imposes responsibilities on the initiate. The processes of rising to leadership positions take the commitment of years of study and apprenticeship.

Becoming

To become initiated in Candomblé is not based on emotion, there is no altar call where someone can walk forward and become a member. Candomblé is not a religion for the masses, Ligiéro stated.[39] Lucas Marques wrote about his own process toward initiation. Marques cited a truism among Candomblé practitioners: no one is here by chance. Instead, initiation is and must be part of an individual's destiny.[40] Destiny is a concept that resonates through AIR and ADR, a life path chosen before birth that can be altered.

Marques described his learning through building relationships; he did not learn in a classroom setting. As a scholar, he was used to the book-bound classroom. He had to begin by changing his mindset: his "yearnings to 'get information'... or worse, to capture 'the whole,' 'the culture,' or 'the native point of view,' were always doomed to failure."[41] He had to learn to learn.

> In Candomblé, learning "is not conceptualized as a perfectly coherent and unified body of rules and knowledge, like a type of overcodified doctrine imposed from above"... The entire trajectory of an initiate is a learning trajectory, where skills and relationships are developed and cultivated through a long process of formation, both of the person and his Orixá.[42]

He became part of a community of practice in the *terreiro*. As an apprentice, he learned "how to do something, that is manipulating certain forces to achieve certain goals. Knowledge, then is a kind of process that creates forces, not just a 'substance.' To cultivate it is to acquire power... in the sense of vital force, of axé."[43] Learning, in this way, was referred to as "gathering leaves," a slow process where small fragments are learned that must then "take root in the depths of your being."[44]

So, through this brief history of African Brazil, the development of Candomblé, and some of its aspects, including processes of initiation, one might wonder why the religion still exists. If enslavement ended in 1888, what has kept it in such a prominent place in Brazil? Afolabi provided some words that lead into the next section:

> The power to venerate African divinities translates into the power to heal, manifest, liberate, subvert, and reinvent. It is also an outlet for persistent frustrations, which urgently seek remedy after many years of deprivation and displacement. Performative rituals, *whether on the sacred or secular plane*, serve to renew lost energies and recuperate memories.[45]

I place emphasis on "sacred or secular plane" because, like the *Lavagem* described above, the many attendees of public rituals are not necessarily initiated into Candomblé—as has been said, it is not a religion for the masses. Social structures and situations set Candomblé in its place of prominence in Brazilian cultures.

Establishing Candomblé

Candomblé is an ADR, but it has a wider impact in Brazil, which began with emancipation. Economic motivation to maintain a relatively cost-free labor force added to the ideologies of racism to free the enslaved but retain a racial hierarchy, ensuring that Black and Brown people were still not full members of Brazilian society. As mentioned in the above discussion of Bahia, oppression and violence against people of color are still experienced in Brazil today. After emancipation, while some of the freed people were still held on farms, others were just left on the streets, especially in urban areas. Examples of mutual support systems already existed; Harding mentioned *libertos* working on behalf of communities. In like manner, *terreiros* opened their doors to bring people in, providing food, education, and sometimes housing. Candomblé exhibited a value for the lives of the community, whether initiated or not.

Like other former colonies with formerly enslaved people, myths of the gentleness and nurturing care of enslavement developed years after emancipation. Ultimately, such myths erased racism. The development of the concept of "racial democracy" also denied the existence of Brazilian racism.

> Brazil would come to be understood as the result of the mixture of three groups—indigenous Brazilians, Europeans, and Africans—who had found a way to live in racial harmony. In other words, according to this vision, there was no racism in Brazil. This mythology, which has become known as "racial democracy," was undergirded by the fact that Brazil, unlike the United States, had never enshrined segregation in law.[46]

Racial democracy was a comforting myth that soothed the powerful while continuing racial oppression and separation. However, this history of separation helped to build the character of Salvador's Africanness since multiple aspects, many drawn from Candomblé, were settled into Brazilian culture. Carnival, which is held in multiple locations, provides one example.

> The carnival can be viewed as the most famous Brazilian celebration, wherein the affinity between the people and Candomblé is expressed with the most freedom. This can be seen in the traditional *Ala das Bainas* (samba school based in Rio de Janeiro) or in the renowned *Afoxé Filhos de*

Gandhi (composed entirely by male Candomblé believers inspired by Gandhi's principles of nonviolence and peace), in the carnival of Salvador.[47]

Samba schools, centers for carnival preparation, and a variety of Candomblé *terreiros* became part of the life of Brazil. Initiation into Candomblé is not required to participate or to receive blessings from the *Pai de santo* or *Mãe de santo*. As one example, the thousands of attendees at the *Lavagem* ritual could not all have been initiates or tourists.

The infusion of Candomblé was particularly aided by Brazilian Popular Music, which is its own genre. There have been consistent efforts to stamp out *"colsas de preto"* or Black people's things, and to Europeanize (read, Whiten) Brazil, but the Africanness did not disappear. Popular music carries references to Orixás and Candomblé that infuse the country and its understanding of its culture. One of the artists who included African religious themes in her music, dress, and performance (she used Orixá dances) was Clara Nunês (1942–1983).

Gilberto Gil is an important artist and activist who also included Candomblé, spiritual, and justice-related themes in his music. He wrote "Andar com Fé" in the 1980s. Gil noted that "the chorus uses the pronunciation '*faiá*' instead of '*falhar*' (the word for faith in Portuguese), 'falhar' is from the head. And faith is from the heart. The song is a hymn that offers perseverance and courage to those who sing and dance to it."[48] Gil and another famous Brazilian musician, Caetano Veloso, were arrested in 1969 and accused of parodying the Brazilian national anthem. They were imprisoned for a few months, then exiled from the country. They went to London, and there, Gil was influenced by reggae and rock. When he returned, he became an active member of *Afoxé Filhos de Gandhi* with a dedication to the environment. As Gil's story demonstrates, Brazilian culture is shaped by the influence of music even as Gil was shaped by Candomblé, human rights, and ecojustice.

Drumming is central to Candomblé ceremonies, just as it is in AIR. Drummers are invaluable in Candomblé society, some of whom are on call for any ritual work at given terreiros. Drummer groups may be found in street performances at any time. Carlinhos Brown is a drummer who brought Candomblé into his music and his commitment to justice.

Brown began drumming as he was selling bottles of water on the street in Candeal as a child; he used the empty bottles as his first drums. Candeal was a poor but historic neighborhood in Salvador. In a 1997 interview,

Brown said that he selected his own last name from James Brown. He invented a small handheld drum, the timbal, eventually launching the band Timbalada, based in Candeal.

> Brazil has no social safety net, and the country has the largest gap between rich and poor in the hemisphere, with millions lacking housing, education, and access to health care. Timbalada's social mission includes educational projects, and aid to street children. "Like many cities in Brazil," says Brown, "we have many many street children. One of our projects is working with these kids, allowing them to work with professional musicians, and play with a wide variety of instruments."[49]

Brown's work with Candeal has changed its character; it's now a tourist destination. He has received national awards for what has been called a "miracle."

Art and monuments can be found throughout Salvador, and the Orixás are everywhere. They are carved into elaborate door frames, they grace the entrance to shops, and they are graffitied on favela walls. One of the more elegant art sites is Dique do Tororó, a lake in the middle of Salvador. There, eight Orixás' sculptures float above the water and, for further effect, are lit at night.

There has been an active arts community in Bahia, from painting to sculpture to installation art. In 2017, "Axe Bahia: The Power of Art in an Afro-Brazilian Metropolis" was an exhibit at the Fowler Museum at UCLA. Some of the works can still be seen online.[50]

Conclusion

The *Irmandade da Nossa Senhora da Boa Morte* highlights many of the aspects of Candomblé that have been discussed in this chapter. The *Irmandade*, like other religious confraternities, was allowed to exist often in conjunction with the Catholic Church. The rulers of Brazil believed that the confraternities calmed Black people, gave them time to worship in a Catholic way, and, perhaps, gave them some space to heal from their work. The *Irmandade da Nossa Senhora da Boa Morte,* begun sometime in the 1800s, was affiliated with different Catholic churches over the years. Today, it is centered in the city of Cachoeira.

Figure 5.1 Festival of the Sisterhood of the Good Death, Cachoeira, Brazil, photo courtesy of Stephanie Mitchem.

Each August, the Sisterhood of Our Lady of the Good Death gathers days before the Catholic feast of the Assumption of Mary into heaven, which is August 8. The Catholic feast celebrates that Mary, Jesus's mother, did not die but was assumed into heaven because of her purity. The Sisterhood understands the day much differently.

The *Irmandade*'s belief is that Mary, at the time she would have been assumed, would not leave as long as there were still enslaved people in Brazil. She stayed and worked to ensure that those who were held in bondage would die "good deaths." The idea of a good death for the enslaved could have meant that they would not die in violence, tragedy, disease, and especially not in bondage. After emancipation was declared, Mary left for heaven. The ritual in Cachoeira marks Mary's sorrow before enslavement in the days before August 8 ended and her joy at emancipation when Mary herself was free to leave. Mary's departure to heaven, her Assumption, is celebrated with a procession of different *terreiros* and community groups followed by a public feast.

The Sisterhood marks these changes with their dress. During the time before emancipation, the women wear somber clothing. On August 8, they are dressed in white, wearing much gold jewelry. They carry a statue of Mary, which is also adorned.

The members are elderly women: they must already be *Mãe de santos* before they can begin a separate initiation to the Sisterhood. Their ages reflect the amount of time it takes to reach their level of expertise within Candomblé.

> "Boa Morte first started in Salvador," said Irma Nilza, a member of the Sisterhood for twenty-one years. "That is where Black women from different groups in Africa who came on slave ships started creating what would become the Sisterhood. They sold clothes; worked outside; did everything they could do to collect money and start something because there was nothing for them in Brazil." . . . It is a radical almost futuristic inclination that led enslaved African women, miles from the Motherland, to create a Sisterhood whose main endeavor was to ensure that Black people could live lives with some semblance of dignity, while wholly aware of how this mission would be affected by the complicated dynamics of gender ad its relationship to violence . . . The sisters set about collecting money that would be used to purchase the freedom of Black slaves . . . [and] some of the money... was used to buy plots of land in which Black people would be buried after death.[51]

The Sisterhood continues its social activism today, addressing injustices and human needs.

The history and activities of the Sisterhood are reminders that Candomblé is complex and that appearances of celebrations hold more meanings. The procession may be enjoyable, but look beneath the surface. The following shows just some aspects that can be gleaned from knowledge about Candomblé.

- *Axé*: like the *Lavagem* mentioned earlier in this chapter, the celebration of Boa Morte on August 8 connects daily life and its struggles to spirituality and practices of justice.

- *Axé*: understood to infuse all life, creating connections among all people, ancestors, and divinities. Therefore, the Sisterhood demonstrated concern for the living and the dead through their actions.
- Women in leadership: biological sex does not determine leadership in Candomblé, as the Sisterhood proves.
- Syncretism: clearly seen in the historic melding of a Catholic Marian story into the plight of enslaved Black people. However, Candomblé syncretism has taken a different shape as the history of the Sisterhood illustrates. While the Sisterhood worked directly through a particular Catholic parish for some time, they were clearly setting their own objectives. Their relationship with the Catholic Church changed over the years, as covering their activities with that institution was no longer necessary. There was also an incident involving the women and their gold jewelry. The gold had been collected over the years by the Sisterhood, dedicated to honoring Mary's Assumption to heaven. The parish with which they were affiliated agreed to hold it for them for safety. Years later, there was some struggle for clear ownership as the parish claimed it; through lawsuits, the Sisterhood retained their traditional jewelry and, in the process, claimed their independence from the parish.
- Procession: reminiscent of carnival as the groups involved in the procession dress in their organizations' colors.
- Addressing social needs becomes integral to Candomblé stories. There are many examples through this chapter, such as *terreiros* after emancipation assisting people in need; as Gilberto Gil working for environmental justice; or Carlinhos Brown using his position to address the poverty in his neighborhood; or a sisterhood working for justice.

The next two ADRs to be discussed will also have a great impact on their respective nations and on the consciousness of many in the Diaspora, showing the variety of ADRs that can be studied.

Notes

1 Patricia de Santana Pinho, *Mapping Diaspora: African American Roots Tourism* (Durham: University of North Carolina Press, 2018), 5.

2. Zeca Ligiéro, trans. Emma Symes, *Initiation into Candomblé: Introduction to African-Brazilian Religion* (New York: Diasporic Africa Press, 2014), 6–7.
3. Ligiéro, *Initiation into Candomblé*, 7–8.
4. Crislayne Alfagali, "Iron, Gold, and Labor in the Eighteenth-Century Ilamba and Minas Gerais," in *Current Trends in Slavery Studies in Brazil*, ed. S. Conermann et al., 32.
5. Gwendolyn Midlo Hall, *Slavery and African Ethnicities in the Americas: Restoring the Links* (Chapel Hill: University of North Carolina Press, 2000), 122–3.
6. Jimin Kang, "In Brazil, a Best-Selling Novel Confronts the Brutal Afterlife of Slavery," *The Nation*, October 25, 2023, https://www.thenation.com/article/culture/crooked-plow-itamar-vieira-junior/.
7. Niyi Afolabi, *Relocating the Sacred: African Divinities and Brazilian Cultural Hybridities* (Albany: State University of New York Press, 2022), 81.
8. Ligiéro, *Initiation into Candomblé*, 18–19.
9. Afolabi, *Relocating the Sacred*, 81.
10. Ibid., 282.
11. Ibid., 283.
12. Kathleen O'Brien Wicker, "Mami Water in African Religion and Spirituality," in *African Spirituality*, 198.
13. José Eduardo Porcher, "The Mythic Narratives of Candomblé Nagô and What They Imply About Its Supreme Being," *Religious Studies* (Cambridge University Press, 2024), https://doi.org/10.1017/S0034412523001129, 3.
14. Ligiéro, *Initiation into Candomblé*, 129–30.
15. Porcher, "The Mythic Narratives," 3.
16. Robert A. Voeks, *Sacred Leaves of Candomblé: African Magic, Medicine, and Religion in Brazil* (Austin: University of Texas Press, 1997), 52.
17. Ibid., 51.
18. Ligiéro, *Initiation into Candomblé*, 19–20.
19. Rachel E. Harding, *A Refuge in Thunder: Candomblé and Alternative Spaces of Blackness* (Bloomington: Indiana University Press, 2000), 46.
20. Ibid., 49.
21. Ibid., 50.
22. Ibid., 53.
23. Robert A. Voeks, "Sacred Leaves of Brazilian Candomblé," *Geographical Review* 80, no. 2 (1990): 120.
24. Ibid., 126.

25 Gladys Mitchell-Walthour, "The Politics of Blackness in Salvador, Bahia," in *The Making of Brazil's Black Mecca: Bahia Reconsidered*, ed. Scott Ickes and Bernd Reiter (East Lansing: Michigan State University Press, 2018), 237.
26 C.M. Rabelo and Luciana Duccini, "Candomblé and the Magic of Bahia," in *The Making of Brazil's Black Mecca*, 258.
27 Bettina E. Schmidt, "Axé as Cornerstone of Candomblé Philosophy and Its Significance for an Understanding of Well-Being," *Religious Studies* (Cambridge University Press, 2024), https://doi.org/10.1017/S0034412523001154, 4.
28 Harding, *A Refuge in Thunder*, 88.
29 Ligiéro, *Initiation into Candomblé*, 43.
30 Porcher, "The Mythic Narratives," 4.
31 Ibid., 4–5.
32 Ligiéro, *Initiation into Candomblé*, 120.
33 Ayodeji Ogunnaike, "What's Really Behind the Mask: A Reexamination of Syncretism in Brazilian Candomblé," *Journal of Africana Religions* (University Park: Penn State University Press, 2020), 146.
34 Ibid., 147.
35 Ibid., 161.
36 Ibid., 162.
37 Afolabi, *Relocating the Sacred*, 85.
38 Ibid., 85.
39 Ligiéro, *Initiation into Candomblé*, 138.
40 Lucas Marques, "Learning to Learn in Candomblé: Notes on Paths, Knowledge, and the 'Education of Distraction,'" *Religion* 52, no. 1 (2022): 131, https://doi.org/10.1080/0048721X.20211087.
41 Ibid., 125.
42 Ibid.
43 Ibid., 126.
44 Ibid., 127.
45 Afolabi, *Relocating the Sacred*, 21.
46 Ana Lucia Araujo, "The Mythology of Racial Democracy in Brazil," *Open Democracy*, June 22, 2015, https://www.opendemocracy.net/en/beyond-trafficking-and-slavery/mythology-of-racial-democracy-in-brazil/, accessed January 2025.
47 Ligiéro, *Initiation into Candomblé*, 24–5.
48 Gilberto Gil's Google Arts & Culture page, "On and Off the Internet: Gil's Most Listened-To Songs," https://artsandculture.google.com/story/

on-and-off-the-internet-gil-s-most-listened-to-songs-instituto-gilberto-gil/mAVxyt_qSHMaFg?hl=en, accessed January 2025.
49 "Dan Rosenberg Talks with Carlinhos Brown," excerpts from *Rhythm Music Magazine*, November 1997, https://www.rootsworld.com/rw/feature/brown.html, accessed January 2025.
50 Fowler Museum at UCLA, "Axé Bahia," https://fowler.ucla.edu/exhibitions/axe-bahia/#:~:text=Axé%20Bahia%20explores%20the%20distinctive,artistic%20practices%20in%20Latin%20America, accessed January 2025.
51 Tarisai Ngangura, "Intimate Portraits of Boa Morte, Where the 'Sisterhood of the Good Death' Honors Afro-Brazilian Ancestors," *Vice News*, September 6, 2018, https://www.vice.com/en/article/boa-morte-festival-sisterhood-images/.

6

Vodou/Haiti and Lucumí/Cuba

Chapter Outline

Vodou/Haiti	144
Vodou	146
Lucumí/Cuba	157
One of Spain's Colonies: Cuba	157
Lucumí's Distinctions	166
Closing Thoughts: Revolution, Revolution	171

Vodou, from Saint-Domingue/Haiti, and Lucumí, from Cuba, have prominence among ADR. When Britain abolished the international trafficking of Africans in 1808, the intra-American trade expanded as labor for sugar and coffee plantations was still in demand. As happened with the original trafficking from the African continent, Black people continued to carry their beliefs with them. Vodou and Lucumí changed and adapted as they moved through the globe, adapting to local needs.

The paths for planting and growing these African-derived religions in Haiti and Cuba reflected types of enslavement, global political situations, and the necessity of the respective nations, France or Spain. While each of these ADR is distinct, there are links in how they developed and, most importantly, how one is often confused with the other. These distinctions, connections, and similarities are best seen when the two are placed next to each other, as in this chapter.

Vodou/Haiti

(Description of a Vodou ceremony from a "trusted Negress:") *They smile, they meet, they jostle rudely and there you have two in crisis, feet in the air, howling like wild beasts, foaming like them . . . one of them was ordered by the leader of the band to take a hot coal that was given to him and it seemed not to burn him . . . another to have strips of flesh removed with iron nails, without noticing the least sign of awareness.*[1]

> *Voodoo means an all powerful and supernatural being . . . That being is a nonvenomous snake . . . under whose auspices gather all who share the faith. Knowledge of the past, the science of the present, foreknowledge of the future, all this the snake possesses, and it consents to communicate its power solely through the medium of a high priest whom the adherents choose, or of a Negress.*[2]

Saint-Domingue

The Western colonizing powers jockeyed among themselves for control of what had been Columbus' so-named Hispaniola. France established settlements in 1625 in a northwest portion that they named Saint-Domingue. But their ownership of that portion was contested by Spain. France had been fighting with Spain and several other European nations, including Britain, during the Nine Years War (1688–1697). It was not until 1697 with the Treaty of Rijswijk that Spain ceded that northwest part of the island to France. Meanwhile, Spain and other European nations continued to jockey over the other portion of the island, known today as the Dominican Republic, which has its own historical development. On either side of the island, those administrators who had followed Columbus had decimated the native Taino and Arawak populations.

Claiming that one portion of the island, the French believed that they sorely needed the trafficked Africans' labor to develop the land for France's benefit. Sugar, lumber, and coffee plantations were France's first developmental focus, beginning with their first settlements in 1625. It could be said that they succeeded for the sake of France: because of the Africans' labor, Saint-Domingue became known as the "Pearl of the Antilles."

But there was no sense of triumph for the laboring Africans. The cost to the enslaved Africans was lethal. John Henley drew from historic records to emphasize this point:

> Economically, French occupation was a runaway success. But Haiti's riches could only be exploited by importing up to 40,000 slaves a year. For nearly a decade in the late 18th century, Haiti accounted for more than one-third of the entire Atlantic slave trade. Conditions for these men and women were atrocious; the average life expectancy for a slave on Haiti was 21 years. Abuse was dreadful, and routine: "Have they not hung up men with heads downward, drowned them in sacks, crucified them on planks, buried them alive, crushed them in mortars?" wrote one former slave some time later. "Have they not forced them to eat excrement? Have they not thrown them into boiling cauldrons of cane syrup? Have they not put men and women inside barrels studded with spikes and rolled them down mountainsides into the abyss?"[3]

To manage the Black population as colonizers' constant fears of rebellion grew, the first *Code Noir* was written in 1685. The *Code* severely restricted the movements of any enslaved person, set punishments for certain offenses, and instructed the plantation owners to feed them. The laws included that all enslaved people be baptized Catholic, and no other religion was allowed. The *Code Noir* was expanded and applied to other French colonies.[4] Both the *Code* and the religious restrictions were theoretical. As will be seen later, these gave way to other realities.

Two groups of Black people in Saint-Domingue did not fit neatly into the "enslaved" category. The *gens de couleur* were mixed-race, free people of color who went out of their way not to be identified with the enslaved. Some of them also became wealthy in trade. They could be annoying to the *blancs*, but they added to the economy, often running taverns and other service businesses. The other group was more worrisome to the French: the Blacks who escaped known as the Maroons. They hid in communities in the mountains. Many of those who ran away were the *bossales*, the recent arrivals, who retained sharper memories of Afrika. "Maroons had a very hard time surviving, as the agricultural yield in the mountains did not come close to feeding anyone." They often raided nearby plantations; even if caught and severely punished, they would continue to attempt escape. "African principles of organization came easily in the fabrication of a new culture that was differentiated from the masters."[5]

The 20,000 *petit blancs* (White employees) and *grand blancs* (plantation owners or administrators) were fewer than the 30,000 *gens de couleur*. Together, they were still significantly fewer than the nearly five hundred thousand enslaved Africans.[6] One author pointed out that this numeric difference aided in the retention of Afrikan practices. These practices also provided the basis for developing resistance groups.[7]

These differences were sharpened by economic stressors in France, which included the financial costs of the Nine Years' War. There were political costs as well. France, often the instigator during the War, had once been considered an international leader. But the aftermath of the War moved it out of dominance. The War's cost in terms of money and life created turmoil at home as the French nobility came to be viewed with greater disapproval. The "Little Ice Age" impacted the northern hemisphere, and severe cold caused many colonial explorations to fail. But Europe experienced the cold as well, with "recurring harvest failures, famines, and epidemics—a crisis that shaped Spanish, French, and English views of colonies and emigration to North America."[8] One clear signal of troubles in France was growing distaste for the monarchy itself, whose financial excesses and exclusion of the merchant class from power created social unrest. The merchants, the wealthy bourgeoisie, were propping up the debt-ridden monarchy with their work. These stressors all made the success of French colonies even more important. The French began "developing large-scale plantations and importing tens of thousands of West African slaves from the Bight of Benin."[9]

The labors of the enslaved Africans did make Saint-Domingue a wealthy colony. The *Grand Blanc* of the Pearl of the Antilles exported sugar, indigo, coffee, copper, and wood. Yet, "the relationship with France had always been considered constraining because of the law of "exclusive trade," which would not permit the sale of colonial goods to any country but France and which set all the prices."[10] This was the world of Saint-Domingue, where Vodou flourished.

Vodou

The captive Africans in Saint-Domingue came from many different groups, "the Fon, Ewe, and Yoruba of Dahomey, the Bambara, Wolof, and

Mandingo of Senegambia, Hausa, Fulani, and Igbo of present-day Nigeria, Akan of Ghana, Kongo, Luongo, and Wangol of the Angola-Congo axis."[11] They gave their collective homelands a mythical name, Guinea, or *Ginen* in *Kréyol* (Creole). But they also knew that they had been sold into their current situation by people in their own homelands. A *Kréyol* saying reflected this sentiment: "*Depi lan Ginen, nèg rayi nèg* (Already in Guinea, the Negro hated the Negro)."[12] At the same time, Guinea was known as the "true birthplace of the spirits, and voodoo was kept alive as a last link with the lost ancestral home of Africa."[13]

The spelling "Voodoo" in this quote refers to the same religion as "Vodou." That spelling is also used to reference the religious tradition in Louisiana and other locations. "Vodún" was used in Chapter 4 to identify the AIR from which these religions grew. For clarity, Vodou, the *Kréyol* spelling, will be used in this chapter to distinguish the religious practices that grew in Saint Domingue.

Vodou was formed from the exchanges of these African groups as well as the remaining Taino people's traditions. Some aspects of Vodou's ceremonies today can be traced to the Taino.[14] The blending of African divinities with Catholic saints continued in Saint-Domingue, but some of this syncretism may have already begun, built into the African systems of fluidly adopting practices or divinities that they believed were effective.

> Vodún's outlook on cultural contact, whether African or European, has been one of assimilation, syncretization, and multiplicity, constantly bringing new ideas and influences into its pantheon as cultural transformations take place, as was the case particularly with Yoruba culture as well as Islam and Christianity. Vodún as a philosophical system thus contains the tools for navigating contradictions and contested worldviews.[15]

From this mixture of peoples and cultures, Vodou identifies itself as having twenty-one nations, one for each of the nineteen African ethnic groups brought there, and one each for Taino and European spirits.[16] Practitioners of Vodou or Vodouisants do not call themselves members of a religion, and will more likely say "*Mwen sèvi Lwa*," that is, I serve the *Lwa*.[17] *Lwa* means divinities in *Kréyol*. The priests in Vodou are called *Mambo* if they are women, or *Houngan* if they are men.

Vodou's supreme Being is Bondye, who created the entire universe, including the *Lwa*. "After creating the world . . . left the management of all earthly matters to the *Lwa* with dominion over specific areas such as fire, water, wind, trees, and plants, including the secrets of their medicinal properties, illnesses, and their cures; in sum, all actions, sentiments, and virtues."[18] Vodouisants know that Bondye is not uncaring or unaware of their actions, but that "Bondye knows and sees all, and no one will get away with evil behavior forever... What you do is what you are, and what you give is what you will receive."[19]

Different divinities, specific to their respective AIR or ADR, have been discussed. Some of them became identified as *Lwa*, such as Eleggua (Èṣù), Ogou (Ògùn), Erzulie (Ọṣùn), Orula (Ọbàtálá), and Chango (Ṣàngo). [See Figure 4–2] But Mambo Tann points out:

> There are thousands and perhaps hundreds of thousands of *Lwa*. Some are Taino *zemi*; some come from Africa, Europe, other parts of the Western Hemisphere, or even Asia ... All the *Lwa* are considered to be "angels of God," working for Bondye to keep the universe in good order and interceding on behalf of those who serve them.[20]

The number includes the different manifestations that each *Lwa* will take on as needed which will be seen below.

Two of the largest African groups trafficked into Saint-Domingue were the Dahomey, who practice Vodún, and the Yorúbà, who practice Ifá. These groups are the basis of the two largest lineages of Vodou. The Dahomey lineage forms the Rada tradition of Vodou; the Yorúbà lineage forms Vodou's Petro tradition. Karen McCarthy Brown (1942–2015) described the Rada and Petro in terms of the differences in their *Lwa*.

Brown wrote that the Rada *Lwa* are known as the *Ginen Lwa* and can be traced back to Dahomey. "The Rada *Lwa* are intimate spirits who surround one with their protection on a day-to-day basis. Their protective power is of a noncoercive sort and is said to reside mainly in their spiritual knowledge.... they are familiar with herbal healing ... they are socially familiar ... they are elders of the family."[21] They are associated with water.

The Petro *Lwa* are sometimes traced back to the Kongo instead of the Yorúbà because of their reputation for fierceness. Brown described the Petro *Lwa* as associated and served with fire, flames, gunpowder, and shrieking police whistles. "Promises to them must be kept and services rendered with care. One does not break or even bend the rules when dealing with the Petro *Lwa*."[22] But another explanation is given by Mambo Tann—"The Petro nation comprises that part of Vodou's spirit world that does not look backward to *Ginen* ... Instead, the Petro as a group represent the history of the island from that first moment of contact ... the Petro live in everyday Haiti from 1492 to today—a world filled with violence, poverty, war, and pain."[23] The Petro *Lwa* are the ones most likely to create a public image of Vodun that is negative and fear-filled. Mambo Tann puts such a view in perspective:

> What those who demonize the Petro do not understand is that Haiti, and Haitian Vodou, occupy both a world of peace and a world of violence, a world of calm and a world of righteous anger, at the same time ... The Rada and the Petro divisions represent two parts of the Haitian experience, neither of which are accurately described as "good" or "evil."[24]

The difference between the Rada and Petro is reflected in the layout of the Vodou *ounjo* or temple. There is a large space, the *peristil*, where the ceremonies take place. At the center of the space is the *poto mitan*, a pole or tree, where the *Lwa* "are said to climb down ... from the heavens and into the floor of the *peristil*, from which they rise up through the bodies of their servants to share in the dance and appear in possessions."[25] The *ounjo* places the altars for the Rada and Petro in separate rooms if possible; otherwise, the space is arranged to keep the altars clearly separated.

The Rada and Petro *Lwa* show another way that Afrikan divinities came to fit the needs of specific communities in Saint-Domingue. They are described as "supernatural beings that can enter the human body, and they are thought to be present in all realms of nature.... [and can] establish a web of linkages between human activities—agriculture, war, courtship ... They create the structure of time and space, and they take control of an individual's life from birth to death."[26] With these understood connections of the *Lwa* in a Vodouisant's (practitioner's) daily life, nothing is seen as accidental or happenstance. It was not just names or the number of nations that would make a difference in Vodou. An example is the Yorùbá/Ifá divinity Ogún who, in Saint-Domingue, became Ogou.

Ogún, within Ifá, is sometimes pictured as a blacksmith. This excerpt of a song from Ketu, Nigeria, highlights this image.

> Ogún, allied to the man with a quick hand ...
> Ogún ties on his cutlass with a belt of cotton
> Ogún of the sharp black cutlass.
> Hoe is the child of Ogún
> Axe is the child of Ogún
> Gun is the child of Ogún.[27]

Ogún, the blacksmith, made iron instruments for cultivating land, hunting, and war. Another important characteristic is his commitment to seek justice—and in this aspect, Ogún is defined as a superior warrior.

In Saint Domingue, Ogou took on characteristics reflecting both Rada and Petro. Brown wrote: "In Haiti, hunting and smithing were no longer crucial to everyday life, while the soldier took on new guises and added significance."[28] There are many manifestations of Ogou. Brown gave an example of a song to Ogou Feray, the head of all soldier Ogou.

> "Ceremonies for Feray are first class.
> Feray the Magnet, who sits on the altar,
> He's firing the cannon. (repeat)"[29]

Ogou, in his multiple guises, became a central Lwa of Vodou. Ogou, such as Ogou Feray, has a fiery nature, aligning with Petro; with ties to *Ginen*, Ogou can be identified with Rada. Therefore, in the *ounjo*, Ogou's altar room is between the Rada and Petro altar spaces.

Vodou Ceremonies

Vodou ceremonies have been the most fictionalized aspects of African spiritualities. Often, depending on the writer or the location, they may be called "voodoo." These misrepresented ceremonies are performed as cannibalistic, zombie creations—in other words, the stuff of nightmares. Are there *ougan* or *manbo* who mislead or take advantage of their members? Yes, as there are in any religion, since seeking spiritual outlets does make the seeker vulnerable to manipulation. However, the ceremonies are not the equivalent of the fictionalized accounts.

Instead, an *ounjo* becomes a site for a sacred ritual, sometimes boisterous, but under the control of a trained priest. Some distinctive aspects of Vodou should be mentioned here, beginning with the safety of the worship space for the participants. "Nothing is left to chance in a voodoo ceremony, even if it gives way to all-out reveling. The *ougan* or *manbo* makes arrangements to watch over and regulate the comings and goings of the *lwa* in the bodies of the faithful. *Lwa* that make unscheduled appearances in the head of a dancer are promptly sent away. . . . the priest . . . [knows] how to restrain or laugh with a *lwa*."[30]

Figure 6.1 Example of Veve, in honor of Lwa Erzulie Freda. Artwork licensed from Alamy Stock, March 12, 2025.

Around the *poto mitan*, *vèvè* (drawings) "praise, summon, and incarnate all at once the vodun deities."[31] The *vèvè* are drawn with a substance, like cornmeal, that does not last past the ceremony as "they are erased by the dancing feet of the devotees."[32] Knowing how to draw these sacred formations becomes part of the training of the priests.

Like other AIR and ADR, drumming, singing, and dancing are central to the ceremonies. "The knowledge and teaching of Vodun are preserved in the songs and dances, which also contain the attributes of the *lwa*. . . . [R]elations between humans and spirits are maintained through exchanges and mutual reinforcement of energies."[33] As the *lwa* arrive at the ceremony, there is often possession of certain Vodouisants who interpret this experience as "communion, an act of communication with an ancestral spirit. The spirit may assist the Vodouisants or *serviteur* in numerous positive ways, such as healing, offering advice, resolving conflicts or providing protection and guidance . . . The ancestral spirits are guides, friends, and healers."[34]

This general description of a ceremony and the definitions of the Rada and Petro lineages are far from the night terrors that the media has created to represent Vodou for the purposes of capital gain. The fierceness of some *lwa*, such as Ogou, reflects needs in the communities. There are connections to Fon and Vodoun in *Ginen* with the Dahomey "Amazons" and the mystical royal lineage that may have added to negative perceptions. But the problems in Saint-Domingue were beyond images that came from Africa. The financial and political pressures from France; the brutal treatment of the enslaved; the privileged lives of the *grand blancs*; the *gens de couleur* efforts to be not treated as "black;" and maroon communities: each added a layer of social fracturing across Saint-Domingue that created irreversible actions.

Becoming Ayiti

As distrust built among the different groups in Saint-Domingue, Vodou swirled through the communities. Among the enslaved, Vodou created safe spaces with connections to *Ginen* while the desire for freedom grew; the importance of the warrior *lwa* Ogou was no accident. The citations at the beginning of this section were among the reports of the horrors of Vodou and the people who participated, furthering negative images.

But the Vodouisants understood their beliefs differently. LaGrace Benson highlighted the power of Vodou, in contrast to the French:

> What the enslaved people understood with their worldview and religion oriented to survival, living well, procreating and becoming honored ancestors were the droits de l'homme—the rights of all human beings. This was and is accepted, even by many who violate it, as a universal idea or ideal. Viewed as words on a page and thought in the mind, the rights of humans were without material existence for the French. For the materially suffering enslaved Africans, this sacred ideal was the biological, ecological condition essential to the continued human physical survival. Thus they acted.[35]

The wider political frame was adding fuel to the fires. The French were combatants in the Seven Years' War, which included fighting over control of the colonies that they had claimed. The American Revolution began stirring in the 1760s; by 1776, the colonies achieved their independence from Britain. The French were inspired: they began to move toward their own revolution. The *gens de couleur* began their own movement—Julien Raimond and Vincent Ogè led a delegation to Paris where the government decreed "that all of Saint-Domingue's free citizens—including *gens de couleur* had the same legal rights to property and elections."[36] The White community of Saint-Domingue, both *petit* and *grand blancs,* rejected the decree. Ogè and Raimond rebelled and marched on Cap Français, where they were defeated by the government forces and put to death in 1791.[37] Of course, the *gens de couleur* were not subdued and their dissatisfactions continued.

Meanwhile, White people's fears of the enslaved community grew as some plantation owners died of poisoning, and they blamed the deaths on Vodou. Their fears grew with their lack of understanding of Vodou. LaGrace Benson continued: "Colonists did not comprehend a danced religion, much less the sensibility of the real presence of transcendent spirits coming down into ordinary people, into animals, tree, water, rocks, and human relationships." Their fears were directed to only one place—religious practice. "They were slow to realize that the growing revolt of the enslaved was forming in what colonists initially saw as weekend parties."[38]

Their fears about the power of African magic were promoted by Maroon leaders and communities. One such leader was François Makandal who, in 1757, "sowed seeds of fear among planters and officials, not only by concocting poisons that killed slowly but also by obtaining talismans . . . [that] were said to make [rebels] invulnerable to weapons and free them from all fear of White people. *Makandal* became a general designation for talismans and poisons."³⁹ François Makandal himself was captured and killed by the French in 1758; but the Maroon communities were not deterred. They would come to play significant roles in the coming upheavals.

A series of events became what we know today as the Haitian Revolution. In 1791, a Vodou ceremony was held at *Bwa Kayima* led by Mambo Mayanet and Houngan Boukman. Much of that ceremony is wrapped in legend and myth. "Regardless of the particulars of the meeting . . . violence broke out all over the Plaine du Nord within a few days . . . Within ten days, the entire northern province of Saint-Domingue was under siege."⁴⁰

The French attempted to regain the colony. Troops were sent that allied with the *gens de couleur* believing that the larger numbers of that group would be strategic in recapturing the colony. But the White community would still not accept the mixed-race community; they called in the British to assist in reclaiming the colony. The Spanish controlled the eastern portion of the island and joined with the British and the White Saint-Dominguans against the French. "In an even more surprising turn of events, [the French] decided to side with the slaves."⁴¹

Historic leaders arose during these battles, General Toussaint L'Ouverture was among them. The General led his troops to expel the British and French, which he achieved in 1798. Then he turned to Santo Domingo, capturing the rest of the island. "L'Ouverture followed his assault by declaring all slaves on Hispaniola free people on January 3, 1801, in the first declaration of emancipation in the Western Hemisphere."⁴² For a time, L'Ouverture was the Governor of the island.

The French Revolution ended in 1799, and Napoleon Bonaparte became First Consul in France's new government. He was not willing to give up Saint-Domingue and sent a huge force back with the demand that the colony return to its previous status, under French control. The newly freed citizens began to turn against each other, with some groups wanting to return to French rule. In the end, L'Ouverture believed he was heading to a French ship to negotiate terms. He was not: he was shipped out to die in a French prison.

Jean Jacques Dessalines took over the leadership. His reputation as a fierce warrior preceded him as he intensified the fighting over the next years. When "he gave the French eight days to evacuate the capital . . . the French military and wealthy colonists took his warning seriously, and most fled the island forever."⁴³ It was Dessalines who, in January 1804, declared the name of the new nation as Ayíti (taken from the Taino name for the land, in *Kréyol*) or Haiti. Dessalines is considered the father of the country.

This island country is significant across the African Diaspora because it is the only nation that has freed itself through a revolt of enslaved Africans. Many of the problems that continue in Ayiti to this day have roots in a forced financial agreement in 1825, where France agreed to recognize Haiti as independent and sovereign for 150 million francs, the equivalent of 21.7 billion in current US dollars.⁴⁴ This debt crippled the new nation's growth; its severe struggles today can be traced to France's bill.

Despite this, there is a song that centers the *lwa's* saving powers: "If it weren't for the lwa, we would have all perished."⁴⁵

Another Condemnation of Vodou: Spiritual Vogue

A Western or capitalist critique arises from the very poverty of Haitians who serve the *lwa*. In the negative narration directed at Haiti, Vodou is a religion for the poor, and the uneducated Vodouisants spend what little money they have on elaborate costumes and expensive rituals. One scholar who has pushed back hard against such a narration is Eziaku Atuama Nwokocha, and her critiques can be applied to the negative views of many Black poor people. She wrote that the views criticizing Haitian poverty ultimately blame the victims of colonialism and neocolonialism for their own conditions. "Underlying these inquiries is a larger concern about Black people's relationship to wealth that colors perceptions about Black communities," she wrote.⁴⁶

Most importantly, Nwokocha coins a new term that better explains the realities of those in African and Diasporan religions and their material expressions of faith: spiritual vogue. The concept names

> [t[he significance of multisensory and material objects and their impacts within the natural and supernatural, the profane and mundane, and the living and the dead. What are seen, felt, and heard in the production and

wearing of religious clothing shape how people engage their faith. . . . The spiritual vogue framework underscores fashion as a key example of the aesthetic ritual practices that animate African Diasporic religions like Haitian Vodou, Brazilian Candomblé, and Cuban Lucumí.[47]

Questioning the expense of items for Vodou worship also underlines the lack of understanding of what happens in the ceremonies. The ceremonies, as described above, celebrate the unity of Vodouisants with *lwa* connected with the ancestors and the universe.

Nwokocha stressed the significance of spiritual vogue:

In Haitian Vodou, the gods care about how they look. African Diasporic gods are not symbols: they are thinking, feeling, drinking, and talking entities in the lives and ritual practices of devotees. Spirits, or *lwa* in Haitian Kreyòl, shape the lives of practitioners through style, aesthetics, and adornment, investing in the physical presentation of their presence. They are, without doubt, vain.[48]

To be creative is to plumb the deepest heart of humanity. To use creativity in worship deepens the humanity of the artist and the community. To promote beauty in ritual is to honor self as a product of divinity. If AIR and ADR understand all life and the universe as connected, why would spiritual vogue not be used? Understanding spiritual vogue is a key to understanding Vodou, Nwokocha explained.

The relentless focus on Haiti's poverty completely misses creative expressions of faith and adornment in service of the spirits. Vodou is about love. Vodou is about self-love. Vodou is revolutionary love. Vodou has created revolutions. Vodou defies gender and sexual boundaries. Vodou is pro-Black. Vodou is anti-White supremacy. It imagines a world beyond the material realities of the anti-Black political present we inhabit, and it venerates the spirits, the people, and the community.[49]

Beyond Haiti

Vodou traveled off the island with Haitian practitioners who often emigrate due to the continued political violence, with the United States being one destination. Voodoo is practiced among other communities in the United States, which is different from Haitian Vodou, as will be seen in the next chapter. In the United States, the Haitian communities of practice can be found in Brooklyn, New York, and in south Florida. These communities continue to view Haiti as a home base.

Eziaku Atuama Nwokocha interviewed Manbo Vante'm Pa Fyem, who travels between the United States and Haiti; her mother, also a Manbo, resides in Haiti. Manbo Vante'm Pa Fyem travels to Haiti to participate in ceremonies or to spend a season there. She compared her time in Haiti and America. "I think growing up and understanding the American culture . . . made Haiti an escape to be honest. It was an escape from social media and everything happening in the US. More I needed that break from feeling trapped, with what's going on in social media, other people's lives, the news."[50] Vodou and Haiti provide this Manbo with a sense of peace, "enthusiastic about connecting with her roots and her ancestors," but she warns that those who leave the country never to return make a mistake. Her comments resulted in the interviewer, Nwokocha, recognizing her own disconnection from her parents' country, Nigeria.[51]

The sense of home, loss, and the search for African spirituality become part of the story of ADR throughout the Diaspora. Not far from French Saint Domingue/Haiti, with the development of Vodou, the ADR Lucumí developed in Spanish Cuba.

Lucumí/Cuba

Each ADR was formed by and reflects a specific era's complex sociopolitical realities. Each one changes as the social situations shift. These statements are true for Cuba's Lucumí. ADR's practices and spiritualities do not form in a vacuum, as has been shown in each one shown in this book. It follows, then, that Lucumí would also develop different shapes. The distinctions begin with Lucumí's development during what has been called the Age of Revolutions.

One of Spain's Colonies: Cuba

Christopher Columbus originally claimed this island for Spain in 1492. By 1502, Africans were trafficked onto the island to work in the copper mines to replace the decimated indigenous Taino population. Like Saint Domingue, the island became one of the disputed territories between Britain and Spain. The disputes were part of the much larger Seven Years' War (1756–1763), as European nations fought for dominance and control of land and people across Europe and the territories they wanted to colonize. The Treaty of Paris ended the Seven Years' War. As part of the settlement, Britain ceded Cuba to Spain. Now, Spain had a colony that had to produce.

Therefore, in 1763, "Cuba went from underdeveloped and underpopulated settlements . . . to communities comprised of large sugar and coffee plantations."[52] The focus on sugar production in particular signally changed the character of Cuban enslavement.

> Sugar plantations . . . required armies of mostly males numbering in the hundreds, if not thousands. They worked eighteen hours a day, six days a week. Most plantation owners, attempting to minimize costs, provided miniscule forms of nutrition and care . . . Death among the enslaved exceeded births, thus necessitating constant acquisitions of bodies for labor. It was considered more cost effective to work an enslaved *negro* to death and purchase a new one.[53]

Thus, the life expectancy for the newly arrived, enslaved African averaged seven years, and "the plantation owner still profited."[54]

The revolution in Saint-Domingue began in 1791 and finally ended in 1804. By 1804, Saint-Domingue's importance in the global production of sugar also ended. Cuban planters quickly moved in to take that lead. "Sugar production increased on the island from 12.5 thousand tons during the 1780s to approximately thirty-two thousand tons by 1805, while almost tripling the population since the 1774 census. Sugar exportation from the port in la Habana quadrupled between 1786 and 1822."[55] Cuba's economy rested on a single product, sugar. The saying "*Sin azúcar no hay país*" ("Without sugar, there's no country") represented the realities of the Cuban economy.

The impact of the Haitian Revolution was beyond the expansion of sugar production.

> Cuban planters rushed in to fill the void left by Saint-Domingue's revolution as if it had been created just for them. But as they worked to expand slavery, the context in which they did so required them always to ponder the possibility of its destruction at the hands of the enslaved . . .

the example of black revolution was not an abstract proposition, but a palpable presence.⁵⁶

When Saint-Domingue's refugees fled at Dessalines' ultimatum, Cuba was a friendly, nearby port. In the final months of Saint-Domingue's existence,

> starting in late June 1803, and over the next few months, thousands of Saint-Domingue residents arrived on the shores of Santiago de Cuba. Men, women, and children of all colors came on French ships that sometimes landed in Santiago . . . [or] dropped passengers on deserted coasts nearby. . . . And so the refugees arrived, on the order of hundreds a day.⁵⁷

However, Cuba did not have the accommodations to absorb such a large number of refugees. Housing and food were in short supply. "The demands placed on cities such as Baracoa and Santiago as a direct result of the influx of people evacuating Saint-Domingue meant that Cubans, in their own way, also experienced the final, dramatic prelude to Haitian independence, that they too encountered the tangible evidence of the defeat of slavery and colonialism at the hands of former slaves."⁵⁸

Because of the sheer numbers, Cuba had to require the refugees to contribute by demonstrating to the authorities how they would contribute to the island. The migrants turned to help build the Cuban society and economy as they contributed to building new plantations, specifically growing coffee. "Before the 1803 influx of . . . refugees, eastern Cuba had a total of eight coffee forms. In 1804, fifty-six new ones were started . . . The coffee boom wrought by the French arrivals brought large-scale, slave-based commercial agriculture to eastern Cuba for the first time."⁵⁹ While the Cuban and Spanish authorities may have reached a workable solution with the migrants, the enslaved population had other ideas and issues: revolution was not over as African religions informed their lives.

Rebellions: Two Examples

The era from 1783 to 1804 is called the Age of Revolutions for good reason: there were three revolutions that redrew maps and strained alliances. Each one impacted the Cuban aristocracy's and enslaved people's images of what could happen. The first revolution was the breakaway of thirteen colonies from the British monarchy, which began with the lofty language of the Declaration of Independence in 1776. The ideas of the Declaration reverberated as people across Europe pondered the concept of "inalienable human rights." In 1783, the American Revolution ended as the United States was formed, and the possibilities of successful revolt were no longer imaginary exercises. The French Revolution took place inside France, not an external colony, and began in 1789. By 1799, the monarchy was violently overthrown, and the Revolution's slogan—"Liberté, égalité, fraternité"—seemed to indicate the aims of a society that sought liberty, equality, and fraternity.

Those who were enslaved could see the disconnections with the United States' and France's slogans—human rights and liberty were not offered to them. So, the Haitian Revolution held up new imagery to Black people, offering them hope. They also had the imagery of their own spiritual and religious traditions on which to draw. While spotty documentation was kept by the Spanish and Cuban officials, some records and memories do indicate the influences of African spirituality and philosophy.

The first widespread Cuban rebellion of the enslaved was in 1812, the Aponte Rebellion. It occurred across the island, and it "was the first movement to seek both Cuban independence and the abolition of slavery. It was led by African descendants in Havana and organized 'internationally' across ethnic boundaries with like-minded groups across the island. A wealth of cultural forms enhanced the rebellion's legitimacy, secrecy, and coordination between African and African-descended *cabildos*."[60] *Cabildos de nación* were ethnic associations, some of which were based on African-derived religious thought. These organizations were permitted by the colonial government to serve as places for the enslaved to entertain themselves, or so the colonizers imagined. The *cabildos* also served as centers for organizing. Some of the *cabildos* held prominence, including those organized by the Abakuá and the Lucumí.

José Antonio Aponte headed a Lucumí *cabildo*, *Chango Tedun*, and he was able to organize across ethnic differences. The colonial name for *Chango Tedun* was *Cabildo Lucumí Sociedad Santa Bárbara*.[61] Lucumí had its roots among the Yorùbá of Nigeria, especially Oyo state.

The Abakuá *cabildo* or ethnic group had its roots in Calabar, Nigeria. Their involvement in the rebellion was supported by "an 1839 police report [that] identified a black militia member who had participated in Aponte's movement as a founding member of an Abakuá lodge, while other police files link Aponte's associates and Abakuá founders to the same social sectors: Freemasons, black and mulatto militiamen, *cabildo* members, free black artisans, and slaves."[62]

This description brings into focus the complex layers of the Cuban colonial society: an image that there were just the enslaved, government officials, plantation owners, and some freed Black people was not true in colonial Cuba, Saint-Domingue, or Brazil. Human beings never structure simple societies. In addition to the social tensions created by the social strata, there were other stress points that led to future events.

The Aponte Rebellion was not successful. All leaders were rounded up and executed. "In 1812, Spanish authorities publicly displayed Aponte's severed head to terrorize a restive populace into submission; they also erased evidence of Aponte's activism, including the documents he created to inform his community about liberation struggles of earlier times and places."[63] Of course, rebellions of enslaved people did not end in 1812. The Lucumí War in 1834 is another example, and the connections with the religion of Lucumí are clearer.

The Cuban colonial military permitted Black men to join their ranks.

> The irony that Cuban officials continuously armed slaves during the Haitian revolution signified how Spanish military perks far outweighed dissension. Black soldiers received a set of privileges and rights . . . which granted use of military and civil courts; exemption from taxes, tributes, and labor levies; and the right to bear arms, apply for loans, and own property, such as houses and slaves.[64]

These militiamen were particularly effective in controlling enslaved populations. One of these militiamen was Prieto.

"Juan Nepomuceno Prieto passed away as a free black man of the Lucumí nation, retired second sergeant of Havana's loyal black battalion, and 'king' of a Lucumí *cabildo* dedicated to Santa Bárbara."[65] This *cabildo* was one of the most prestigious. Santa Bárbara is the same as the Òrìṣà Ṣàngó, a fierce warrior divinity of thunder and lightning. The name of the *cabildo* was *Changó Tedún*, the same one that Aponte had led. Prieto led the community with his wife Camejo. Prieto's religious role led to his arrest after the Lucumí Wars.

Prieto was born around 1773 in Benin on the African continent but was captured by a Dahomey army that sold him into enslavement; he was shipped out from Badagry, eventually arriving in Cuba. He enlisted in the Cuban military in 1791 and earned his freedom. Prieto's service included policing the arrival of enslaved Africans and suppressing the Aponte Rebellion. His involvement in the Lucumí War or uprising is not clear; he was arrested in 1835, nearly two years after its suppression.

The uprising itself began at a plantation west of Havana. "Of the alleged participants, 265 were Lucumí." On a mid-August evening, a group of rebels seized and set fire to the plantation house. They proceeded to destroy three more plantations, then looted the town of Banes. They moved on to destroy three more plantations. Because of cholera's weakening effects on their troops, the Cuban military was unable to quickly respond as they had to send for reinforcements. When they did, the rebellion was crushed. "The main leaders, along with another fifty men, were killed; several more committed suicide; and others tried to hide in the coffee plantation, the swamp, or up the cliffs."[66] What followed these events was a ratcheting up of the fears of the White population. The military enacted a systematic suppression of Black people in Cuba.

During these uprisings, Prieto's wife was ill with cholera and died. Prieto was not directly a part of the War. But in 1835, a few Lucumí fought with some Whites in Havana. "Given Prieto's relative authority over a large Yorùbá-speaking community in Havana, it was a matter of time before officials pointed fingers at his *cabildo* and questioned his motives. Since the fracas occurred close to his home ... Prieto was guilty by association."[67] He was arrested and brought to trial. There are no records of what happened to Prieto after the trial, whether he was sentenced or released.

Lucumí and Cuban Society

These two examples of the unrest among Black people in Cuba highlight the interworking of race and class in colonial Cuban society that shaped Lucumí. Cuban society and Spain were dependent on the success of plantations to build their wealth. But they were also dependent on enslaved labor to work the plantations. The number of the Black population, enslaved and freed, was greater than that of the White population. As a result, fear was ever-present in White communities as they reflected on the experiences of Haiti. "'The fear of the negros,' according to José Maria Calatrava, Prime Minister of Spain from 1836 to 1837, 'is worth an army of 100,000 men, and it will prevent the Whites from making any revolutionary attempts.' 'Antes españoles *que* africanos' ('Spaniards before Africans') became a rallying cry."[68]

The push of the plantocracy to quickly get trafficked Africans to work their fields also meant that large groups were brought in from the same area of Africa. Prior to the Lucumí War, a large number of Yorùbá were trafficked from the same area, some of whom had military backgrounds. They were trafficked to meet the demands of Cuba's sugar production. With their shared background and the distances between the various plantations and urban centers, the Yorùbá were able to establish some sense of community, even under the harsh demands of enslavement.

While there were paths for Black people, such as Prieto, to be freed, they were still not fully accepted into Cuban society. They did establish their own communities and sometimes had businesses in the urban areas. But there were also opportunities for Black people to travel between plantations and between urban centers; such movement was necessary to maintain the Cuban flow of goods and services.

> The insatiable needs of sugar required a select group of black people to be mobile, and sometimes highly so. Such mobility in turn enabled select groups of male slaves in particular to reconfigure the spatial and social limits of the traditional estates, to nurture the growth of an organic rural leadership, and to facilitate the spread of revolutionary ideas within their districts.[69]

In other words, there were Black people able to travel, whether freed or on plantation business, and to use that mobility to build networks among themselves.

As in other colonies, the memories of Afrika and spiritualities that affirmed their humanity provided support for Black people to structure alternate societies, which was not understood by most Whites. *Cabildos de nación* were more than social clubs. *Changó Tedún* was an important *cabildo*, with both Aponte and Prieto as leaders at different times in history. Its importance was emphasized by John Mason, "an African American community historian, descended from a Cuban family, who is a leader within Lukumí lineages of New York City."[70] Mason traveled to Cuba and interviewed members who were able to give a history of *Changó Tedún*. The *cabildo* is the oldest in Havana, established in the 1700s. "All the Yorùbá belonged there, Àtàndá, Adésínà, Ifá Lobí, and 'Tata' Gaitán all belonged there, yet there were also other Africans who were not Yorùbá. . . . They all tried to raise money so that they could liberate their brothers who were slaves."⁷¹ The history of Black people, of African religions, had been masked, erased, unknown, or altered by Cuban colonial powers. The interview by Mason provided critical insight into the real history. Not only was the establishment of the *cabildo* dated differently in the people's memory than in the official Cuban records (1800s), but the former members' names that were cited indicate important and powerful African leadership throughout the history of the *cabildo*.

The different dates and missing information from Cuban historical records have led scholars, such as Mason, to find ways to gather data. It has not helped that some previous scholars' work about Lucumí oversimplified it, stating that it was merely a continuation of Yorùbá-Ifá. The prominence of Lucumí cabildos, the use of some Yorùbá language, and the reference to divinities that sound like those of Ifá—each point made the assumptions more solid. But more extensive research indicated that information had been glossed over as other scholars have found evidence of other traditions, as in those involved in another rebellion, La Escalera. La Escalera brought different traditions of Palo, which are derived from BaKongo traditions, to the attention of Aisha Finch.

Between 1841 and 1843, the repression of the enslaved became brutally cruel. "With the uprisings of the 1840s, brutal whippings became more and more frequent across the rural landscape, and inflicted on more and more people. From the spring of 1843 to the summer of 1844, they reached perhaps an unprecedented height, as hundreds of estates across the region witnessed punishment after punishment for resistance."⁷² La Escalera Rebellion ran from March to November 1843. It was named La Escalera, the ladder, because this was where prisoners were tied for the administration of lashings.

During this time frame, several uprisings boiled over onto different plantations. The largest of these uprisings was on November 5. Finch identified the forms and sources of African spiritual practices that were critical sources for those who rebelled.

> The ritual expertise of the black plantation world was nurtured and maintained through the consciousness and the memories of thousands of Africans who came to Cuba over the course of the nineteenth century. Having survived the Middle Passage, knowledgeable men and women

would reconstitute the institutions of priesthood, divination, and ritual healing on the rural plantations as best they could. This black sacred culture had to be maintained by whatever slaves could find in their daily lives—in the cabins, fields, woods, taverns, general stores, and by what lived in their own minds.[73]

Their reconstitution of their sacred practices was often fragmented, as will be shown in the next section.

Finch identified evidence of Palo through artifacts that were found or practices named in official documents. Among these were various amulets for protection; *Muñecos de Palo*, also known as *Nkuyo*, *Nkonsi*, and *Kinikini*, and all were quite feared as spiritual weaponry; *nganga* or ritual pots that could communicate with the *Kalunga*; accounts of the use of gunpowder, critical for Palo practice.[74] "This body of knowledge became known as Regla de Congo or, more commonly, Palo. Palo has four different branches—Palo Monte, Palo Mayombe, Palo Briyumba, and Palo Kimbisa—with the first two being the most widely practiced."[75]

Part of the reason that there is such incoherence between what occurred in Black Cuba and the White Spanish colonists is due to an influential thinker who promoted a colorblind Cuban society: José Marti (1853–1895). Unlike Brazil's use of "racial democracy" to cover continuing racism with aspirational language, Marti, as a political philosopher, was successful in implanting ideas of the unimportance of race. His writings continue to be taught in Cuban schools today, and he is considered Cuba's national hero.

But there was a dichotomy in his thinking that is still reflected in the divisions in Cuba. A documentary by Margaux Ouimet, *Walking the Cuban Tightrope*, traces Marti's history and thought and how it has ultimately been used to repress Black Cubans.[76] Marti's influence on Cuba began during his lifetime. He had a vision of a unified Cuba, but that unification depended on the elimination of race. In Marti's own words, a wonderful vision was promoted:

> In Cuba, there is no fear of a racial war. Men are more than Whites, mulattos or Negroes. Cubans are more than Whites, mulattos or Negroes. On the field of battle, dying for Cuba, the souls of Whites and Negroes have risen together into the air. In the daily life of defense, loyalty, brotherhood and shrewdness, Negroes have always been there, alongside Whites. Negroes, like Whites, are divided by their character-timid or brave, self-

sacrificing or selfish-into the diverse parties in which men group themselves.[77]

Miguel De La Torre sharply critiqued such a view because, for Martí, White people have suffered as much as, or more than, Black people. According to Marti, if Black people attempt to develop Black consciousness, "they are the true racists."[78]

This was the world in which Lucumí was formed.

Lucumí's Distinctions

Lucumí is called by several titles: "In Cuba, it is sometimes called *la religion* or *la religion lucumí*. Some refer to it as *la regla de Ocha* or simply *la ocha*. Others will call it Ifá, claiming that it is through Ifá that everything else is born. The least common name, however, has become the one most commonly used by outsiders: *Santería*."[79] The term *Santería* is not used as often, for practitioners want to emphasize the African roots of the religion. The term Lucumí is also given multiple translations, sometimes meaning "my friend" or sometimes referring to Oyo as the home of the Yorùbá.

Ivor Miller pointed to the blending of African divinities with Catholic saints within Lucumí. Saints were used

> [t]o visually disguise their fundamentally Yorùbá rites in a repressive Catholic society. Some Cuban *babaláwo* go even further than this by telling me that "Ifá speaks all languages," which is their way of saying that the Ifá divination system can deal with the complete spectrum of human experience, and thus can encompass all belief systems it encounters. They say Ifá has encompassed the Catholic Church in Cuba, making it a subsidiary belief system.[80]

Miller pointed to another distinctive aspect of Lucumí, understanding and honoring ancestors. Ancestors, generally, are important across ADR and AIR, with hopes of those living today becoming honored ancestors themselves. Miller stated that ancestor worship was transformed into *Espiritismo* (Spiritism) in some of the Cuban Lucumí communities. Spiritism came from the French mystic Allan Kardec (1804–1869). His mysticism was popular among the Spanish upper classes, and his thought traveled to Cuba through Amalia Soler. Eventually, Spiritism worked its way into Lucumí. This form is called Kardecist Spiritism. Allan Kardec wrote several books, some of which are required reading for those seeking Lucumí initiation today.

There are other forms of Spiritism as well, some directly related to Black communities. Spiritism, in general, believes in reincarnation and that it is possible to contact the spirits of those who have died. For instance, a séance is a form of Spiritism. In Spiritism, the practitioner works to become a medium, that is, a person who can make contact with spirits. In some forms of Spiritism, mediumship is a gift that only some will hold rather than something that can be learned. Overall, Spiritism seeks more direct contact with ancestors and others who are on another plane of existence.

Egúngún is the Yorùbá name for an individual or a community's ancestors. Miller wrote: "The Egúngún society was not recreated in Cuba ... Cuban Espiritismo ... a complex mixture of European and African ancestor reverence, has influenced the Egúngún system in some houses."[81]

The development of Lucumí happened over time. Many refer first to the influence of the Yorùbá. An important Yorùbá *babaláwo* ("father of secrets") trafficked to Cuba was Ño Remigio Herrera Adésínà Obara Meyi (1811–1905). (Ño is a sign of respect, Remigio Herrera were names given to him upon arrival in Cuba.) He was born in Osun State, Nigeria. Already a priest in 1830, he was warned of his upcoming capture. So, he swallowed his Orisha Orula and some Ikin that he would later defecate so that he could continue his service as priest.[82] He was in leadership for a while at Changó Tedún, but in 1866, he was the co-founder of *Cabildo Yemaya*. The Orisha to whom this Cabildo is consecrated, Yemayá, demonstrates how the Orishas themselves changed as the Africans traveled to different situations.

In Nigeria, Yemayá is an Òrìsà or Divinity of a river. As Africans were transported to different colonies, it was believed that Yemayá traveled with them: "Yemayá rules travel over salt water, and Lucumí credit her with delivering Yorùbá captives safely across the Atlantic during the Middle Passage, protecting them from fatal illnesses on voyages that frequently lasted many months. In Cuba her association with the institution of slavery runs deep."[83] Stories are told that she was raped; this experience defined her womanhood. *Regla* means rule, but it also means period, "encouraging the belief that Yemayá governs the cyclical flow of blood from women's bodies."[84]

The Orisha Yemayá, for whom Adésínà dedicated the cabildo, is also known as the Virgin of Regla; Regla is a Cuban seaside town. She had not been as popular as the Virgin la Caridad—Regla is Black and la Caridad is depicted with lighter skin. Perhaps it was because Adésínà himself had been a captive who survived his own passage over the Atlantic that Orisha Yemayá became so important for him to honor. The *cabildo* that Adésínà founded has grown over the years. "In the 1880s *cabildos de nación* started to die out a result of repressive legislation, while those in Regla only increased in vigor and number."[85] This cabildo remains important in Cuba, with his family still leading the community.

Yemayá is another example of how an Orisha changed in the process of traveling with the captive Africans, changing to meet their needs. Figure 4–2 lists some of the Lucumí Orishas next to those from Candomblé, Ifa, Vodou, and Vodun. The names may be similar, but it is not simply a change in language; there will be changes in the divinity's character and power. Such differences can be found in other belief patterns.

The distinctions of Lucumí went beyond beliefs about divinities or ancestors. The time frames in which Africans were transported to Cuba, as shown above, determined the formation of this ADR. For example, the famous *babaláwo* Adésínà was not transported to Cuba until the 1800s, but enslaved Africans had been there for centuries already. The influx of Yorùbá priests happened as wars on the African continent led to more captures and transports; Adésínà was caught in those groups. During this time, as Cubans increased their sugar production, their massive need for enslaved labor increased their human trafficking.

Yet, this influx was not until the 1800s. Africans had been enslaved, laboring in the copper mines as well as the plantations since the late 1500s. Simply put, the Africans who had been in Cuba for those centuries were not waiting until the famous *babaláwo* arrived to express their spiritualities. The Palo communities and *Espiritismo*, mentioned above, show that there are other religious strands happening across Cuba.

Lucumí had been creolized as Ysamur Flores-Peña, who is a priest of the tradition, explained: "As the Lucumí community evolved during slavery and after the founding of the republic in Cuba, it became polarized. Priests of Ifá, the *babalao*, claim a divine right to religious supremacy,

Figure 6.2 Callejon de Hamel, Havana, Cuba. Photo licensed from iStock.

based on their close links to Africa and the course of old Oyo in Nigeria. By contrast, the *obá oriaté*, a Creole institution, vigorously disputes such claims."[86] He continued that these religious forms predated *cabildos*. Lucumí was a new religion as it developed that was created "out of the parallel recollections of Congo and Yoruba cults."[87]

The differences were not cosmetic. The *obá oriaté* developed a different a divination system, the *dilogún*. "The *dilogún's* innovative approach separated the systems to the point of antagonism... [it] helped the *santeros* (priests) to organize the religion and culture in the absence of Ifá and its priests."[88] Different folk tales and histories, both for divination and about the Orishas, were developed within a Creole context. The *obá oriaté* is in charge of ceremonies, especially initiations, the Cuban *babalawo* holds a secondary place. "The *oriaté* can and does eliminate the *Babalawo* from his ritual practice; yet the *Babalawo* cannot do the same ... The mortar that unites the blocks of Lucumí culture—Ifá included—is the *obá oriaté*."[89]

Cuban practices of Lucumí continue today. Sites can be found, such as the Callejon de Hamel, one of the sections considered by some to be a temple.

Lucumí into the Diaspora

With the migration of Cubans fleeing Castro's revolution in 1959 and subsequent migrations, South Florida has become a center for Lucumí in the United States. The tensions of Cuban society traveled with them. The first group of migrants were "early resisters of the Castro regime. They were largely—though not entirely—well-off professionals seeking temporary refuge in hopes of Castro's failure."[90] This group worked to minimize or erase the "Africanness" of their roots. A later group of migrants came with the Mariel boat lift in 1980, as Castro opened the port of Mariel and told anyone who was dissatisfied with his regime to leave. "Largely poor and often black, these Cubans were prime practitioners of the unorthodox and African-derived religious traditions that the original exiles were so determined to suppress."[91]

It should be noted that Fidel Castro insisted that racism should no longer exist in Cuba. To this end, he promoted the Africanness of Cuba, promoting Black arts. Cuban musicians were prime examples, becoming symbols whose work, at times, reflected African themes and, of course, drumming. Some of these musicians were Celia Cruz, the Afro-Cuban All Stars, Ibrahim Ferrer, and Irakere (Yoruba for vegetation). That Cuba identified as Communist and secular did not matter; the religious themes were identified as cultural and therefore acceptable.

The 1980 migrants to Florida from Cuba continued the practice of animal sacrifice in their worship at the Church of the Lukumi Babalu Aye, and well-heeled Cubans pursued legal action through the city of Hialeah. Three laws of the City Council forbade animal sacrifice.[92] The clash between these strands of worship ended up before the Supreme Court, and in 1993, the decision was reversed. While this one group of Cubanos held onto their African-based practices, their victory does not indicate that ADR or AIR are generally accepted.

Lucumí is not restricted to South Florida or Cuba. Like other ADR, it travels and may attract practitioners in any location. John Mason, mentioned earlier, demonstrates that ADR and AIR are not confined to any one location. The ability of the African Diasporans to travel also expands possibilities for making connections and deepening understandings of their spiritual heritage.

Closing Thoughts: Revolution, Revolution

ADR in both Haiti and Cuba demonstrates how differences and similarities can develop. But there is one common thread: the struggles of people to get free from the long-term results of colonization.

France's and the United States' language of liberty, equality, and fraternity or inalienable human rights rang hollowly among Black people across the Diaspora who continued to be oppressed. In a speech in 1852, Frederick Douglass asked a question that was not answered by those revolutions: "What to the slave is the fourth of July?" The American Revolution, the French Revolution, Cuba's independence from Spain (1902), and Castro's Revolution (1959) did not encompass the longings of the enslaved or free Black people to heal from the past. Haiti's Revolution succeeded, only to be caught in a trap of financial serfdom to France—but this one success continues to have great resonance among Black people who had been oppressed.

Both Lucumí and Vodou could provide religious and spiritual forms that undergird a philosophical framework for understanding oneself against those who would continue oppressions. It is healing to identify as fully human within the circles of like-minded communities. The first of the ADR discussed was in the United States, MST and PAOCC, with many similar sentiments for freedom and healing core to their development. The stories of ADR in the United States reflect the differences of that country, as will be seen in the next chapter.

Notes

1 Michel-Étienne Descourtilz, 1791, cited in Laënnec Hurbon, *Voodoo: Search for the Spirit*, trans. Lory Frankel (New York: Harry N. Abrams, 1995), 131.
2 L. E. Moreau de Saint-Méry, 1791, cited in Laënnec Hurbon, *Voodoo: Search for the Spirit* (New York: Harry N. Abrams, 1995), 132.
3 John Henley, "Haiti: A Long Descent to Hell," *The Guardian*, January 14, 2010, https://www.theguardian.com/world/2010/jan/14/haiti-history

-earthquake-disaster, accessed January 2025. The cited description of enslavement is from Henri Christophe's personal secretary.
4   William Renwick Riddell, "Le Code Noir," *The Journal of Negro History* 10, no. 3 (July 1925): 322–3.
5   Hurbon, *Voodoo, Search for the Spirit*, 37–8.
6   Mambo Chita Tann, *Haitian Vodou: An Introduction to Haiti's Indigenous Spiritual Tradition* (Woodbury, MN: Llewellyn Publications, 2012; 9th printing, 2021), 21–2.
7   A. S. Weber, "Haitian Vodou and Ecotheology," *The Ecumenical Review* 70, no. 4 (December 2018): 683.
8   Sam White, *A Cold Welcome: The Little Ice Age and Europe's Encounter with North America* (Cambridge: Harvard University Press, 2017), 252.
9   Weber, "Haitian Vodou and Ecotheology," 683.
10 Hurbon, *Voodoo*, 42.
11 Gerdès Fleurant, "The Music of Haitian Vodun," in *African Spirituality*, 418.
12 Hurbon, *Voodoo*, 21.
13 Ibid.
14 Tann, *Haitian Vodou*, 52.
15 Politz, *Transforming Vòdún*, 3–4.
16 Tann, *Haitian Vodou*, 53.
17 Ibid., 55.
18 Fleurant, "The Music of Haitian Vodun," 420.
19 Tann, *Haitian Vodou*, 61.
20 Ibid., 88.
21 Karen McCarthy Brown, "Systematic Remembering, Systematic Forgetting: Ogou in Haiti," in *African American Religion*, ed. Timothy E. Fulop and Albert J. Raboteau (New York: Routledge, 1997), 437.
22 Ibid., 438.
23 Tann, *Haitian Vodou*, 107.
24 Ibid., 108.
25 Ibid., 58.
26 Hurbon, *Voodoo*, 66.
27 Thompson, *Flash of the Spirit*, 53.
28 Brown, "Systematic Remembering, Systematic Forgetting," 435.
29 Ibid., 442.
30 Hurbon, *Voodoo*, 112.
31 Thompson, *Flash of the Spirit*, 188.
32 Ibid., 191.

33 Fleurant, "The Music of Haitian Vodun," 420–1.
34 Weber, "Haitian Vodou and Ecotheology," 686.
35 LaGrace Benson, "Meeting Grounds in Saint-Domingue and the Emergence of Haitian Vodou: An Ecological Approach," in *Indigenous and African Diaspora Religions in the Americas*, ed. Benjamin Hebblethwaite and Silke Jansen (Lincoln: University of Nebraska Press, 2023), 77.
36 Tann, *Haitian Vodou*, 22.
37 Ibid., 22.
38 Benson, "Meeting Grounds in Saint-Domingue," 77.
39 Hurbon, *Voodoo*, 40.
40 Tann, *Haitian Vodou*, 24.
41 Ibid., 25.
42 Ibid., 26.
43 Ibid., 27.
44 Ibid., 31.
45 Fleurant, "The Music of Haitian Vodun," 427.
46 Eziaku Atuama Nwokocha, *Vodou en Vogue: Fashioning Black Divinities in Haiti and the United States* (Durham: University of North Carolina Press, 2023), xi.
47 Ibid., 7.
48 Ibid., 1.
49 Ibid., xii.
50 Ibid., 167–8.
51 Ibid., 169–70.
52 Miguel A. De La Torre, *Reading José Martí from the Margins* (Lanham, MD: Rowman & Littlefield, 2024), 62.
53 Ibid., 64.
54 Ibid., 64.
55 Ibid., 63.
56 Ada Ferrer, *Freedom's Mirror: Cuba and Haiti in the Age of Revolution* (New York: Cambridge University Press, 2014), 44.
57 Ibid., 173.
58 Ibid., 174.
59 Ibid., 181–2.
60 Ivor Miller, "Aponte's Legacy in Cuban Popular Culture," *Afro-Hispanic Review* 37, no. 2 (Fall 2018): 126.
61 Ibid., 131.
62 Ibid., 128.
63 Ibid., 126.

64 Henry B. Lovejoy, *Prieto: Yorùbá Kingship in Colonial Cuba During the Age of Revolutions* (Chapel Hill: The University of North Carolina Press, 2019), 60.
65 Ibid., 135.
66 Ibid., 118.
67 Ibid., 123.
68 De La Torre, *Reading José Martí*, 65.
69 Aisha K. Finch, *Rethinking Slave Rebellion in Cuba: La Escalera and the Insurgencies of 1841–1844* (Durham: University of North Carolina Press 2015), 54.
70 Miller, "Aponte's Legacy in Cuban Popular Culture," 133.
71 Cited from John Mason's 1983 interview with Babaláwo "Tin", in Miller, "Aponte's Legacy in Cuban Popular Culture," 134.
72 Finch, *Rethinking Slave Rebellion in Cuba*, 227.
73 Ibid., 200.
74 Ibid., 204.
75 Ibid., 201.
76 Margaux Ouimet, *Walking the Cuban Tightrope* (Oley, PA: Bullfrog Films, 2024).
77 José Martí, "My Race," *Patria*, April 16, 1893, http://www.historyofcuba.com/history/race/MyRace.htm, accessed February 2025.
78 De La Torre, *Reading José Martí*, 79.
79 Curtis Lanoue, *Reading José Martí, Handbook for the Aborisha: A Beginner's Guide to the Lucumí Tradition* (Curtis Lanoue, s.p., 2019), 1.
80 Miller, "Aponte's Legacy in Cuban Popular Culture," in Abimbola, 105.
81 Ivor Miller, in Wande Abimbola, *Ifá Will Mend Our Broken World* (Roxbury: Aim Books, 1997), 107.
82 Farida Dawkins, "Remigio Herrara," *Face2Face Africa*, April 17, 2018, https://face2faceafrica.com/article/remigio-herrera-the-nigerian-slave-who-heavily-influenced-cuba-as-a-mystic-in-the-1800s, accessed February 2025.
83 Perez, "The Virgin in the Mirror," 207.
84 Ibid.
85 Ibid., 212.
86 Ysamur M. Flores-Peña, "Mofá and the Oba: Translation of Ifá Epistemology in the Afro-Cuban Dilogun," in *Ifá Divination, Knowledge, Power, and Performance*, ed. Jacob K. Olupona and Rowland O. Abiodun (Bloomington: Indiana University Press, 2016), 212.
87 Ibid., 213.
88 Ibid., 216.
89 Ibid., 219.

90　Joseph M. Murphy, "The Many San Lazaros of Hialeah: Material Practice in the Celebration of a Cuban American Saint," *Material Religion* 13, no. 4 (2017): 490.
91　Ibid., 491.
92　"Animal Sacrifice Suit Called Fight for Religious Freedom," *Sun-Sentinel* (Fort Lauderdale), March 28, 1989, 5B, https://www.proquest.com/newspapers/animal-sacrifice-suit-called-fight-religious/docview/389351010/se-2, accessed March 2025.

7

Widening the Lens
ADR in the United States

Chapter Outline

Groundworks of ADR in the United States	177
Bodies	180
Music and Dance	182
Hoodoo and Voodoo	185
Back to Dance	187
Oyotunji Village	189
Black Religious and Spiritual Life, Making Afrikan Connections	190
Education	193
Conclusion: AIR and ADR in the United States	197

Groundworks of ADR in the United States

In fact, the Negro has not been christianized as extensively as is generally believed. The great masses are still standing before their pagan altars and calling old gods by a new name.

Z. N. Hurston[1]

> *Oppression makes the strangest things radical. Imagination, for example, to a society that commodifies human life, imagination is a threat to the bottom line. Free labor makes slavery profitable, but slaves who spend their time daydreaming waste profit . . . For the money to keep flowing, their imagination must be suppressed. This suppression of imagination takes many forms and occurs in many contexts.*
>
> N. K. Jemison[2]

ADR in the United States developed along distinctive paths. The northeastern colonies were predominantly British ruled, some southern areas were held by the Spanish, and some areas by the French. While there were varieties of Christian confessions practiced by British settlers, anything African, such as drumming or dancing, was viewed negatively and therefore prohibited in those territories. The Catholic Spanish and French held negative views but provided a bit more leeway for Black people to hold some scraps of their own cultures. These French and Spanish colonies would eventually be incorporated into the new country.

The original thirteen colonies expanded south and west and eventually became states. But there was no consistency in the ways that Black people were constrained, for each state had its own laws for the treatment of Black enslaved or free populations. As the country expanded, each newly minted state argued for or against the legality of enslavement within its own borders. That determination was often settled by economic drivers for an expendable labor force or by political pressure from Southern states to maintain the balance of slaveholding territories. The transatlantic trafficking of Africans was abolished in 1808 in the US, although there would have been some who flouted the law and continued to receive human cargo. But interstate trafficking took the place of the transatlantic captures under the chattel principle:

> Any slave's identity might be disrupted as easily as a price could be set and a piece of paper passed from one hand to another. Of the two thirds of a million interstate sales made by the traders in the decades before the Civil War, twenty-five percent involved the destruction of a first marriage and fifty percent destroyed a nuclear family—many of these separating children under the age of thirteen from their parents. Nearly all of them involved the dissolution of a previously existing community. And those are only the interstate sales.[3]

The expansion of the country meant that as Black people were carted to different places, families and communities were broken. But identity was reshaped, as Michael Gomez stated it, from multiple African ethnicities to "an amalgam of the ethnic matrix; that is, the African American identity is in fact a composite of identities."[4] He points out that the "composite" was at times fragmented; some ethnic identifications were retained, such as the Gullah Geechee. Yet, even without a seamless blending, a new sense of "us" was created in the face of oppression, reflected in a folk song: "Got one mind for white folks to see, 'Nother for what I know is me, He don't know, he don't know my mind."[5]

Together, some members of the Black community sought healing spaces grounded in spirituality, in other words, a holistic consideration of whole persons and communities. For these healing spaces, they used their memories and shared stories. How did memories and stories become spaces that could not be legislated? How can ADR be understood in the United States? The two quotes that began this chapter show different perspectives that answer those questions.

The first, from the collected works of Zora Neale Hurston, signals the spiritual flexibility that is part and parcel of Black cultural forms. Hurston, the anthropologist and rhetorician, identified creative and free Black spiritualities. The second, written nearly one hundred years later, is from the renowned science fiction writer, N.K. Jemisin. As part of the development of the field of Afrofuturism, she highlights how Black creativity flies in the face of colonial/capitalist societies. AIR and ADR do not "fit" the framing of Western religions. Therefore, it is easy for a Western-trained religious thinker to apply to any AIR/ADR the words of Christopher Columbus, who wrote of the Taino he encountered in 1492: "They have no religion."

That African-derived religions are established and continue across the Diaspora is often based on indirect but powerful realities. Yet, being in the United States was its own reality. "As practiced in North America, Protestantism tended to be rigid and inflexible, hostile to the kind of association between African deities and Christian saints found in a number of Catholic societies elsewhere in the New World."[6]

There was a wide range of indirect influences that touched Black people's lives in the United States. The underlying philosophies of AIR/ADR were named and expressed in multiple ways. Twentieth-century efforts such as the Moorish Science Temple indicated to wider communities that something else, something of their own, was possible in a formal institutional setting. Marcus and Amy Garvey's Pan-Africanist works had a global influence, providing new images and structures. However, efforts to find healing spaces did not begin after Emancipation.

For the African captives and their descendants, how they cared for their bodies provided information about who they were, despite oppressions. Music and dance, centrally important in AIR, played roles that communicated spiritual content from captivity, through oppressions, into the present. Each of these—bodies, music, and dance—provided the foil for the development and expansion of ADR in the United States.

Bodies

Cultural and home-based practices with commonly held knowledge, such as folk wisdom, form a substantial groundwork to inform spiritual beliefs. AIR is holistic; therefore, the material conditions of the people were always important. In this, the knowledge of herbs and healing became centrally important. Even as these forms of knowledge, incomplete in many cases, traveled through the Diaspora, they were revised by people to fit the frames of their new oppressive conditions. While their knowledge may have been incomplete, whatever they did stood in clear contrast to the lack of care Africans in the Diaspora received from the colonizers. Healing practices that offered care, drawn from familiar cultural bases, held promises of life.

Childbirth is a human experience, not an illness, but working with the delivery of a child is a healing practice. It was common for Black women, often enslaved themselves, to serve as midwives for other enslaved women. "In the New World, racial slavery and colonialism dictated the hierarchy of labor, and midwifery was no exception. African and African-descended midwives in rural and urban areas served populations throughout the Americas... As the primary health care providers, especially on plantations, women of color performed a range of tasks."[7] Across Latin America, these midwives were called *parteras* and they "gained experience through traditional cultural practices"[8] as one author stated. These women learned their craft from other midwives and utilized knowledge of herbs and plants.

Funlayo O. Wood wrote about the importance of healing:

> One of the traditions that developed during and right after slavery is known as Conjure or Hoodoo, which is also often referred to as "root work" because of its connection with herbal medicines—a prominent feature of many African religions. . . . The people who were the most revered conjure doctors, as they were called, were often what was called "saltwater" Africans or those who had been born in Africa and who had come over on the ships . . . Among the enslaved people, these conjure doctors took the place of medical doctors because enslaved peoples did not have access to medical doctors.[9]

Zora Neale Hurston's interviews of Black people gathered information on folkways and hoodoo beliefs. She conducted this research, it is estimated, between 1925 and 1936.[10] Hurston left some records of stories told about conjure doctors: Father Abraham, Mother Catherine, and Uncle Monday.[11] Hurston gathered data on some folk cures as well. So, for headaches, "rub table salt onto the 'mould' of the head."[12] Conjure and hoodoo were ways to connect with the healing power of the earth, of herbs, and of its substances such as salt, all integral to African spirituality. Bunseki Fu-Kiau's list of possible therapies in BaKongo belief, with the centering of healing as sacred, provides an indirect line where conjure, hoodoo, and rubbing salt on the head are logical extensions. (A longer discussion of Hoodoo, with Voodoo, as ADR is below.) Other aspects of Black cultural life across the Diaspora have foundations drawn from Afrikan religious thought.

As shown in earlier chapters, ancestors are centrally important in Afrikan worship. Ancestors are part of the cohesive realities of the cosmos that include the divinities, nature, and humans. It follows that funerals mark the movement of a deceased person from one plane of existence to another. Laura Jarmon emphasized the importance of funerals. "The funeral is the ultimate worshipful act, the essence of which eludes articulation. As an elaborate ritual, a traditional African funeral may span several years and encompass a variety of expressive forms, and the African American funeral tends to vary in its replication of features of the traditional African form."[13] Whether or not Black people in the Diaspora recognize the African connections, the flavor still lingers in funerary practices. I remember being called about a family member's funeral at a Christian church, which would include a communion rite. The caller emphasized the importance of attending because it "would be the last time you can eat with her."

The mergers between spiritualities and cultures can be seen in Black Americans' folk healing practices, which defy reduction to simple superstition.[14] The care of Black bodies, from womb to tomb, was in the hands of midwives and root workers, and spiritual practices of closure, such as funerals. Much of the healing practice was wrapped in folk wisdom or proverbs, which also indicated a spirituality, such as "A baby born near midnight will be able to see ghosts."[15] Community was created, and Black humanity was affirmed. These practical matters ensured the transmission of conceptual frameworks that were derived from Africa: the care of bodies is integral to a definition of spirituality. These caring practices may not have spread a defined AIR or ADR, but reflect their general characteristics as described in the Introduction.

Music and Dance

"In traditional African cultures, one is born, named, and initiated through music into various levels of existence—puberty, marriage, life, and death. Music is a vital part of domestic chores as well as religious and social events.... People of African heritage in America bear the cultural seeds of musicians, poets, and dancers."[16] The arts of the Africans did not look like those of their captors and were, in fact, called "heathenish" or "pagan." The music and dance were decidedly different, rhythmically alien to the Europeans. Yet, both Black music and dance shaped the cultures of the colonies and the countries that they became. Both music and dance carried African culture and, by extension, overt or covert spiritualities.

While the following citation identifies characteristics of African American musical expression, many of these can be applied across the Diaspora:

> There is no clear line of demarcation between secular and sacred in language and performance; a strong sense of communal togetherness is evoked; existential situations provide the subject for the poetic language; and the common means of transmission are by way of the oral tradition.... The songs emanating from the earliest poet-musicians were created and employed in "praise houses," in fields, and in other work arenas characterized by a strong sense of corporate identity and cooperation.[17]

The years from 1950 to 1970 were volatile for Black people globally as different liberation movements grew. Amiri Baraka (1934–2014) was a poet and playwright, one of the founders of the Black Arts Movement in the United States in the 1960s. Baraka was a prolific writer and provided analysis and history of Black music in America with his first book.

Baraka wrote that Africans used drums for more than a kind of Morse code, but reproduced words, "the result being that Africans developed an extremely fine and extremely complex rhythmic sense . . . Also, the elaborately developed harmonic system used in the playing of percussion instruments . . . was not immediately recognizable to the Western ear . . . [which were] used to less subtle musical devices."[18] He delved into the history of work songs sung by field hands. The lyrics to one song Baraka cited clearly indicated African spiritualities: "After the planting, if the gods bring rain/My family, my ancestors, be rich as they are beautiful."[19] But after the plantation owners came to understand the meanings of the song, they forbade it, along with drums, because they "could mean that those particular Africans were planning on leaving that plantation as soon as they could . . . and that drums could be used to incite revolt as well as to accompany dancers."[20]

The power of music shaped religious and political lives. The flow of religious music and meaning into everyday life was seen through the American Civil Rights Movement. During the 1950s and 1960s, songs, especially gospel songs and spirituals, provided a way for people to keep marching. Sweet Honey in the Rock was a group that became well known for its a cappella singing. The leader, Bernice Johnson Reagon (1942–2024), told the story of the group in her book, *We Who Believe in Freedom*.[21] The lyrics to their songs were not all directed to a divinity but sometimes sung in honor of the community's ancestors who had died or been murdered in the Freedom Movements, such as Fannie Lou Hamer[22] or Reverend Herbert Lee[23]—in other words, ancestors in struggle. Music became the message, a justice focus wrapped in spirituality. As Arthur Jones stated:

> It is clear that the religious experience of the creators of the spirituals was full and creatively comprehensive. It offered African American believers a varied repertoire of spiritual resources for their everyday confrontations with the forces of oppression, while at the same time providing an internal framework of sanity and justice in an insane and unjust environment. . . .

the experience of the divine was powerful and highly personal, and certainly not confined to weekly . . . worship services.[24]

Dance was and remains central to prayer life within African and African Diasporan spiritualities. Europeans generally had negative views of human bodies, with binary philosophies of body/soul. African dance was defined as sexually suggestive at best, as Sterling Stuckey noted: "That whites considered dance sinful resulted in cultural polarization of the sharpest kind since dance was to the African a means of establishing contact with the ancestors and with the gods. Because the emotions of slaves were so much a part of dance expression, the whole body moving to complex rhythms—what was often linked to the continuing cycle of life, to the divine—was thought to be debased."[25] As the enslaved were seemingly Christianized, such dancing was seemingly forbidden. "The deemphasis on dance meant more stress on the words, a development associated with the introduction of choirs and 'audiences.'"[26]

The idea of "art for art's sake" is European; for the Afrikan, art is woven into daily life. However, Afrikans adapted, learning to express dance cultures in new formats. Rumba and salsa are danced in Cuba among other Latin countries; the samba is celebrated in Brazil. Each of these blends African with European forms, and some consider these dances sacred. Break dancing in the United States looks very much like Brazilian Capoeira, which is now called a dance form. But Capoeira was transported with captives from the Western African area known today as Angola; there, Capoeira was a form of combat.

Africans learned to adapt their dance to stage performances. Tap dance put complex African rhythms into their feet. Black popular dance became a powerful twentieth-century influence. Langston Hughes (1901–1967) collected information on Black performing arts over the centuries in the book *Black Magic*. He noted the significance of dance in Harlem, New York, in the 1920s: "In the Twenties it seemed as if all Harlem was dancing—and Harlemites set the rest of the world to dancing, too."[27] He included mention of other dances such as the Charleston (which originated in Harlem), the Black Bottom, and the Lindy hop. As these popular dance expressions developed, the presentation of Black dance on stages developed as well.

African dance was presented in 1893 at the Chicago World's Fair with a troupe of Dahomey dancers. But this was not a breakthrough for acceptance of African dance: this was still 1893, and negative views of people of color continued. They were displayed on the Midway: "Living humans—Native Americans, Africans, Pacific Islanders, Middle Easterners, and Southeast Asians—were displayed to a buying public in ethnological zoos and widely perceived as representing various lower stages of ascending human social evolution."[28] The records of perceptions of the Dahomeans were negative and dehumanizing. "One journalist asserted that 'a Dahomean mother is, in feature and figure, the incomparable nightmare of the human race,' while another asserted that the Dahomeans were 'blacker than buried midnight and as degraded as the animals which prowl the jungle of their dark land. It is impossible to conceive of a notch lower in the human scale.'"[29] The images of African dance in the American mind did not begin to change with this 1893 exhibition. But these negative images did not necessarily reflect the minds of Black people who still sought healing and expression of their own humanity. The earliest forms of ADR, Hoodoo and Voodoo, were part of that healing. Pioneers in dance brought Afrikan expressions to many audiences. Both were integral to the development of ADR.

Hoodoo and Voodoo

Hoodoo is more than the care of Black bodies and is one of the first ADRs in the United States. Most people may not recognize hoodoo as a religion. Katherine Hazzard-Donald responded that not recognizing the religious dimensions of hoodoo was a continuation of negative beliefs about Black people as primitive and ignorant, with no real religion. She identified the "old" hoodoo religion, which included midwives, morticians/gravediggers, and root workers, in contrast to contemporary hoodoo that has expanded into commercial areas. Belief makes sense of life, and so she contends:

> The old Hoodoo religion contained those African elements that would later give birth to numerous religious practices that would be labeled "superstition" because they were outside of acceptable mainstream Christian practice. It would also give birth to numerous practices that would become secularized and move into African American popular culture, particularly in music and dance, but into other areas and into the black church as well.[30]

Hoodoo, also known as conjure, focused on correcting issues of money, luck, and love, as well as health. Hoodoo doctors or conjurers used herbs and roots in their cures, which were sometimes made into teas or ointments. The patient may be instructed to use the prescribed herbs for a certain period of time. The conjurer's knowledge about the correct use of herbs may have been learned from others, including Native people. Charms and amulets were also part of their trade, each charm crafted specifically for the person seeking help. Other elements, such as pebbles or coins, could be added to charms. Some hoodoo practitioners also worked with removing or placing evil spells, and this is where the negative images of the practices arise. In spite of such a reputation, the conjurer's work was often mixed with Christian symbols.

Zora Neale Hurston described the practice of Father Abraham, who healed illness but included charms.

> Abraham often gave his patients a white muslin packet known as a "Christian letter" to be carried on the person at all times. These letters cost from $5 to $25 and were supposed to bring good luck and ward off evil spells and any form of disaster. To lose the letter meant that one was liable to fall under an evil influence and be tormented.[31]

Voodoo is also an ADR in the United States. While Haitian Vodou has been carried to places in the United States, the first form, usually associated with New Orleans and Louisiana, is different. Mambo Chita Tann distinguished between the Voodoo of New Orleans and the Vodou of Haiti. The Africans transported to Louisiana significantly originated from areas of Benin, Tann indicated, especially between 1719 and 1808. She continued that upon arrival in New Orleans' ports, those "who arrived as a family group were legally required to be sold as a group. Thus . . . the African heritage . . . was more likely to be preserved." Conditions in Louisiana, while brutal, were not as terminal as those in Haiti. "Because of this, there were actual African elders in Louisiana living out their natural lives among descendants without separations [and] . . . were able to keep the traditions and cultural information of their homeland alive."[32] Therefore, New Orleans Voodoo was able to keep many African traditions alive. The changes came more from influences in Louisiana, such as their local indigenous groups and European Spiritism.

But Voodoo itself was a continual target of the press, especially after the Union occupation of New Orleans during the Civil War. Danielle Boaz, with thorough research of various news reports, argued that this presentation of the depravity of Black folk "was intricately tied to debates about the extension of citizenship and voting rights to African Americans. These (often made up or exaggerated) descriptions of Black spiritual practices served as purported evidence that persons of African descent needed to be firmly controlled by whites.... This general argument would slightly shift but never disappear."[33]

Back to Dance

There were two significant figures who brought African dance into wider acceptance in American arts in the 1930s and 1940s. Consequently, they each contributed to the growth of ADR.

Asadata Dafora Horton (1890–1965) was from a well-connected and well-educated Sierra Leone family. "Dafora received musical training in Europe, including operatic studies at La Scala between 1910 and 1912."[34] When he moved to Harlem, he encountered the disconnect between the ways that Africa had been portrayed by White Americans and the desire for a timeless, pure Africa held by African Americans. His artistic work can be credited with breaking open the theater world for the acceptance of African dance, but there were problems. He often had to revise his work and himself to be more primitive, to fit patterns of perception of "African." He edited the Horton from his name, using only the African-sounding portions.

In 1934, Asadata Dafora's dance-opera opened in New York. "*Kyunkor: A Native African Opera*, told a story set in a Mende village of a young man wooing his bride ... until an evil rival sends a 'witch woman' to cast a spell on the prospective groom; a 'witch doctor' finally lifts the spell and the marriage proceeds."[35] *Kyunkor* was a great success and Dafora's fame spread. He was the choreographer and musician for Orson Welles' 1936 Federal Theater Project production of *Voodoo Macbeth* with an all-Black cast that toured nationwide.

> Not only were Dafora and his troupe confined to performing Welles' ideas of primal evil, Dafora and his colleagues were presented in promotional ploys ... as actual voodoo priests. Although versions vary, the central story

tells of the Africans drumming all night in the rehearsal room to cast a spell on a hostile critic, who soon died of pneumonia.³⁶

Perhaps these two steps—the Chicago Exposition and Dafora's fame—were necessary to clear the way for the success that Katherine Dunham would achieve.

While American Katherine Dunham was not the first African dancer in the US, she broke through barriers of stage and film in her presentations of Black dance. She established the Dunham Dance Company in 1931. Dunham was a pioneer and an anthropologist,

> who[w]ent to both library and living sources for her materials before bringing them to the stage. On a Rosenwald fellowship, she travelled far afield in search of Afro-Caribbean and American negro rituals, rhythms, and patterns of movement... For more than twenty years, she kept together a dance company that performed in most major cities of the world and periodically returned to Broadway.³⁷

Dunham was not just a researcher of African dance. She herself was initiated into Vodun in Haiti. Her long relationships with those Haitian communities spilled over into her studies of other Caribbean countries such as Jamaica. But none of those studies were as significant as her work with Haiti.

Dunham wrote of her initiation and the sense of being split as a researcher:

> It is hard to describe to an uninitiated the process of becoming initiated. Harder still when one remains for years on a fringe border of belief and nonbelief, because the two are so close. A thing happens, you experience it often without seeing it, and it is true. From then on, the bitter battle with society begins, whether the thing that happened was acceptable in the society judging it. There must have been, I have since reflected with my jaded observer's mind, drugs of some mild kind administered, incense and herbs burnt that added to the trance feeling that made me see with startling clarity the meaning of this marriage to Damballa.³⁸

As part of her stage performances, Dunham performed some of the sacred dances. One for which her troupe was well known was the *Yanvalou*, which means "come to me." "It is both invocation and a supplication dance/music, which must be played first at all ceremonies for the Rada rite ... It is danced on bent knees.... It is through the singing, playing, and dancing of the *yanvalou* that vodunists establish contact with the ancestors in *Lafrik Ginen* or Guinea, Africa."³⁹ Many of the members of the dance troupe were initiated from Cuba, Brazil, or Haiti. In the performance of sacred dance, even on stage, some of the dancers could become possessed by *orichas*.

> Trance possessions were seemingly common at Dunham's performances, and according to Nigerian drummer, Babatunde Olatunji, "It happened one time to a whole dance company from Jamaica that came to perform with us. . . . The entire dance company got possessed on me, right on stage. . . . We had to stop the show . . . I had to stop my drumming and call for an intermission."[40]

Dunham's influence on Afrikan religious life extended in another direction as well. The Oyotunji Village was a definite expansion of ADR in the United States.

Oyotunji Village

Walter King was born in Detroit, Michigan, in 1928. His biographer, Tracey Hucks, recounts his question to his mother at the age of fifteen: "Who is the African God? That's what I want to know."[41] This question became a driving focus of his life. In Detroit, he was influenced by Marcus Garvey's ideas and the Moorish Science Temple as he set out on his own journey of discovery. While in high school, King began to study African dance, which he continued in Chicago and Los Angeles after graduation. He then auditioned for the Katherine Dunham Dance School in New York and was accepted. The time with Dunham provided King the beginning of the answer to his question, as he stated in his own words, his "first exposure to something genuinely African. . . . She had some Cubans in the company; she had some Brazilians in the company; and she had some Haitians and these were all dark-complexioned people. . . . Each was showing what they knew or doing what they knew well."[42]

King had traveled to Haiti with Dunham, and this fired his intention to become initiated. He left Dunham's company in 1950, moving to New York, where he established the Order of Damballah Hwedo Ancestor Priests in 1956.[43] In 1957, the Order moved to Harlem, and King renamed himself. He would "now be known to others and to himself as Nana Oseijeman Adefunmi I. Nana he translated as 'honorable chief'; Oseijeman, an Akan name he understood as 'savior of the people';

Adefunmi, a Yorùbá name that asserted royal lineage meaning 'a crown for me'; and I, which designated the first in this new African lineage in America."[44] His title for this new lineage was His Royal Highness.

In 1970, His Royal Highness Adefunmi I established Oyotunji African Village on several acres of land in the low country of South Carolina. Oyotunji is named for the Oyo Empire, which fell in 1836. This empire covered parts of today's Nigeria and Benin and was central to the Yorùbá people and Ifá. A treaty signed in July 1888 and still on display in Oyo today signaled that "all Yorùbá speaking peoples" would "forever maintain friendly relations" with England and provide that country exclusive rights to trade. Nigeria would not gain complete independence from Britain until 1960. So, Oyotunji Village was so named to signal a coming renaissance of Afrikan centrality. His Royal Highness Adefunmi I died in 2005, but Oyotunji Village continues today. As Tracey Hucks noted:

> Oyotunji has made a broad appeal to African Americans across class and education lines. . . . Statistically, Oyotunji consists of some twelve families, with a total population of close to three dozen people. In the past, the village has housed as many as 250 African American residents at the height of black-nationalist enthusiasm. Oyotunji's numbers, however, in no way indicate the vast influence and symbolic meaning the village has held since 1970. . . . in 1992, Adefunmi estimated that some 435 people had been initiated into the Yoruba priesthood through Oyotunji. By the mid-1990s, that number had grown to nearly 600.[45]

The question of the young Walter King that came to be expressed in the establishment of Oyotunji Village is but one example of a religious seeking that draws on history with attention to present realities. It is a question that many have asked, and Adefunmi found his answer, which led other people to find their own. Oyotunji Village was one way that Africa was recognized among those in the Diaspora.

Black Religious and Spiritual Life, Making Afrikan Connections

With few exceptions in the United States, such as in Louisiana and some locations in Florida or Georgia, the captives' native dancing and use of drums were outlawed. The languages and customs of those who were enslaved were, on many levels, forbidden. Some among the plantocracy argued against making Christians of the enslaved—that would entail having Sunday off. Others argued that Black people would not be allowed into heaven with White folks. Finally, making the Black folks become Christian was seen as a method to control them, since biblical scriptures, they argued, clearly supported enslavement.

Each state with legal enslavement had a set of laws that defined the roles and limits of Black people, called Black codes. Such codes continued through the Jim Crow years of de facto and de jure segregation, by law and by practice. American laws were studied as prototypes by Hitler's regime as they developed their own to exclude and execute Jews.[46]

With all the barriers set up in American society, Black people recognized that they were not "home" and that there were many things wrong in the places they lived in the United States. From one former self-identification of Black people in the colonies as "Anglo-Africans" to the naming of Christian denominations—African Methodist Episcopal or African Methodist Episcopal Zion—Africa has been in the minds of Black people. Paralleling the expansion of Pan-Africanism, music and dance, with formal or informal education, Black Christian churches claimed their own cultures in the realities of their faith lives. They were "Christian." However, as Melva Costen stated:

> Those in bondage receiving religious instruction were liberated by the power of God to sing to the hypocrisy of the slaveholder's preacher whose sermon exhorted to "sinlessness" as a ticket to heaven. Thus, the slave could sing "Everybody talkin' 'bout heaven ain't going there . . ." The community could admonish Mary (Magdalene) not to weep and mourn "'cause Pharoah's army got drownded" . . . The singers did not allow chronology to hinder matters of the faith and hope were pertinent to contemporary existence. . . . The community could ask "Were you there when they crucified my Lord?" . . . Jesus can be seen talking with Noah . . . just as easily as he is seen walking and talking with the slave.[47]

Such fluid reinterpretation of specific religious ideas fit well within Tracey Hucks' analysis of Black communities "blurring religious boundaries and traversing multiple sacred cosmologies in ways that are self-authorizing."[48]

Black American struggles for justice continually operated on multiple levels, from the Underground Railroad to Civil Rights and Black Power.

From the naming of Black denominations to spirituals, there was also ferment in Black Christian churches: how to reconcile the idea of a loving God with ongoing oppression? Out of this history, Black theology developed. In 1969, the National Committee of Black Churchmen met and issued a statement that began with this paragraph:

> Black people affirm their being. This affirmation is made in the whole experience of being black in the hostile American society. Black theology is not a gift of the Christian gospel dispensed to slaves, rather it is an appropriation which black slaves made of the gospel given by their white oppressors. . . . Black theology has dealt with all the ultimate and violent issues of life and death for a people despised and degraded.[49]

James H. Cone (1938–2018) was a Methodist minister with the National Committee of Black Churchmen. He was a leading influence in the development of this statement. He is credited with the development of the field of Black theology, as he authored several books that centered Black Christian theology in the life experiences of Black people. He emphasized this point as he wrote: "Truth cannot be separated from the people's struggle and the hopes and dreams that arise from that struggle. Truth is that transcendent reality, disclosed in the people's historical struggle for liberation, which enables them to know that their fight for freedom is not futile."[50]

Some Black Christian churches began to incorporate African aspects into services and decor. For instance, Adinkra symbols began to be more widely used. These symbols are from Ghana and surrounding regions. Some, such as Sankofa (symbolized by a bird looking back) or "looking back to go forward," were used to emphasize the importance of Black history, including that in Christian churches. The most popular Adinkra is the Gye Nyame symbol which means "Except for God," signaling that God is above all; this symbol is often used in jewelry. Kente cloth, which is also from Ghana, began to be used in official church services, from altar covers to ministerial robes.

The inclusions and celebrations of Africa were not limited to churches. In some ways, Black theology was a formalized expression of what was happening in the streets and among people. But Black Christian religions, across many denominations, began to embrace their own identities, no longer hamstrung by the need to hide from or appease White Christians. So Gayraud Wilmore could write that

The freedom toward which the religious experience of the people tended was rooted and grounded in the ancestral African environment. It was freedom as existential deliverance, as liberation from every power or force that restrains the full spontaneous release of the dynamism of body, mind and spirit—freedom from every bondage that is not recognized as contributing to the development of the whole person in community . . . the freedom of the person as a child of God.[51]

Self-care and community care for Black bodies; music that expressed African-derived thought in work or prayer; dance, socially or on stage, with African rhythms and movements: through all these, Black spiritual and religious life sought the African God. Sometimes, these were not clearly defined ADR. But the limiting definition of "religion," as something clearly defined with a structure that aligns with Western thinking, does not meet the challenge of the authors that I cited in the Introduction to this book: "The word 'religion' itself has lost its usefulness and that a new vocabulary needs to be developed for naming the various attitudes and activities that the word 'religion' is sometimes used to describe."[52]

There were other signs of the Afrikan presence or its adaptation among Black people in the United States that cannot be covered in this Introduction. These include, but are not limited to, the Gullah Geechee communities in parts of South Carolina and Georgia; the Black or Mardi Gras Indians in New Orleans, Louisiana; African American Spiritualist churches, such as Mother Leafy Anderson's Universal Hagar Spiritualist Church; the United House of Prayer for All People, whose leader "Daddy Grace" was believed to be divine by his followers; and the Five Percenters or Nation of Gods and Earths. Adenfunmi's question, "Who is the African God?" has been a driving force for many Black Americans.

The roots of ADR in the United States were held within Black people's underlying philosophies and cultures, their memories. Education, at both formal and informal levels, was a way that more information about Afrika and ADR spread.

Education

Through the 1950s and 1960s, with music, dance, Pan-Africanism, and the political movements of Civil Rights and Black Power, many Black

Americans were searching for ways to express African ideals. Finding expressions that were not tied to Christian or Western constructs and expressed Black cultural values became a motivation. So, in late 1965, the California-based Us Organization began discussing cultural practices, with an emphasis on holidays. The group, led by Maulana Karenga, researched African festivals and developed Kwanzaa, a seven-day holiday that celebrates an African value system. Kwanzaa is held during the month of December, either as a substitute or an addition to the celebrations of Christmas or Hanukkah. The seven days are based on the Seven Principles or the Nguzo Saba that Karenga introduced in 1964.[53] The Seven Principles are Umoja (Unity); Kujichagulia (Self-Determination); Ujima (Collective Responsibility); Ujamaa (Cooperative Economics); Nia (Purpose); Kuumba (Creativity); and Imani (Faith). Swahili is the African language used in naming the Principles. Each day ritually celebrates one of the Principles in a community or family setting. Kwanzaa has spread among many groups in and beyond the United States.

Ritual is, by its nature, educational. But especially so in Kwanzaa's case, as community or family groupings meet to discuss lives informed by African principles, using sources from Black cultures for the group's reflection. It is notable that there are many children's books that teach the meaning of Kwanzaa. Kwanzaa is not a formal ADR, but it might inform other religious practices, and this needs further study.

John Mason, mentioned in the previous chapter for his connections with Lucumí, is an initiated Babálorìsha who has held a significant role in the study of African religious cultures in the United States. In 1973, he and Cristobal Oliana founded the Yorùbá Theological Archministry in Brooklyn, New York, which was also incorporated as a church in 1978. Becoming a church allowed the Archministry, under Baba Mason, to offer classes at all levels. On the Archministry's website, Mason aimed "to meet the need to form a religious institution to fill spiritual and cultural voids, while nurturing, enhancing productive study, research, and trusted documentation of West African religious culture and its development, growth, and influence in the American diaspora."[54]

Baba Mason is a serious scholar of Afrikan religious traditions who has written several books. Mason outlined his intentions to provide "a new world to English-speaking initiates and devotees in the religion . . . with four classes: Òrìṣà Cooking; Òrìṣà Studies; Òrìṣà Songs; and Yorùbá Language."[55] He stated that these particular classes fostered students' understandings on deeper levels and, effectively, demonstrated that forms of hybrid Yorùbá derived religions, such as Lucumí, did not need "the influence of the Catholic saints, the holy water, etc. [which] had no real effect on the core message related in prayers, praise poems and songs. This approach has been called 'Yorùbá Reversionism.'"[56] Mason among others, identified the separation of Yorùbá practices from the accumulation of Western religious signs and symbols tied to study, practice, and belief. He and other Lucumí practitioners have been dedicated to removing the non-African aspects, which has been a motivation to avoid the designation Santería.

There are other community-based education centers throughout the US, which provide information on African religious thought. Many have educational programs that include speakers' series and classes in African dance or drumming. The availability of these educational centers might be called "self-help" programs and, as one author stated: "It can be argued that self-help education was both a building block and a facilitator of Pan-Africanist thinking. . . . Cooperative efforts at education from both sides of the Atlantic inevitably generated interest and awareness in the common plight of African people."[57] I would argue that building blocks and cooperative efforts are not past tense; in fact, the conversations across the Diaspora and into Africa are expanding through community-based programs.

College and university educational programs in the United States also expanded conversations and connections. Historically Black Colleges and Universities (HBCUs) have played roles in providing spaces for more programs dedicated to advancing Black history and activism.

Black Studies programs across the country especially aided cross-Diasporan conversations around religions and politics. Abdul Alkalimit has written a history of Black Studies. Black Studies, he wrote, is community-connected and community-based. Black Studies

> Advances knowledge about the Black experience. This involves the production, distribution and use of texts and cultural creativity. This involves the resurrection of previous knowledge, which sparks new consciousness . . . One of the mandatory starting points of the Black freedom struggle is the reclaiming of Black history . . . Part of this is to establish pride in what Black people have accomplished over historical time.[58]

Religions and spiritualities are certainly integral to Black experiences and often become part of Black Studies. Exchanges of African and Diasporan scholars advance the studies and the conversations.

One other strand that can provide formal and informal educational experiences are museums that specifically focus on Black history and culture. When any museum focused on Black history and culture is operated by people who have a scholarly background in Black studies, something powerful happens: Black people tell their own stories. An example is the National Museum of African American History and Culture (NMAAHC) with the Smithsonian museums in Washington, DC. Before opening, curators of the museum engaged African American people across the country, going from community to community, asking for artifacts, stories, and memorabilia. They also provided educational materials to assist those who attended the meetings in preserving their own families' historical documents and artifacts. From this collection process, the curators built the exhibits. One of the areas focuses on Black religions. The museum opened in 2016 and has become an oft-visited educational tourist attraction. The museum states its mission to "capture and share the unvarnished truth of African American history and culture. We collect stories, scholarship, art, and artifacts from the past and present to illuminate the contributions, struggles, and triumphs that have shaped our nation. We forge new and compelling avenues for audiences to experience the arc of living history."[59] The NMAAHC begins telling its stories of African Americans on the continent of Africa.

Black Americans' curiosity about all of Africa and the entire Diaspora has only grown through histories, museums, arts, music, and dance. Travel has become important to feed that curiosity.

ADR Travel Stories

The question "who is the African God?" still motivates some Black people in the Diaspora. They may respond by traveling in search of an answer. There are different opportunities to travel. Some agencies specialize in programs for African and Diasporan people to explore related countries. Spirituality can turn a trip into a pilgrimage. A BBC documentary explored the homecoming for several African Americans whose DNA tests revealed links to Sierra Leone.[60] Some of the comments from those travelers were: "It restores a stolen legacy." "I've been on a journey of self-discovery." "I'm the one to reunite our family to the homeland." Coming to a sense of one's history, when so many Diasporans" family roots were broken through trafficking, is a deep healing that is spiritual.

Some Black Americans hunger for new understandings and practices of spirituality. Religious tourism to the African continent or Brazil or Jamaica has grown. Some come to various African or Diasporan countries for initiation. In my travels, I met a woman who had been "initiated" seven times, in different countries, as she sought a "true" African spirituality. There are risks in seeking initiation without a trusted guide: those who seek spiritual upliftment are vulnerable, and some who call themselves guides do not have the knowledge or skill to provide what the seeker needs.

Wándé Abímbọlá, while he was spokesperson for Ifá in the world, stated that Yorúbà religion was spreading. But, he cautioned, "I am concerned that people have distorted the meaning and message of our culture for their own ends. People are not serious about the religion, and they are commercializing it. Some claim to be babaláwo . . . yet they don't know how to cast Ifá, and even if they know how to cast, they cannot chant a single verse of Ifá."[61]

Yet, these ADRs grow and continue in the United States. Despite the difficulties, Afrikan spiritual practices can become a haven, even as they challenge seekers to step outside their comfort zones.

Conclusion: AIR and ADR in the United States

The continuation and growth of AIR and ADR are highlighted in a collection of narratives from those who have been initiated. Each person tells their religious journey through "travel, learning, adaptation, apprenticeship, and initiation."[62] The narratives are not the sweeping testimonies from noted individuals such as Malidome Somé or Katherine Dunham. The people with these narratives are everyday folk from all walks of life across the globe who have found their ways into AIR or ADR. Martin Tsang affirmed that "More and more people are searching for tangible connection and initiation to the divine and are traveling to embrace and learn, transforming their lives and in turn amplifying religious global connections."[63] In part, he continued, this searching reflects that the views of African spiritual practices have shifted today:

> No longer are these religious traditions, systems, and lifeways considered "primitive," nor are they treated as having their foundations enshrined within a pristine and static past. Within the last two decades, discussions of diasporic Afro-Atlantic religions have increasingly become situated within the context of complex and dynamic politics, scales of economies, and international networks of communication and movement that serve to disrupt nation-state boundaries.[64]

Years ago, Gayraud Wilmore, as a Christian minister, indicated needs that the present day is beginning to address.

> We have a great deal more work to do on both sides of the Atlantic if we are genuinely interested in the recovery and enhancement of values, particularly those that reflect the affirmation of life . . . the unity of all life in the unquenchable desire for liberation, the freedom to be *Muntu*, man and woman, in the most penetrating sense of that profound Bantu word.[65]

Notes

1 Zora Neale Hurston, *The Sanctified Church* (Berkeley: Turtle Island, 1981), 105.
2 N. K. Jemisin, "There's a Reason," in *Afrofuturism: A History of Black Futures*, ed. Kevin M. Strait and Kinshasha Holman Conwill (Washington, DC: Smithsonian Books, 2023), 88.
3 Johnson, *Soul by Soul*, 19.
4 Michael A. Gomez, *Exchanging Our Country Marks: The Transformation of African Identities in the Colonial and Antebellum South* (Chapel Hill: University of North Carolina Press, 1997), 13.
5 Ibid., 10.
6 Ibid.
7 Michelle Reid-Vásquez, "Tensions of Race, Gender, and Midwifery in Colonial Cuba," in *Africans to Spanish America: Expanding the Diaspora*, ed. Sherwin K. Bryant, Rachel Sarah O'Toole, and Ben Vinson III (Urbana: University of Illinois Press, 2012), 188.

8 Ibid., 189.
9 Funlayo E. Wood, "A Brief History of Diasporic Religions in the United States," in Ẹlẹ́rìí Ìpín Brochure, Annual World Ifá Festival (International Council for Ifá Religion, June 2015), 44.
10 Toni Cade Bambara, "Some Forward Remarks," in Zora Neale Hurston, *The Sanctified Church* (Berkeley: Turtle Island, 1981), 9.
11 Zora Neale Hurston, *The Sanctified Church* (Berkeley: Turtle Island, 1981), 23–37.
12 Ibid., 19.
13 Laura C. Jarmon, *Wishbone: Reference and Interpretation in Black Folk Narrative* (Knoxville: University of Tennessee Press, 2003), 244.
14 Stephanie Y. Mitchem, *African American Folk Healing* (New York: New York University Press, 2007).
15 Hurston, *The Sanctified Church*, 22.
16 Melva W. Costen, "Singing Praise to God in African American Worship Contexts," in *African American Religious Studies*, ed. Gayraud S. Wilmore (Durham: Duke University Press, 1989; 2nd printing, 1992), 393.
17 Ibid., 393–4.
18 Amiri Baraka, *Blues People: Negro Music in White America* (New York: William Morrow and Company, 1963), 33.
19 Ibid., 26.
20 Ibid.
21 Bernice Johnson Reagon, *We Who Believe in Freedom* (New York: Anchor Books, 1993).
22 Ibid., 161.
23 Ibid, 160.
24 Arthur C. Jones, *Wade in the Water: The Wisdom of the Spirituals* (Maryknoll, NY: Orbis Books, 1993), 83.
25 Stuckey, *Slave Culture*, 25.
26 Ibid., 58.
27 Langston Hughes and Milton Meltzer, *Black Magic: A Pictorial History of the African American in the Performing Arts* (New York: Da Capo Press, 1967; repr., 1990), 91.
28 Micaela di Leonardo, *Exotics at Home: Anthropologies, Others, American Modernity* (Chicago: University of Chicago Press, 1998), 6.
29 Ibid., 7.
30 Katherine Hazzard-Donald, *Mojo Workin': The Old American Hoodoo System* (Champaign: University of Illinois Press, 2012), 3.
31 Hurston, *The Sanctified Church*, 17–18.

32 Tann, *Haitian Vodou*, 64.
33 Boaz, *Voodoo*, 26.
34 Philip Serge Zachernuk, "Contemporary Africans Meet Timeless Africa: The Conflicted Impact of Asadata Dafora's 'African Operas' on Pan-African Work in the United States, 1930–1950," *Journal of West African History* 8, no. 1 (Spring 2022): 62.
35 Ibid., 63.
36 Ibid., 68.
37 Hughes and Meltzer, *Black Magic*, 266.
38 Katherine Dunham, *Island Possessed* (Chicago: University of Chicago Press, 1969; repr., 1994), 105.
39 Fleurant, "The Music of Haitian Vodun," 429.
40 Tracey E. Hucks, *Yoruba Traditions and African American Religious Nationalism* (Albuquerque: University of New Mexico Press, 2012), 70.
41 Ibid., 50.
42 Ibid., 70.
43 Ibid., 73–4.
44 Ibid., 75.
45 Ibid., 173–4.
46 Cf. Isabel Wilkerson, "The Nazis and the Acceleration of Caste," chap. 8 in *Caste: The Origins of Our Discontents* (New York: Random House, 2020), 78–88.
47 Costen, "Singing Praise to God," 398.
48 Hucks, "Habitations of the Sacred," 44.
49 Cited in Wilmore, *Black Religion and Black Radicalism*, 215.
50 James H. Cone, *God of the Oppressed* (New York: Seabury Press, 1975), 17.
51 Wilmore, *Black Religion and Black Radicalism*, 219.
52 Ibid., 13.
53 "Expanding Our Understanding of the Kwanzaa Creation Story," *Kwanzaa Creators*, https://creators.kwanzaa.org/, accessed April 2025.
54 *Yoruba Theological Archministry*, http://www.yta-mason.com/ytawebpages-2018.htm, accessed February 2025.
55 John Mason, *Òrìṣà: New World Black Gods* (Brooklyn: Yorùbá Theological Archministry, 2016), vi.
56 Ibid., vii.
57 William H. Watkins, "Pan Africanism and the Politics of Education: Towards a New Understanding," in *Imagining Home: Class, Culture, and Nationalism in the African Diaspora*, ed. Sidney Lemelle and Robin D. G. Kelley (London: Verso, 1994), 235.

58 Abdul Akalimat, *The History of Black Studies* (London: Pluto Press, 2022), 90.
59 "About the Museum," *National Museum of African American History and Culture*, https://nmaahc.si.edu/about/about-museum, accessed February 2025.
60 "Paths of Return," *The Documentary*, BBC News World Service, released January 2025, https://www.bbc.co.uk/programmes/w3ct7lcc.
61 Wándé Abímbọ́lá, *Ifá Will Mend Our Broken World* (Roxbury: Aim Books, 1997), 25.
62 Martin Tsang, ed., *Spirited Diasporas: Personal Narratives and Global Futures of Afro-Atlantic Religions* (Gainesville: University of Florida Press, 2023), 4.
63 Ibid., 3.
64 Ibid., 5–6.
65 Wilmore, *Black Religion and Black Radicalism*, 240.

Conclusion
Horizons

Chapter Outline

Sources	204
Revisioning the African Diaspora	206
World Religions	208
Healing Communities	208
Concluding . . .	209

Studies of ADR/AIR have been journeys across time, nations, and cultures. But the journeys we've seen so far are not the endpoints for studying these spiritualities. There is much more to discover. However, our views of these horizons are often blocked because old ways of thinking about AIR and ADR remain. For instance, in some models of religious scholarship, all African and Diasporan religions are lumped into an "indigenous" category, are deemed primitive, superstitious, and therefore not considered real religions. When the religions or spiritualities are identified as primitive, they can be viewed through a hierarchical lens and, thus, not evolved. Further, when these African spiritualities are not understood, they are viewed as mere superstitions, taken out of their historical and cultural contexts. Despite these negative views, Africana Studies that focus on African and Diasporan spiritualities are growing. Ways to study African cultures and history are expanding across the Diaspora. The internet can provide greater access to information, such as Isaac Samuel's African History Extra.[1]

At the same time, awareness of and interest in ADR and AIR grow. This conclusion is an invitation to explore some of the other horizons of these traditions. Here are four windows that briefly look into the horizons of these rich spiritual traditions and practices: locating sources; revising the African Diaspora; defining world religions; and healing communities.

Sources

There are multiple ADR traditions that have not been covered in this introductory text. I mention here the rich vein of already developed textual materials that shed light on some of these traditions. Some of those texts have been written by authors who emphasize scholarship, while others take the viewpoint of practitioners of various spiritualities, and some blend the two perspectives.

One tradition not covered in this text is Rastafarianism. Dianne Stewart includes information within the wider context of ADR in Jamaica.[2] Gullah Geechee spirituality and traditions are the focus of Rhonda Manigault-Bryant's text.[3] Tracey Hucks provides an extensive study on Obeah in Trinidad.[4] Yvonne Daniel analyzed dance and ADR in Cuba, Haiti, and Brazil.[5] Luisah Teish is a chief in the Lucumi tradition and has written several celebratory books, which sometimes include rituals.[6]

In some places across the Diaspora as well as on the continent of Africa, there are community organizations that promote and explore African culture and history, including forms of religion. Some of the organizations will have speakers' series and may even record the lectures. One example is a recorded lecture on YouTube that was given at the Caribbean Cultural Center African Diaspora Institute (CCCADI) by Dr. Bunseki Fu-Kiau[7] who was a leading scholar on BaKongo AIR.

Other expressions of African Diaspora spirituality grow, sometimes in creative and surprising ways. As an example, Yirser Ra Hotep is a teacher and promoter of Kemetic Yoga. Taken from the website of Kemetic Yoga Skills, Yirser Ra Hotep is described as "a master instructor of Yoga and the creator of the YogaSkills Method.... Yirser was involved with the original research and documentation of Kemetic Yoga (Ancient Egyptian or African Yoga)."[8] This system was developed in the 1970s amid the ongoing growth of Kemetic studies and under the influence of Pan-Africanism. Kemetic Yoga is described as "a healing and regenerative Yoga system that is characterized by a series of geometrically progressive postures ... Kemetic Yoga emerges from one of the oldest known civilizations which is ancient Egypt . . . [and] is both a philosophy and a practice."[9] While Kemetic Yoga is not a religion, it is informed by Afrikan spirituality. Its continuation since the 1970s demonstrates that AIR and ADR continue to be flexible to meet the moment.

Of course, today the internet and social media provide important routes for gathering information. These sources are invaluable in the retrieval of news articles or historical documents, and they are important ways to flesh out information. Other sites identify as botanicas or marketplaces for hoodoo, voodoo, or Santeria items. There are some social media sites seeking people to become members or practitioners. Whether seeking information, sales, or personal study, there are several cautions about these or other services.

Recognizing that religion itself is a complicated issue in our world, careful selection of sources is necessary. Take the issue of items for sale. Most items claim to offer some material benefit through a spiritual source—seven-day candles to draw money or true love; floor washes to keep bill collectors away; voodoo dolls to use against enemies; or herb pouches to win in court. But the items themselves are often disconnected from a spiritual community, and some of the people producing them are disconnected from a related spiritual tradition.

Religion and spirituality may be monetized, and this is not exclusive to AIR/ADR. A prime example of this marketing focus can be found in many prosperity religions where members may be encouraged to "put this blessed dollar bill in your wallet and it will grow into thousands!" Of course, the blessed dollar bill is for sale. Part of these practices can be traced back to the concept of personal property and capitalism where anything can be bought or sold, including religious beliefs.

AIR and ADR are not exempt from those leaders who are unethical and part of those who give all religions bad names. The ethical problems may range from large-scale financial or sexual scandals to disrespectful treatment of members. Those who are spiritual seekers are vulnerable as trust is placed in a religious leader. Jim Jones and the People's Temple tragedy are extreme examples.[10] Those who have been abused by a religion, its leaders, or the community, while on their sacred search for spiritual growth, can become cynics or embittered, which requires other layers of healing. Those who are spiritual seekers should research the organization and its leadership. However, there is another aspect that must be mentioned.

As has been referenced in several chapters, there are no microwave speeds in getting information on AIR or ADR. Both still depend on gradual degrees of oral transmission. This entails an investment of time with a willingness to learn. The traditional method of learning AIR or ADR necessarily involves communities of believers who impart knowledge. While internet connections can assist the educational process, it is still imperative to have personal involvement with a community of believers.

Revisioning the African Diaspora

As stated in the Introduction, the African Diaspora is a complex term. There, I stressed that African Diasporan religions and spiritualities came from the African continent, but I have only traced a few of the lineages. The array, variety, and geographical locations of ADR open to other horizons.

For instance, Islam broadens our views of ADR. Islam was practiced on the continent of Africa from the eleventh century. Despite restrictions from Muslims capturing other Muslims for the transatlantic trade, some were sold into bondage. Like others who carried their beliefs with them into bondage, so did Muslims. I have mentioned several ways that Islam was integral to the growth of what we know today as ADR: the Amazighs' establishment of the empire Andalusia; the Moorish Science Temple which splintered to become the Nation of Islam; or evidence of Islamic influence in Candomblé. But there is an important point to make here: there is an African Islam, one that is seldom recognized today because of current scholarship and religious politics. That scholarship defines Islam primarily as related to Arabic nations; as a result, African expressions of Islam are ignored or perceived as derivatives of the Arabic. Rudolph T. Ware has defined this problem well: "The field has been constructed as though one cannot be authentically African and authentically Muslim at the same time."[11]

Ware focuses on the traditional West African Qur'an schools where memorization and strict discipline are intended to have students become "walking Qur'ans." "That one could embody the Book is a notion deeply rooted in the Muslim societies of West Africa."[12] Tracing the history before and after transportation, Ware lifts up other African aspects in the education and lives within these Muslim societies. Other scholars also look closely at the African or Diasporan developments of Islam.[13] These have not broken through studies of Islam, but for those who are studying ADR, there is need to consider this horizon.

The distribution of African descendants across the globe is also constitutive of defining "Diaspora," and too often this breadth is ignored. The presence of Africans in Asia is one example. It is speculated that, millennia ago, the tectonic plate known as Gondwana shifted a large land mass to make the separate continents of Africa and Asia; the argument follows that there would have been biological and racial connections among the inhabitants.[14] But the two continents are not that far apart. Tracing these connections, Michael Thornton found: "Ethiopia and Yemen are separated by less than one hundred miles—it is not surprising that there has been an African presence in western Asia for many thousands of years."[15] He continued: "The descendants of Africans are still to be found in many parts of India, though they are primarily concentrated in three areas. They are linked to their African heritage by language and physical appearance."[16]

In addition to geographical links, the history of African trade routes and human trafficking included Asia. The Moors or Amazigh were already trading partners with India, thereby becoming the link where Indian goods could be transported to Spain. The desire to reach Indian trade routes after the Moors were expelled without crossing African territory was one motivation to fund Columbus, trying to get to the East by going West. The human trafficking routes from the African continent (see Figure 1.2) were not only to the Caribbean and the Americas; the trafficking routes to Asia may add to an African Diasporan presence and forms of ADR. Whether through geography or captivity, there are African descendants in India. Certainly, some forms of ADR will surface.

For example, "Muslim Sidis, Indians of African ancestry living in the state of Gujarat and the city of Mumbai in western India," Jazmin Graves Eyssallenne wrote, have a Sidi Sufi tradition. This tradition "centers on the veneration of three African Rifai Sufi saints of fourteenth-century Gujarat . . . the veneration of these saints involves the performance of devotional songs . . . preserved over generations."[17] Such evidence of wider horizons of ADR indicates that more study is needed.

World Religions

Even without these wider horizons, ADR/AIR should be considered a world religion; this is not a novel idea.[18] As has been discussed throughout this book, there are multiple forms of AIR/ADR, which is true of any religious tradition. As Wándé Abímbọ́lá stated, AIR/ADR have "significant features . . . which are perhaps different from some of the other well known 'world' religions, especially Judaism, Christianity, Islam, Buddhism, and Hinduism."[19] Yet, there is no single form of Christianity, Buddhism, Judaism, or any other religion that exists. Each one has shifted over time and place; after all, cultures shape religions. Additionally, theological splits and arguments among any one world religion create tensions and splinters. For instance, there are Protestant denominations that claim Roman Catholicism is not really Christianity; yet, that disagreement would not be basis for claiming Christianity is not a world religion. So why are ADR/AIR generally not identified as a world religion?

We cannot avoid recognizing the global nature of AIR/ADR, and it is time that we think of them in this manner. Martin Tsang emphasized the changes in contemporary meanings of "global": "The forces of global trade and information exchange have caused a de-emphasis of the African diaspora as being comprised of neat, geographically bounded units of culture to be studied in isolation."[20] Each of these points underlines the reality: AIR/ADR is a world religion.

Healing Communities

AIR/ADR can become locations for healing as Malidoma Somé, Adefunmi, and others indicated in their journeys through Afrikan spiritualities. Healing is a core constituent of the spirituality. The aim of healing, in these traditions, is for the whole person.

In addition to personal growth, Afrikan spiritualities can become bridges among African and Diasporan people, possibly healing old separations, as the following example shows.

Despite the lingering issues of negative identification of Vodou/Voodoo/Vodun, Benin recognized Vodun as an official religion in 1996. That year, the Vodun Festival was established. The festival annually takes place on January 10 in Ouidah and other locations around the country. Ouidah is a coastal town, one that was a Door of No Return for transporting some of the captured Africans. With the festival, Benin welcomes Vodou/Voodoo/Vodun practitioners from around the globe, as well as those from across the Diaspora. Several people who attended in 2023 identified their own motivations for coming to the festival, from honoring the earth to rediscovering the spirituality practiced by their grandparents. "'Our ancestors foresaw this return of Afro-descendants. They are eagerly awaited by the ghosts of our ancestors,' said Hounnongan Viyeye Noumaze Gbetoton, one of the Vodoun dignitaries in Ouidah. 'When they return, it is to take blessings and recharge their batteries to move forward. . . . Our major objective is that the indigenous culture never fades away . . . Sooner or later, all Afro-descendants will return to the fold. This is what our ancestors say.'"[21]

Understanding the complexities of AIR/ADR has the added benefit of healing views of history. African and Diasporan history is part of world history, which is incomplete without it.

Concluding . . .

This text has considered history and sociopolitical realities, crossing the globe. There has been a focus on the Afrikan continent and some of the indigenous traditions—BaKongo, Ifá, and Vodun. Some ADR have been explored, including the Moorish Science Temple and the Pan-African Orthodox Christian Church. We have considered aspects of Vodoun, Candomblé, Hoodoo, Voodoo, and Lucumí.

What happens from here? I pointed in a few directions to turn our sights to other horizons. These four areas for further exploration of ADR were finding sources, extending Diaspora, naming world religions, and healing community. Yet, these are not exclusive of other directions.

The bottom line: the journey has not ended. More stories are yet to be told.

Notes

1. Isaac Samuel, *Africa History Extra*, https://www.africanhistoryextra.com/.
2. See Dianne M. Stewart, *Three Eyes for the Journey: African Dimensions of the Jamaican Religious Experience* (New York: Oxford University Press, 2004), covers more than Rastafarianism and situates it within Jamaican ADR.
3. LeRhonda S. Manigault-Bryant, *Talking to the Dead: Religion, Music, and Lived Memory among Gullah/Geechee Women* (Durham: Duke University Press 2014).
4. Tracey M. Hucks, *Obeah, Orisa, and Religious Identity in Trinidad* (Durham: Colgate University Press, 2022).
5. Yvonne Daniel, *Dancing Wisdom: Embodied Knowledge in Haitian Vodou, Cuban Yoruba, and Bahian Candomblé* (Urbana: University of Illinois Press, 2005).
6. For example, Luisah Teish, *Carnival of the Spirit, Seasonal Celebrations and Rites of Passage* (New York: Harper San Francisco, 1994).
7. Kimbwandende Kia Bunseki Fu-Kiau, "The Ancestors and Our Connection to Them," Caribbean Cultural Center African Diaspora Institute (New York: n.d), https://www.youtube.com/watch?v=ncJTH6tJdiY, accessed March 2025.
8. Yirser Ra Hotep, https://kemeticyogaskills.com, accessed March 2025.
9. "What is Kemetic Yoga?" https://kemeticyogaskills.com/what-is-kemetic-yoga/, accessed March 2025.
10. For example, see David Chidester, *Salvation and Suicide: Jim Jones, the Peoples Temple, and Jonestown*. Rev. ed. (Bloomington, IN: Indiana University Press, 2003).
11. Rudolph T. Ware and Rudolph T. Ware III, *The Walking Qur'an: Islamic Education, Embodied Knowledge, and History in West Africa* (Chapel Hill: University of North Carolina Press, 2014), 5.
12. Ibid., 9.
13. For example, Sherman A. Jackson, *Islam and the Problem of Black Suffering* (New York: Oxford University Press, 2014); Michael Muhammad Knight, *Metaphysical Africa: Truth and Blackness in the Ansaru Allah Community* (Penn State University Press, 2022); Su'ad Abdul Khabeer, *Muslim Cool: Race, Religion, and Hip Hop in the United States* (New York: New York University Press, 2016, reprint).
14. Cf. W. S. McKerrow, C. R. Scotese, and M. D. Brasier, "Early Cambrian Continental reconstructions," *Journal of the Geological Society* 149,

no. 4 (1992): 599–606 or Ana D. Gibbons, Joanne M. Whittaker, and R. Dietmar Mueller, "The Breakup of East Gondwana: Assimilating Constraints from Cretaceous Ocean Basins around India into a Best-Fit Tectonic Mode," *Journal of Geophysical Research* 118, no. 3 (2013): 808–22.

15 Michael C. Thornton, "African Diaspora Passages from the Middle East to East Asia," in *Routes of Passage: Rethinking the African Diaspora*, volume 1, ed. Ruth Simms Hamilton (East Lansing: Michigan State University Press, 2007), 125.

16 Ibid., 139.

17 Jazmin Graves Eyssallenne, "Voices from the African Diaspora in India: Lyric Poetry in the Sidi Sufi Devotional Tradition," in *Comparative Studies of South Asia, Africa and the Middle East* 44, no. 3 (Duke University Press, December 2024), 508.

18 See for example, Jacob K. Olupona and Terry Rey, editors, *Òrìṣà Devotion as World Religion: The Globalization of Yorùbá Culture* (Madison: University of Wisconsin Press, 2008).

19 Abímbọ́lá, *Ifá Will Mend Our Broken World*, 1.

20 Tsang, *Spirited Diasporas*, 6.

21 "Benin's Famed Voodoo Festival Draws Afro-Descendants," *Africa News*, 2023, https://www.africanews.com/2023/01/11/benins-famed-voodoo-festival-draws-afro-descendents//, accessed January 2025.

Bibliography

Abímbọ́lá, Wándé. *Ifá Will Mend Our Broken World*. Aim Books, 1997.
Afolabi, Niyi. *Relocating the Sacred: African Divinities and Brazilian Cultural Hybridities*. State University of New York Press, 2022.
Akalimat, Abdul. *The History of Black Studies*. Pluto Press, 2022.
Alexander VI, Pope. "Demarcation Bull." May 4, 1493. The Gilder Lehrman Collection, GLC04093. https://www.gilderlehrman.org/sites/default/files/inline-pdfs/04093_FPS.pdf.
Araujo, Ana Lucia. "The Mythology of Racial Democracy in Brazil." *Open Democracy*, June 22, 2015. https://www.opendemocracy.net/en/beyond-trafficking-and-slavery/mythology-of-racial-democracy-in-brazil/.
Arizona State University. "Celebrate 2024, A Year for Human Origins." Institute of Human Origins. https://iho.asu.edu/Lucy50.
Ashby, Muata. *The 42 Precepts of Maat and Their Foundation in the Philosophy of Righteous Action of the Wisdom Text Sages of Ancient Egypt Study Guide*. Sema Institute of Yoga, 1998.
Ausar Auset Society. *Website of the Ausar Auset Society Atlanta, GA Branch*. https://ausarausetatl.com/ra-un-nefer-amen-i.
Badejo, Deidre. *Ọṣun Ṣèègèsí, The Elegant Deity of Wealth, Power, and Femininity*. Africa World Press, 1996.
Baraka, Amiri. *Blues People: Negro Music in White America*. William Morrow and Company, 1963.
Bassey, Nnimmo. *To Cook a Continent: Destructive Extraction and Climate Crisis in Africa*. Kraft Books Limited, 2013.
Benson, LaGrace. "Meeting Grounds in Saint-Domingue and the Emergence of Haitian Vodou, An Ecological Approach." In *Indigenous and African Diaspora Religions in the Americas*, edited by Benjamin Hebblethwaite and Silke Jansen, 61–82. University of Nebraska Press, 2023.
Bernal, Martin G. *Black Athena: The Afroasiatic Roots of Classical Civilization*. Vols. 1–3. Rutgers University Press, 1987.
Boaz, Danielle. *Voodoo: History of a Racial Slur*. Oxford University Press, 2023.
Brown, Karen McCarthy. "Systematic Remembering, Systematic Forgetting: Ogou in Haiti." In *African American Religion*, edited by Timothy E. Fulop and Albert J. Raboteau, 434–61. Routledge, 1997.

Budge, E. A. Wallis. *The Book of the Dead*. From a 1920 edition. The Floating Press, 2008.

Burkett, Randall K. "Religious Ethos of the Universal Negro Improvement Association." In *African American Religious Studies: An Interdisciplinary Reader*, edited by Gayraud S. Wilmore, 60–81. Duke University Press, 1989; 2nd printing, 1992.

Buxton, Thomas Fowell. *African Slave Trade*. London: John Murray, Albemarle Street; reprinted American Anti-Slavery Society, 1840.

Cannon, Katie Geneva. "Christian Imperialism and Transatlantic Slave Trade." *Journal of Feminist Studies in Religion* 24, no. 1 (2008), 127–34.

Césaire, Aimé. *Discourse on Colonialism*. Monthly Review Press, 1972, 2000.

Charles, Mark, and Soong-Chan Rah. *Unsettling Truths: The Ongoing, Dehumanizing Legacy of the Doctrine of Discovery*. InterVarsity Press, 2019.

Cleage, Albert B. *Black Christian Nationalism: New Directions for the Black Church*. Luxor Publishers of the Pan-African Orthodox Christian Church, 1987; originally 1972.

Collins, Lisa Gail. "Historic Retrievals." In *Venus 2010, They Called Her Hottentot*, edited by Deborah Willis. Temple University Press, 2010.

Cone, James H. *God of the Oppressed*. Seabury Press, 1975.

Conermann, S., P. M. Dias, P. R. Hofmeister, and T. P. Cruz, eds. *Current Trends in Slavery Studies in Brazil*. Walter de Gruyter, 2023.

Costen, Melva W. "Singing Praise to God in African American Worship Contexts." In *African American Religious Studies*, edited by Gayraud S. Wilmore, 392–404. Duke University Press, 1992; 2nd printing 1989.

Curtis IV, Edward E. "Debating the Origins of the Moorish Science Temple." In *The New Black Gods: Arthur Huff Fauset and the Study of African American Religions*, edited by Edward E. Curtis and Danielle Brune Sigler. Indiana University Press, 2009.

De La Torre, Miguel. *Reading José Martí from the Margins*. Rowman and Littlefield, 2024.

DeGruy, Joy. *Post Traumatic Slave Syndrome: America's Legacy of Enduring Injury and Healing*. Joy DeGruy Publishing, Inc., 2017; 2nd ed., 2005.

Denfulani, Umar Habila Dadem. "Pa Divination: Ritual Performance and Symbolism among the Ngas, Mupun, and the Mwaghavul of the Jos Plateau, Nigeria." In *African Spirituality*, edited by Jacob K. Olupona. Crossroad Publishing Company, 2000.

di Leonardo, Micaela. *Exotics at Home: Anthropologies, Others, American Modernity*. University of Chicago Press, 1998.

Diop, Cheikh Anta. *The African Origin of Civilization: Myth or Reality*. Lawrence Hill Books, 1974.

Diouf, Sylviane A. *Servants of Allah: African Muslims Enslaved in the Americas*. Fifteenth Anniversary ed. New York University Press, 1998; 2013.

Douglas, Kelly Brown. *Stand Your Ground: Black Bodies and the Justice of God*. Maryknoll, NY: Orbis Books, 2015.

Douglas, Kelly Brown. *What's Faith Got to Do with It? Black Bodies/Christian Souls*. Orbis Books, 2005.

Du Bois, W. E. B. *The Souls of Black Folk*. Bantam Books, 1989; originally 1903.

Dunham, Katherine. *Island Possessed*. University of Chicago Press, 1994; originally 1969.

Edozie, Rita Kiki, with Glenn A. Chambers and Tama Hamilton-Wray. "Diasporas of the Blackworld: Re-sculpting Themes, Expanding Scopes, and Recreating Disciplinary Representations." In *New Frontiers in the Study of the Global African Diaspora: Between Uncharted Themes and Alternative Representations*, edited by Rita Kiki Edozie et al. Michigan State University Press, 2018.

Eluwa, G. I. C., M. O. Ukagwu, J. U. N. Nwachukwu, and A. C. N. Nwaubani. *A History of Nigeria for Schools and Colleges*. Onitsha: Africana First Publishers, PLC, 1988. Reprint, 2016.

Ephirim-Donkor, Anthony. *African Spirituality: On Becoming Ancestors*. Africa World Press, Inc., 1997.

Fanon, Frantz. *The Wretched of the Earth*. Grove Press, 1963.

Ferrer, Ada. *Freedom's Mirror: Cuba and Haiti in the Age of Revolution*. Cambridge University Press, 2014.

Finch, Aisha K. *Rethinking Slave Rebellion in Cuba: La Escalera and the Insurgencies of 1841–1844*. University of North Carolina Press, 2015.

Fleurant, Gerdès. "The Music of Haitian Vodun." In *African Spirituality*, edited by Jacob K. Olupona. The Crossroad Publishing Company, 2000.

Flores-Peña, Ysamur M. "Mofá and the Oba: Translation of Ifá Epistemology in the Afro-Cuban Dilogun." In *Ifá Divination, Knowledge, Power, and Performance*, edited by Jacob K. Olupona and Rowland O. Abiodun, 212–22. Bloomington: Indiana University Press, 2016.

Ford, Clyde W. *The Hero with an African Face: Mythic Wisdom of Traditional Africa*. Bantam Books, 1999.

Fu-Kiau, Kimbwandende Kia Bunseki. *African Cosmology of the Bantu-Kongo: Principles of Life and Living*. Clifton, NJ: African Tree Press, 2001 reprint.

Fu-Kiau, Kimbwandende Kia Bunseki. *n'Kongo ye Nza Yakun'zungidila*, 1969. Cited in John M. Jantzen and Wyatt MacGaffey, *An Anthology of*

Kongo Religion: Primary Texts from Lower Zaire. Lawrence: University of Kansas, 1974.

Gerbner, Katherine. "Rebellion and Religion: Slavery and Empire in Early America." In *Religion and U.S. Empire: Critical New Histories*, edited by Tina Wegner and Sylvester A. Johnson. New York University Press, 2022.

Goldstein, Bernard R. "Astronomy as a 'Neutral Zone': Interreligious Cooperation in Medieval Spain." In *Al-Andalus, Sepharad and Medieval Iberia: Cultural Contact and Diffusion*, edited by Ivy Corfis. Leiden: Brill, 2010.

Gomez, Michael A. *African Dominion: A New History of Empire in Early and Medieval West Africa*. Princeton: Princeton University Press, 2018.

Gomez, Michael A. *Reversing Sail: A History of the African Diaspora*. 2nd ed. Cambridge: Cambridge University Press, 2020.

Hall, Gwendolyn Midlo. *Slavery and African Ethnicities in the Americas: Restoring the Links*. University of North Carolina Press, 2000.

Harding, Rachel E. *A Refuge in Thunder: Candomblé and Alternative Spaces of Blackness*. Indiana University Press, 2000.

Hazzard-Donald, Katherine. *Mojo Workin': The Old American Hoodoo System*. University of Illinois Press, 2012.

Henley, John. "Haiti: A Long Descent to Hell." *The Guardian*, January 14, 2010. https://www.theguardian.com/world/2010/jan/14/haiti-history-earthquake-disaster. Accessed January 2025.

The Holy Koran of the Moorish Science Temple of America. Divinely Prepared by the Noble Prophet Drew Ali.

hooks, bell. *Killing Rage: Ending Racism*. Henry Holt and Company, 1995.

Hucks, Tracey E. "Habitations of the Sacred." *Harvard Divinity Bulletin* 41, nos. 3–4 (Summer/Autumn 2013): 43–7.

Hucks, Tracey E. *Yoruba Traditions and African American Religious Nationalism*. Albuquerque: University of New Mexico Press, 2012.

Hughes, Langston, and Milton Meltzer. *Black Magic: A Pictorial History of the African American in the Performing Arts*. Da Capo Press, 1990; reprint, 1967.

Hurbon, Laënnec. *Voodoo: Search for the Spirit*. Translated by Lory Frankel. Harry N. Abrams Inc., 1995.

Hurston, Zora Neale. *The Sanctified Church*. Turtle Island, 1981.

Ickes, Scott, and Bernd Reiter, eds. *The Making of Brazil's Black Mecca: Bahia Reconsidered*. Michigan State University Press, 2018.

Idowu, E. Bolaji. *African Traditional Religion: A Definition*. Orbis Books, 1973.

Jacobsen, Douglas, and Rhonda Hustedt Jacobsen. *No Longer Invisible: Religion in University Education*. Oxford University Press, 2012.

Jantzen, John M., and Wyatt MacGaffey. *An Anthology of Kongo Religion: Primary Texts from Lower Zaire*. University of Kansas, 1974.

Jarmon, Laura C. *Wishbone: Reference and Interpretation in Black Folk Narrative*. University of Tennessee Press, 2003.

Johnson, Sylvester A. *African American Religions, 1500–2000: Colonialism, Democracy, and Freedom*. Cambridge University Press, 2015.

Johnson, Sylvester A. "The Rise of Black Ethnics: The Ethnic Turn in African American Religions, 1916–1945." *Religion and American Culture: A Journal of Interpretation* 20, no. 2 (2010): 125–63.

Johnson, Walter. *Soul by Soul: Life Inside the Antebellum Slave Market*. Harvard University Press, 1999.

Jones, Alice Eley. "Sacred Places and Holy Ground: West African Spiritualism at Stagville Plantation." In *Keep Your Head to the Sky: Interpreting African American Home Ground*, edited by Grey Gundaker, 93–108. University Press of Virginia, 1998.

Jones, Arthur C. *Wade in the Water: The Wisdom of the Spirituals*. Orbis Books, 1993.

Kôkô, Koffi. "What Is Vodun?" *Performance Research* 25, nos. 6–7 (2020): 163. https://doi.org/10.1080/13528165.2020.1909956.

Lane-Poole, Stanley. *The Story of the Moors in Spain*. Black Classic Press, 1990 edition; originally published 1886.

Lanoue, Curtis. *Handbook for the Aborisha: A Beginner's Guide to the Lucumi Tradition*. Curtis Lanoue, s.p., 2019.

Ligiéro, Zeca. *Initiation into Candomblé: Introduction to African-Brazilian Religion*. Translated by Emma Symes. Diasporic Africa Press, 2014.

Lincoln, C. Eric. "The Muslim Mission in the Context of American Social History." In *African American Religious Studies: An Interdisciplinary Anthology*, edited by Gayraud S. Wilmore, 340–56. Duke University Press, 1989.

Lovejoy, Paul E. "The African Diaspora: Revisionist Interpretations of Ethnicity, Culture and Religion under Slavery." *Studies in the World History of Slavery, Abolition, and Emancipation* 2, no. 1 (1997). http://www.h-net.msu.edu/~slavery/essays/esy97011ove.html. Cited in *New Frontiers in the Study of the Global African Diaspora*, edited by Rita Kiki Edozie et al., 9.

Lovejoy, Henry B. *Prieto: Yorùbá Kingship in Colonial Cuba During the Age of Revolutions*. University of North Carolina Press, 2019.

Marques, Lucas. "Learning to Learn in Candomblé: Notes on Paths, Knowledge, and the 'Education of Distraction.'" *Religion* 52, no. 1 (2022). https://doi.org/10.1080/0048721X.20211087.

Mason, John. *Òrìṣà: New World Black Gods*. Yorùbá Theological Archministry, 2016.

Medsger, Betty. "Just Being Black Was Enough to Get Yourself Spied on by J. Edgar Hoover's FBI." *The Nation*, January 22, 2014. https://www.thenation.com/article/archive/just-being-black-was-enough-get-yourself-spied-j-edgar-hoovers-fbi/.

Mets, Thaddeus, and Motsamai Molefe. "Traditional African Religion as a Neglected Form of Monotheism." *The Monist* 104, no. 3 (2021). https://academic.oup.com/monist/article/104/3/393/6305009.

Miller, Ivor. "Aponte's Legacy in Cuban Popular Culture." *Afro-Hispanic Review* 37, no. 2 (Fall 2018), 126–51.

Mitchem, Stephanie Y. *African American Folk Healing*. New York University Press, 2007.

Montgomery, Eric James. "Vodún/Vodu, Resistance, and North/South Relations in Undemocratic Togo." *Journal of Religion in Africa* 50, nos. 3–4 (2020), 224–48.

Moorish Science Temple of America. *Federal Bureau of Investigation BU File 62-25889*. September 12, 1931. https://vault.fbi.gov/Moorish%20Science%20Temple%20of%20America/Moorish%20Science%20Temple%20of%20America%20Part%201%20of%2031/view#bypass-fullscreen.

Morgan, Edmund S. "Columbus' Confusion about the New World." *Smithsonian Magazine*, October 2009. https://www.smithsonianmag.com/travel/columbus-confusion-about-the-new-world-140132422/.

Ngangura, Tarisai. "Intimate Portraits of Boa Morte, Where the 'Sisterhood of the Good Death' Honors Afro-Brazilian Ancestors." *Vice News*, September 6, 2018. https://www.vice.com/en/article/boa-morte-festival-sisterhood-images/.

Nkrumah, Kwame. *Africa Must Unite*. Frederick A. Praeger Publisher, 1963.

Nwokocha, Eziaku Atuama. *Vodou en Vogue: Fashioning Black Divinities in Haiti and the United States*. University of North Carolina Press, 2023.

Ogunnaike, Ayodeji. "What's Really Behind the Mask: A Reexamination of Syncretism in Brazilian Candomblé." *Journal of Africana Religions* 8, no. 1 (2020), 146–171.

Okemuyiwa, Ṣọlágbadé Pópóọlá Fákúnlé Oyèsànyà Gbolahan. *Ifa: Its Core Values, Vol. 1: What Is Ifa?* Phoenix: Ifaworks, LLC, 2016.

Oyèwùmí, Oyèrónkẹ́. *The Invention of Women: Making an African Sense of Western Gender Discourses*. University of Minnesota Press, 1997.

P'Bitek, Okot. *Decolonizing African Religions: A Short History of African Religions in Western Scholarship*. Diasporic Africa Press, 2011 reprint; originally 1971.

Peek, Philip M. "The Silent Voices of African Divination." *Harvard Divinity Bulletin* 41, nos. 3–4 (Summer/Autumn 2013), 34–42.

Perez, Elizabeth. "The Virgin in the Mirror: Reading Images of a Black Madonna Through the Lens of Afro-Cuban Women's Experiences." *The Journal of African American History* 95, no. 2 (Spring 2010): 202–28.

Pew Research Center. "A Brief Overview of Black Religious History in the U.S." February 16, 2021. https://www.pewresearch.org/religion/2021/02/16/a-brief-overview-of-black-religious-history-in-the-u-s/.

Pew Research Center. "Black Americans' Experiences with News." September 26, 2023. https://www.pewresearch.org/journalism/2023/09/26/black-americans-experiences-with-news/.

Pinho, Patricia de Santana. *Mapping Diaspora: African American Roots Tourism*. University of North Carolina Press, 2018.

Porcher, José Eduardo. "The Mythic Narratives of Candomblé Nagô and What They Imply About Its Supreme Being." *Religious Studies* (Cambridge University Press, 2024). https://doi.org/10.1017/S0034412523001129.

Reagon, Bernice Johnson. *We Who Believe in Freedom*. Anchor Books, 1993.

Reid-Vasquez, Michelle. "Tensions of Race, Gender and Midwifery in Colonial Cuba." In *Africans to Spanish America: Expanding the Diaspora*, edited by Sherwin K. Bryant, Rachel Sarah O'Toole, and Ben Vinson III. University of Illinois Press, 2012.

Report of the Working Group of Experts on People of African Descent on its Mission to the United States of America. United Nations Working Group of Experts on People of African Descent. Geneva: United Nations, 2016. https://digitallibrary.un.org/record/848570?ln=en&v=pdf.

Retamero, Fèlix, and Josep Torró. "One Conquest, Two Worlds: An Introduction." In *From Al-Andalus to the Americas (13th–17th Centuries): Destruction and Construction of Societies*, edited by Thomas F. Glick, Antonio Malpica, Fèlix Retamero, and Josep Torró. Leiden: Brill, 2018.

Riddell, William Renwick. "Le Code Noir." *The Journal of Negro History* 10, no. 3 (July 1925), 321–29.

Safran, Janina M. *Defining Boundaries in Al-Andalus: Muslims, Christians, and Jews in Islamic Iberia*. Cornell University Press, 2013.

Somé, Malidoma Patrice. *Of Water and the Spirit: Ritual, Magic, and Initiation in the Life of an African Shaman*. G. P. Putnam's Sons, 1994.

Stringfellow, Thornton. "A Scriptural View of Slavery." In *Slavery Defended: The Views of the Old South*, edited by Eric L. McKitrick. Englewood Cliffs: Prentice-Hall, Inc., 1963.

Stuckey, Sterling. *Slave Culture: Nationalist Theory and the Foundations of Black America*. Oxford University Press, 1987.

Tann, Mambo Chita. *Haitian Vodou: An Introduction to Haiti's Indigenous Spiritual Tradition*. Llewellyn Publications, 2012; ninth printing 2021.

Thompson, Robert Farris. *Flash of the Spirit: African and Afro-American Art and Philosophy*. Vintage Books, 1984.

Touati, Samia. "Lalla Fatma N'Soumer (1830–1863): Spirituality, Resistance and Womanly Leadership in Colonial Algeria." *Societies* 8, no. 4 (2018): 126. https://doi.org/10.3390/soc8040126.

Voeks, Robert A. *Sacred Leaves of Candomblé: African Magic, Medicine, and Religion in Brazil*. University of Texas Press, 1997.

Walker, Cardinal Aswad. "Princes Shall Come Out of Egypt: A Theological Comparison of Marcus Garvey and Rev. Albert B. Cleage Jr." *Journal of Black Studies* 39, no. 2 (2008), 194–251.

Walker, David. *Appeal in Four Articles to the Coloured Citizens of the World*. Introduction by Sean Wilentz. Hill and Wang, 1965; 1995.

Watkins, William H. "Pan Africanism and the Politics of Education: Towards a New Understanding." In *Imagining Home: Class, Culture, and Nationalism in the African Diaspora*, edited by Sidney Lemelle and Robin D. G. Kelley, 222–42. London: Verso, 1994.

Weber, A. S. "Haitian Vodou and Ecotheology." *The Ecumenical Review* 70, no. 4 (December 2018), 679–94.

Wicker, Kathleen O'Brien. "Mami Water in African Religion and Spirituality." In *African Spirituality: Forms, Meanings, and Expressions*, edited by Jacob K. Olupona. Crossroad Publishing Company, 2000.

Wilmore, Gayraud. *Black Religion and Black Radicalism: An Interpretation of the Religious History of Afro-American People*. 2nd ed. Maryknoll, NY: Orbis Books, 1983.

Wiredu, Kwasi. "Reflections on Cultural Diversity." *Diogenes* 52, no. 1 (2005), 117–28.

Wood, Funlayo E. "A Brief History of Diasporic Religions in the United States." In *Ẹlẹ́rìí Ìpín Brochure*, Annual World Ifá Festival. International Council for Ifá Religion, June 2015.

Woodson, Carter G. *The Mis-education of the Negro*. Africa World Press, 1988; tenth printing.

Zachernuk, Philip Serge. "Contemporary Africans Meet Timeless Africa: The Conflicted Impact of Asadata Dafora's 'African Operas' on Pan-African Work in the United States, 1930–1950." *Journal of West African History* 8, no. 1 (Spring 2022), 53–86.

Zahan, Dominique. "Some Reflections on African Spirituality." In *African Spirituality*, edited by Jacob K. Olupona. The Crossroad Publishing Company, 2000.

Index

Abímbọ́lá, Wándé 90
Adefunmi, Nana Oseijeman I/Walter King 189–90
Adinkra symbols 192
African and Diasporan religions and spiritualities
   African 56, 60
   general charactcristics 2–3, 53–4
   metaphysical 9, 54, 82, 109, 111
   spiritual science 87, 92
African Diaspora
   defined 11–12
   revisioning 206–7
African Orthodox Church 64, 67
Afrika/Africa
   Amazigh/Berbers/Moors 25
   Kanuri/Kanem-Bornu Empire 23–4
   Mali, Mansa Musa 24
   spelling 22
Afrofuturism 74, 179
Agyeman, Jaramogi Abebe/Albert Cleage 67–9
Ajayi, *see* Crowther, Samuel
Al-Andalus 25–8
Ali, Noble Drew 61–2
Alkalimit, Abdul 195
Amen, Ra Un Nefer 91, 94
ancestors 85–6
Ani, Marimba 101
Ashby, Muata 92, 94
Ausar Auset 91–5
   Laws of Ma'at 92
   NTR, NTRU, NU 94

BaKongo 100–5
   circle 103, 105
   Dikenga Yowa cross 104
   Kalûnga 104
   Mûntu 104
   Nzambi Mpungu 102
Baraka, Amiri 183
Black Christian Nationalism, *see* Pan African Orthodox Christian Church
Black codes 191
Black Madonna, Shrine of 67–8
Black Studies 195–6
Black theology 67, 192
Boaz, Danielle 109–10
Brown, Karen McCarthy 148–9
Budge, E. A. Wallis 69
Buxton, Thomas Fowell 40

Candomblé 121–38
   Axé 128–9
   Bahia 127–8
   Irmandade da Nossa Senhora da Boa Morte 136–8
   libertos 126
   meaning of 124
   Olorum 129
   origin stories 125–6
   Orixás 129–30
   possession 130
   syncretism 124, 130–1
   terreiro 125
Capoeira 127–8, 184

Christianity
    African Americans 56, 67, 191-3
    African churches 41-2
    African Methodist Episcopal Church, African Methodist Episcopal Zion Church 191
    component of colonization 39, 42, 57
    converting enslaved 45
    images of 56-7
    mission work, Africa 40-2
    Protestant Reformation 9-10, 33
    Roman Catholic 9, 31-2
Cleage, Albert, see Agyeman, Jaramogi Abebe
colonization
    Age of Colonization 34
    Columbus, Christopher 28-30
    impacts of 36
    Inquisition 27, 32-3
    Partitioning of Africa, Berlin Conference 38, 41-2
    patterns of 34, 36-8, 44-6
    postcolonial control 39
    private ownership 30
    Treaties 34
Community 83
Cone, James H. 192
Conjure, see Hoodoo
Cosmology 82
Crowther, Samuel/Ajayi 40-1
Cullen, Countee 59

Dance 45, 105, 182, 184-5, 187-9
Dash, Julie 86
De Gruy, Joy 84
De La Torre, Miguel 166
Destiny 131-2
Diop, Cheikh Anta 72, 74
divination 87-8
divinity 2, 53, 84-5, 168
Doctrine of Discovery 9, 33-5
Drew, Timothy, see Noble Drew Ali

drumming 42, 102, 126, 135, 152, 170, 183, 191
Du Bois, W. E. B. 58
Dunham, Katherine 188-9

Egyptian Book of the Dead 69-70

Finch, Aisha 164-5
folk, folkways 11, 14, 88, 179-82
Fu-Kiau, Kia Bunseki 101, 104

Garvey, Marcus Mosiah 65-6
Gilkes, Cheryl Townsend 114
Gomez, Michael A. 23, 179

Harlem Renaissance 58-9
Hazzard-Donald, Katherine 185
healing 14, 88, 90, 102, 105, 109, 113, 129, 165, 171, 181-2, 208-9
Higginbotham, Evelyn Brooks 14
High john de conquer 57-8
Historically Black Colleges and Universities (HBCUs) 195
Holy Koran of the Moorish Science Temple, Circle 7 Koran 61-2
Hoodoo 16, 181, 185-6
    conjure doctors 181, 186
    as religion 185
Horton, Asadata Dafora 187
Hotep, Yirser Ra 204-5
Hucks, Tracey E. 87-8, 189-90
Hughes, Langston 184
Hurston, Zora Neale 57, 88
hybridization 11, 63, 89, 100, 113, 195

Idowu, E. Bolaji 83-4, 89
Ifá 106-9
    Àṣẹ 108
    destiny 108
    good character 109
    Olódùmarè 106
    Òrìṣà 107
    Yorùbá 106

initiation   43, 101–2, 116, 130, 132
Islam   60
   in ADR   61–3, 126, 147, 206–7
   in history of Africa   23–4

Jarmon, Laura   88

Karenga, Maulana   194
Kemet   69
   42 Laws of Ma'at   70
   Kemetic principles   81, 92–5
   Kemetic yoga   204–5
Kôkô, Koffi   111–12
Kwanzaa   194

Ligiéro, Zeca   125
Lucumí   143, 157–70
   amulets   165, 186
   Cabildos de nación   160–1
   Chango Tedun   160, 163, 167
   Church of the Lukumi Aye   179
   la regla de Ocha   166
   obá oriaté   169
   Santería   166
   Spiritism   166–7
Lucy   23

Maat, Sekhmet Ra Em Kht (Cher Love McAllister)   94
Marti, Jose   165–6
Mason, John   163, 170, 194–5
McGuire, George Alexander   66–7
Miller, Ivor   166–7
Mills, Charles W.   47
Moorish Science Temple   60–4
   FBI surveillance   64
   members   63–4
   Pan African   63
music   46, 127, 134, 170, 182–4, 187–8

National Committee of Black Churchmen   192

National Museum of African American History and Culture (NMAAHC)   198
Nguzo Saba   194
Nkrumah, Kwame   38–9
Nwokocha, Eziaku Atuama   116, 155–7

orality   115–16
Oyèwùmí, Oyèrónkẹ́   114–15
Oyotunji African Village   189–90

Palo   164–5
Pan African Orthodox Christian Church/Black Christian Nationalism   67
Pan Africanism, defined   58–9
P'Bitek, Okot   81

Race
   defined   13
   history   13–14, 65, 127, 162, 165
   negative uses of   5–6, 13–14, 47–8, 56, 84, 89–90
racial democracy, defined   133
Reagon, Bernice Johnson   183
Rebellions   37, 46
   Aponte rebellion   160–3
   La Escalera rebellion   164
   Maroons   46, 145, 153–4
   Queen Nanny of Jamaica   46
   Quilombos   46
   S'oumer, Lalla Fatma   37
   Stono Rebellion   47
   Zumbi   46
religion, general
   as cultural   8, 14, 28
   limits of   9–10
Reynolds, Sarah M.   111
ring shout   45
Ritual   105, 113

sacrifice   113–14
Samuel, Isaac   24

Somé, Malidoma Patrice 42–3
Spirit Attenuation Well 43–4, 46, 113
spirituals 183
Stuckey, Sterling 105

Tann, Mambo Chita 148–9, 186
Thompson, Robert Farris 104, 109
travel, ADR 196–7

United Negro Improvement
 Association (UNIA) 65

Vodou, Haiti 147–52
 Ayiti 152–5
 Code Noir 145
 Guinea/ *Ginen* 147
 Lwa 147–8
 Petro, Rada 148–50
 Saint-Dominigue 144–6
 spiritual vogue 155–6

Vodún, Benin 109–12
 Dahomey 110
 Fa 112
 Mawu Lisa 111–12
 Prince Agasu 110
 Vodún Festival 209
Voodoo, New Orleans
 Black cultural life 185
 Louisiana 186–7
 negative perceptions of 6

Walker, David 10
Wilmore, Gayraud S. 63
Wiredu, Kwasi 82, 85
women and gender in AIR and
 ADR 114–15
Wood, Funlayo O. 181
Woodson, Carter G. 7–8, 56

Yorùbá Theological Archministry 194–5